SOUTHERN LITERARY STUDIES
Louis D. Rubin, Jr., Editor

# JAMES BRANCH CABELL

James Branch Cabell

# JAMES BRANCH CABELL

## CENTENNIAL ESSAYS

Edited by M. Thomas Inge
and Edgar E. MacDonald

Louisiana State University Press
Baton Rouge and London

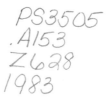
Designer: Joanna Hill
Typeface: Linotron Baskerville
Typesetter: Graphic Composition
Printer: Thomson-Shore
Binder: John Dekker and Sons

*Library of Congress Cataloging in Publication Data*
Main entry under title:
James Branch Cabell, centennial essays.

  (Southern literary studies)
  The majority of essays in this volume were presented at a symposium held Oct. 14–17, 1979, in Richmond, Va. sponsored by the Virginia Commonwealth University.
  Bibliography: p.
  Includes index.
  1. Cabell, James Branch, 1879–1958—Addresses, essays, lectures.
2. Authors, American—20th century—Biography—Addresses, essays, lectures.
I. Inge, M. Thomas.  II. MacDonald, Edgar E.
III. Virginia Commonwealth University.  IV. Series.
PS3505.A153Z628 1982    813'.52    82–7821
ISBN 0–8071–1028–0        AACR2

Publication of these essays was assisted by a generous grant from the Associates of the James Branch Cabell Library, Virginia Commonwealth University.

# CONTENTS

 PREFACE

A program commemorating the centennial of the birth of James Branch Cabell took place in Richmond at Virginia Commonwealth University on October 14–17, 1979. The observance began on October 14 with a lecture by Louis D. Rubin, Jr., and continued on subsequent days with lectures by Joseph M. Flora on October 15, William Leigh Godshalk and Edgar E. MacDonald on October 16, and Leslie A. Fiedler on October 17. A panel discussion by Rubin, Flora, and Nelson Bond, chaired by MacDonald, was held at the Richmond Public Library on October 15. The five lectures delivered at the centennial are all published here for the first time, along with additional new essays by Dorothy McInnis Scura, Mark Allen, and Ritchie D. Watson, Jr. The whole constitutes a fresh appraisal, or in some cases a second look, at a writer who has been neglected by the modern literary critical establishment.

The symposium was made possible through a generous grant from the Associates of the James Branch Cabell Library and was sponsored by Virginia Commonwealth University. The program was administered by Maurice Duke with the assistance of Edgar MacDonald and Dorothy Scura. Others who rendered valuable assistance were Gerard McCabe, George C. Longest, Ellington White, Walter Coppedge, Josephine Clark, Cathy Churchill, Clinton Webb, Peter C. Toms, and the members of the Associates of the James Branch Cabell Library. The support of this project by Louis D. Rubin, Jr., at an early stage was especially helpful. This volume serves as a tribute both to their labors and to the accomplishments of James Branch Cabell.

Edgar E. MacDonald also wishes to thank Mrs. Cassius Moncure Chichester of Richmond for details of Moncure family history, Miss Mary Cary Moncure of Williamsburg, half sister of Gabriella Moncure, for family memories, Mrs. William Ronson of Melbourne, Florida, Gabriella's sister-in-law, for a wealth of material and unstinting aid, Mrs. William Moncure of Woodstock, New York, for making Cabell's manuscript poems available, and Margaret Cabell for granting her permission to quote from them. The letter of December, 1898, from Cabell to Gabriella Moncure is quoted through the courtesy of Mrs. William Moncure and with the permission of Mrs. James Branch Cabell. The frontispiece and the pictures in the photographic essay, except where noted, are used through the courtesy of the James Branch Cabell Library of Virginia Commonwealth University.

Dorothy McInnis Scura wishes to thank Edmund Berkeley of the Alderman Library, University of Virginia, and Mrs. James Branch Cabell for permission to quote from the letters of Cabell and Guy Holt in her essay.

# CHRONOLOGY

1879    April 14, James Branch Cabell born at 101 East Franklin Street, Richmond, Virginia

1894    Matriculated College of William and Mary at age fifteen

1898    Graduated from college, where he had taught French and Greek as an undergraduate

1898–
1900    Worked as a newspaper reporter in New York

1901    Reporter in Richmond; first stories accepted for publication; suspected of murder in Richmond

1902    Seven stories published in national magazines

1904    *The Eagle's Shadow*

1905    *The Line of Love*

1907    *Branchiana* (genealogy); *Gallantry*

1909    *The Cords of Vanity*; *Chivalry*

1911    *Branch of Abingdon* (genealogy)

1911–
1913    Employed in office of the Branch (his uncle's) coalmines in West Virginia

1913    *The Soul of Melicent* (later title *Domnei*); November 8, married Priscilla Bradley Shepherd

1915    *The Rivet in Grandfather's Neck*; August 25, Ballard Hartwell Cabell born; *The Majors and Their Marriages* (his wife's genealogy)

1916    *The Certain Hour*; *From the Hidden Way*

1917    *The Cream of the Jest*

1919    *Beyond Life*; *Jurgen* (suppressed January 14, 1920, cleared October 19, 1922)

1920    *The Judging of Jurgen*

1921    *Figures of Earth*; *Taboo*; *Joseph Hergesheimer*; *The Jewel Merchants*; edited October, November, and December issues of the *Reviewer*

1922    *The Lineage of Lichfield*

1923    *The High Place*

1924    *Straws and Prayer-Books*

1926    *The Silver Stallion*; *The Music from Behind the Moon*

1927    *Something About Eve*

1928    *The White Robe*; *Ballades from the Hidden Way*

1929    *Sonnets from Antan*; *The Way of Ecben*

1927–    The Storisende Edition of *The Works of James Branch Cabell* with
1930    prefaces, in eighteen volumes

1930    *Some of Us*; *Between Dawn and Sunrise* (selections edited by John Macy)

1932    *These Restless Heads* (dropped James from name)

1933    *Special Delivery*

1934    *Smirt*; *Ladies and Gentlemen*

1935    *Smith*

1936    *Preface to the Past* (prefaces from the Storisende Edition)

1937    *Smire*

1938    *The King Was in His Counting House*

1940    *Hamlet Had an Uncle*

1942    *The First Gentleman of America*

1943    *The St. Johns* (with A. J. Hanna)

1946    *There Were Two Pirates*

1947    *Let Me Lie*

1948    *The Witch-Woman*

1949    *The Devil's Own Dear Son*; March 29, death of Priscilla Bradley Cabell

1950    June 15, married Margaret Waller Freeman

1952    *Quiet Please*

1955    *As I Remember It*

1958    May 5, died at 3201 Monument Avenue, Richmond, Virginia

# JAMES BRANCH CABELL

# A VIRGINIAN IN POICTESME

## Louis D. Rubin, Jr.

Concerning authorial personality James Branch Cabell once remarked "the so amply attested fact that the only books which ultimately count, for their permitted season, are ultimate expressions not of any ideas just then in the air (to use that delightfully two-edged phrase), but of the individual being who wrote that particular book. And personality seems a remarkably haphazard affair. You are born, for one inexplicable reason or another, as such and such a person, as a person endowed with private and especial faults and hallucinations. And if your book is ultimately to count, however transiently, you will in your book have managed to expose that person."[1]

Setting out to consider the life and art of James Branch Cabell upon the approximate centenary of his birth, one is compelled to recognize at the outset that he is not like most other writers. His way of dealing with life in literature was and is sufficiently at variance with the literary practices of his day and ours as to create certain difficulties in dealing with him. These difficulties include form, language, audience, reputation, historical significance, and several other elements that affect his stature within both the literary community and the social community of his residence and ironic affiliation.

The fourteenth of April, 1979, marked the one hundredth birthday of an American author, who has been dead now for twenty-one years. Though for a period of about ten years, just over half a century ago, this writer's

---

1. James Branch Cabell, *Straws and Prayer-Books: Dizain des Diversions* (New York: Robert M. McBride, 1924), 244.

works were best sellers, and the author was the subject of widespread journalistic and critical discussion, he has not been paid very much attention since then—since about 1930. Only a single major textbook anthology of American literature with which I am acquainted contains selections from his work. A very few of his many books are now in print but are not widely circulated. Most of us who read James Branch Cabell's writings do so in long out-of-print editions, purchased at used-book stores. Insofar as the general reading public of our day is concerned, his works are as one with those of the late James Oliver Curwood, Maria Cummins, and Constance Fenimore Woolson. In the province of American literary scholarship he customarily merits some brief mention as a phenomenon of the exotic cultural climate of the 1920s. Occasionally his work is discussed in terms of its putative influence upon that of other writers—as for example Cleanth Brooks's comments on *Jurgen* and William Faulkner—or, more topically, as a precursor of the currently fashionable novel of fabulation, or even of science fiction. But for the most part veracity forces the admission that we are trafficking in a little-remembered American author.

On or about the date of his one hundredth birthday, no notice whatever was taken of his centennial in the newspapers of the city of Richmond, Virginia, which in his fiction he denominated as "Lichfield." During his lifetime in that city he was of a social stratum located at the very top of the pile. He was in almost all ways proud of this, and ironically proud, too, of the genealogical finesse he employed in elevating the social position of his first wife from the somewhat threadbare Charles City County gentry to the more lofty reaches of Richmond's elite.

However secure his social position, as a writer of fiction Cabell was little read and seldom honored in his native city. In one of his numerous allusions to this phenomenon, writing of himself in the third person, he remarked that "his books were not purchased in Virginia; they were not often talked about except, just in passing, shruggingly; nor at all often were they even borrowed gratis from his birthplace, which through time's purification, had been converted alike into a free public library and a shrine to the cultural achievements of Major James H. Dooley in the stock market and in the enlargement of railways."[2] To some writers—Hemingway, say, or William Faulkner—this would have made little difference, but Cabell placed considerably more stock in his role within the community

---

2. James Branch Cabell, *Quiet, Please* (Gainesville: University of Florida Press, 1952), 12.

than did such writers, and I think it not a distortion to say that all things being equal (which they were not), he would have preferred a little more local renown than was his fate. In any event, he did not get it, or very much of it. At no time, he declared, were his books "spoken of in the same breath as were the ingenious Mr. So-and-So and the scholarly Dr. Somebody-or-Other, or as were the all-gifted Mrs. What's-Her-Name and the perhaps yet more widely famous Miss Thingumbob, whensoever their ever-living genius was acclaimed by the exiguous yet exigent 'reading public' of Virginia."[3] (The reader is invited to penetrate those aliases.)

So it may seem something of an anomaly to set out to observe the centennial of a writer now possessed of no popular reputation and only minor scholarly renown, who lived in a community where he received very little recognition or readership during his lifetime and is scarcely remembered today outside the walls of the library bearing his name on the campus of a downtown university.

Yet I propose to pay homage to James Branch Cabell. And for good reason. For there are some of us who have read Cabell's work, have enjoyed it, and who constitute a self-appointed coterie which refuses, gently but firmly, to acquiesce in any kind of popularity contest, whether of scholars or citizenry, that would relegate his books either to the paper pulp mills or to the library stacks. In the writings of Cabell, we say, whether in fiction or nonfiction, there is that kind of intellectual felicity and an uncommon imaginative keenness that may *not* be set aside. We do not consent to play critical games—to contend that he is better than this writer, not as good as that one, that he is major, or minor, that he is worth reading because he is like this or that writer, or unlike this or that one, that he is precursor to writers or successor to others. We will take him as he is.

We reject, too, any notion that the celebration of his life and work is principally a ritual of local or regional literary history: that an interest in Cabell is that of the cultural historian who undertakes antiquarian research into the life and times of a once-renowned author whose books posterity has adjudged as of no enduring merit. Cabell's position is not of that sort. He is not to be grouped with a writer such as the late Thomas Nelson Page. By 1953, the centenary of Page's birth, his work was dead; it was, and it remains, of historical significance. Cabell's work, however select its circle of admirers, remains entirely alive. Very likely it will be read (assuming certain things about national, cultural, and linguistic survival that cannot be certified one way or the other) a hundred years hence

3. *Ibid.*, 12–13.

as well. Its ultimate popularity, one guesses, may be neither much greater nor notably less than exists nowadays. But there will quite probably be an interest in the work, and the interest will be not merely archaeological in nature. That, it seems to me, is quite as much as one ought to claim today, and neither more nor less than that.

In the spring of 1956, just over two years before James Branch Cabell died, I visited him at his home on Monument Avenue in Richmond in order to write an article about him for the editorial page of the Baltimore *Evening Sun*—that was my excuse. It was a pleasant enough afternoon. I asked him about what he was reading, how he felt about Edmund Wilson's then-recent "rediscovery" of his work in the *New Yorker* (April 21, 1956), how the *Jurgen* censorship affair looked from the perspective of thirty-five years, what he thought of his contemporaries of the 1920s and 1930s, what were his methods of composition, and so on. The piece I wrote for the *Evening Sun* (July 6, 1956) was in no way a major work of literary journalism, though Cabell wrote afterward to thank me for writing it and expressed an envy of my memory, since I had taken no notes and yet, as he remarked, had included in the interview (I quote from memory here) "nothing that I did not say or at any rate think."

Examining today the interview that I wrote in 1956, I find it decently enough done, though in retrospect I am somewhat chagrined at the realization that most of the questions I propounded had already been answered by Cabell in his numerous books of nonfiction, relatively little of which I had read at the time. Yet I have no doubt that Cabell was long since accustomed to that. Toward the close of my interview, however, I find these two paragraphs:

> You thought of what Mr. Cabell was saying, and how he said it. You had wondered whether in conversation he would talk the way he wrote— the involved, complex phrasing, with the nuances, the little ironies, the bittersweet jests. For the most part he did not speak that way; his answers had been direct, simple.
>
> You thought of the six or seven drafts his books went through. More than almost any other writer you could think of, you decided, James Branch Cabell had created his personality with words. "Words are the only thing we have to work with," he had remarked earlier. The Cabell of the books was the real Cabell, not merely a facet or an attitude of the author. There was no element whatsoever of a pose in them, he had communicated himself in his style as best he could, and his books contained the man.

Though I am not sure I would express the matter exactly that way today—there *was*, for example, an element of pose involved sometimes—it seems to me that the young interviewer who wrote those paragraphs was doing rather better than he had any right to expect to be able to do, in getting at the particular nature of Cabell's genius. For the more I think about it, the more I am inclined nowadays to believe that as a man of letters James Branch Cabell was neither importantly a novelist, as that term is ordinarily used, nor a romancer, nor yet a moralist, so much as a virtuoso performer, a literary personality—somewhat after the manner of, say, Stendhal or Mark Twain. I mean by this that, rather hesitantly at first but with continuously growing assurance, he spent his days and his talents creating a public literary presence known as James Branch Cabell, and that the interest we take in his work today is principally an interest in that created personality.

Now beyond doubt all good writers do something of the sort. There is really no such thing as an effaced author (and least of all, I might add, one named Henry James); elsewhere I have argued this at some length. The difference is that with a writer such as Cabell, the presence of the implied author, the storytelling persona, isn't a way of narrating a story, so much as the narrating of the story is a way of exhibiting the author. Consider, for example, three kindred books of his maturity, *Jurgen, Figures of Earth*, and *The Silver Stallion*. Is the reader drawn to these narratives because he or she wishes to find out what happens to Jurgen, or to Dom Manuel, or to the aging Fellowship of the Silver Stallion? To an extent, perhaps—yet there is scarcely enough suspense involved to keep one reading on merely because of the plot and characterization. What one enjoys, rather, is watching the author put them through their paces. That is also what *he* enjoys. And, apprehending that, the reader is highly pleased to be invited to share in the enjoyment.

Such, it seems to me, is the principal function of Cabell's famous style, which functions equally delightfully—when it does—with works of fiction, so-called, and of nonfiction, equally so-called. Those who have objected to Cabell's way of telling a story as overly mannered and unduly self-conscious miss the nature of the art form, I think. Do we read Cabell for what he has to say, any more so than we read the *Lives of the Poets* for the literary criticism, or *Urn-Burial* for the anthropology, or *Old Times on the Mississippi* for instruction in the craft of piloting a steamboat? All in all, I doubt it very much.

Consider, for example, this passage from *The Silver Stallion*, wherein old Coth of the Rocks, having grown disgusted with the pieties being attached to the memory of Dom Manuel, sets out in search of his former chieftain, and dallies here and there in search of information and of pleasure while en route:

> So he went on, always westward, with varied and pleasant enough adventures befalling him, at Leyma, and Sheaf, and Adrisim. He had great sorrow at Murnith, in the land of Marked Bodies, on account of a religious custom there prevalent and of the girl Felfel Rhasif Yedua; and—at San Reigan,—the one-legged Queen Zélélé held him imprisoned for a while, in her harem of half a hundred fine men. Yet, in the main, Coth got on handily, in part by honoring the religious customs everywhere, but chiefly by virtue of his maps and his natural endowments. These last enabled him amply to deal with all men who wanted a quarrel and with all women whom he found it expedient to placate and to surprise: and as far as to Lower Yarold, and even to Khaikar the Red, his maps served faithfully to guide him, until Coth perforce went over the edge of the last one, into a country which was not upon any map; and in this way approached, though he did not know it, to the city of Porutsa.[4]

This is not an especially notable passage; it is, as the Cabell fiction goes, pretty much straight narration. Surely, though, we do not find ourselves consumed with suspense over the outcome of Coth's journey. We feel sure that something droll will occur when he reaches his destination, yet we are in no way impatient for him to get where he is going. Rather, our attention is drawn to the improbable delights of the alleged narrative. Where on earth are Leyma, Sheaf, Adrisim? What might the Land of Marked Bodies be? Who, indeed, is Felfel Rhasif Yedua? What about that one-legged queen and her fifty-man harem? (The mind boggles at the imagery.) And so on. All this is related to us in passing, as it were; further explanations will obviously not be forthcoming. What we enjoy is the author as he tosses off those names and makes those insinuations. The pleasure, thus, is that of watching the author-impresario spinning out his texture of fact, fancy, and fine surmise, the meantime that the essential joke goes on—the essential joke being always that mythical heroes and heroines are being made to behave in incorrigibly human guise. In short, James Branch Cabell is at work in Poictesme. The splendid virtuoso performance, not the plot or the characterizations, is what we crave.

It is my contention that Cabell was, from his young manhood onward,

---

4. James Branch Cabell, *The Silver Stallion: A Comedy of Redemption* (New York: Robert M. McBride, 1926), 98–99.

urgently impelled to perform in public as an author. For him, the art of fiction was also the art of being self-evidently an author and—as were Stendhal and Mark Twain among others—he was eager to be quite as self-revelatory as he dared, in order to effect that transaction. *Look at me!* his style demands. We may move from his fiction to his nonfiction with only the minimum of adjustment in reader expectation, for in both forms he is concerned principally with being himself. To enhance the impact and point the role-playing, he adapts persona after persona, often one within the other, calls himself Townsend, Charteris, Kennaston, Harrowby, changes his name from James Branch Cabell to Branch Cabell, and then back again. His protagonists are almost all of them artists, however *manqué*. He draws upon his bag of tricks repeatedly, introduces all manner of mythological, anthropological, occultish allusions and references. "The tale tells," he commences; and he is the teller of and in the tale.[5] One of his protagonists, an author, whose story is told by another author, clutches furtively a portion of the Sigil of Scoteia, that mysterious talisman with the odd hieroglyphs that, turned upside down, reads "JAMES BRANCH CAB-ELL MADE THIS BOOK."[6] He composes a trilogy based on dreams, and the dreams are those of a married Episcopalian author of distinguished family living in Richmond-in-Virginia. Frequently he interviews himself, with the younger Cabell addressing the older Cabell as to what will be involved in the profession of authorship. Always the author is at center stage. "For man alone," he reminds us so often in what I think is a revealing image, "plays the ape to his dreams."

This is not to say that in so portraying himself in public, the author is under obligation to tell the truth, the whole truth, and nothing but the truth, so help him God. For as Cabell likewise insists, "These egotists who write perpetually about themselves are under no bond, and under no temptation whatever, to write the truth. . . . in pretending to commemorate himself the self-respecting artist, who is also an egoist, substitutes an edited and a considerably embellished effigy. He immortalizes, in fine, somebody else."[7] Along with the compulsion to be oneself in public, therefore, goes the urge to touch up the image just a trifle.

It is, however, a delicate business, for in so doing, sometimes the author shows more or other than what he means to show. A reader, if sufficiently attuned to the Cabell canon, can sometimes recognize certain occasions

5. James Branch Cabell, *The Cream of the Jest: A Comedy of Evasions* (New York: Robert M. McBride, 1917).
6. *Ibid.*, flyleaf.
7. Cabell, *Straws and Prayer-Books*, 259.

when the author is at work touching up things. I, for example, very much doubt the complete veracity of all those assertions of very active premarital philandering that reputedly went on at the Rockbridge Alum Springs in the days of Cabell's young manhood. I detect, the more often that it is repeated, the note of what is today termed "overkill." Observe, the author seems to be saying, what a concupiscent and lusty specimen of entire masculinity I used to be in my salad days. Do not ever mistake me for one of your weak, effeminate author-types. It is true that I am a writer of tales and verses rather than one of your men of action and practicality, but I am most emphatically not the less virile and swashbuckling for having selected as a career the pursuit of words rather than deeds and money. And as for certain nasty rumors that may have circulated locally in the wake of that unfortunate scandal in Williamsburg during my last year in college, let it be observed that clearly I was not that way inclined.

Please observe that I am not suggesting that Cabell was either overtly or latently a homosexual, but only that I suspect he feared being mistaken for one. Yet I believe, too, that he recognized within his makeup sufficient sexual ambivalence as to make him like most men, however predominantly masculine; so that in the years following his marriage he felt at sufficient liberty in his fiction obliquely to say as much—as for example in that rather odd conclusion to one of Kennaston's dreams in Chapter 30 of *The Cream of the Jest*. For at bottom, one might say, James Branch Cabell was impelled to reveal almost everything about himself; to quarrel with his own formulation, he did *not* "immortalize, in fine, somebody else." That is one important reason why, given the kind of writer he was, he was so good a writer, and why his prose will live. He was every whit as honest as—to cite an author whose work he detested—the late James Joyce.

Some years ago I ventured, in a little book, to dispute the then-prevalent contention that the bulk of the fictional writings of James Branch Cabell, in their preoccupation with goings-on in the mythical land of Poictesme, bore no relationship to the time and place of Cabell's own occupancy, save that of assiduous escape. I noted that the deification of Dom Manuel by his heirs and assigns, and the rather free way in which those who came after him proceeded to revise history so as to convert Dom Manuel and his lieutenants into a saintly and high-minded pantheon of legendary heroes, reminded one strikingly of what was being made, during the days of Cabell's boyhood, of a group of fighting men who not many years earlier had worn the Confederate gray throughout four years of sweaty civil war. "Between the myth of the Redeemer of Poictesme and that of the stainless heroes of the South's Lost Cause," I declared, "there seems little difference. Mr. Cabell had created the one; he had during his childhood observed the other in the process of being created. In neither instance did the final product seem to bear more than a nominal relationship to the truth."[8]

What I was attempting to do was to establish the linkage, as I saw it, between Cabell's allegedly "escapist" romancing and the literature of the South of Cabell's day and thereafter, a literature that whatever its sins could not remotely be described as "escapist." I was quarreling with the too-frequently received notion of Cabell as a world-weary, jaded holdover from the *fin de siècle*, the effete Virginia aristocrat who retreats from the post-Appomattox vulgarity into a bright, cloud-cuckoo land of tinselly fabrication and fabulation. I did not think it was so simple as that, even though H. L. Mencken had lauded just that aspect of Cabell's work and Cabell himself had also proclaimed as much.

I have no wish to modify my formulation; it seems sound, if I do say so myself. But it now seems to me that there is a more elementary and perhaps important way than through subject matter whereby James Branch Cabell's writings derive from their time and place—from a southern city during the years when the Confederate veterans were still holding their well-attended reunions and Harry Flood Byrd was known as the enterprising young son of the Speaker of the Virginia House of Delegates.

For it strikes me that from *The Eagle's Shadow* onward, down to the very last volume of memoirs, there is a notable and even extraordinary concern shown for role—public role, social role, literary role. What do one's contemporaries think? seems constantly to occur to almost everyone, including the author himself; and at the same time, there is considerable satisfaction taken in the private flouting of such roles. I get the impression of a kind of double life, one part involving the flagrant pursuit of art, the other the acceptance of one's impressive social status within the greatly nonartistic community, which by the time of *The Rivet in Grandfather's Neck* is made into a principle of absolute division of role as between John Charteris and Rudolph Musgrave. These two Lichfieldians, once roommates at college, possess respectively the artistic temperament, which is seen as utterly self-serving and unmoral, and the chivalric temperament, which ostentatiously believes in honor, genealogical prestige, and the public virtues. To essay the one role would appear to rule out the

8. Louis D. Rubin, Jr., *No Place on Earth: Ellen Glasgow, James Branch Cabell, and Richmond-in-Virginia* (Austin: University of Texas Press, 1959), 64.

possibility of the other. With *The Cream of the Jest* we observe the maturation of a character who begins to approach the current situation of the
author himself, for Felix Bulmer Kennaston has become a highly domes-
ticated Episcopalian vestryman and satisfactory member of Lichfield society, yet one who also retreats into his library, grasps the magic Sigil of
Scoteia, and is straightaway transported into a magical and wondrous
eternity of nonmortal romancing. Noteworthy, too, is the fact that by virtue of this secret life, Kennaston is enabled to elevate his literary artistry
from mediocrity and to write a novel that makes him famous, and also
makes him notorious because of the wild suggestivity of sexual misbehav-
ior contained therein. All this, mind you, some few years before the publication of *Jurgen*, upon which publication just that took place.

Such imaginative goings-on in literature, and all offenses against the
public ideal of probity and respectability, must stay unnoticed and un-
mentioned in the assuredly polite society of Lichfield, where, the author
of *Preface to the Past* assures us, "such improprieties, however widely known,
or however freely discussed in private conversation, were nevertheless
assumed, as a social rule of thumb, simply not to exist among the well-
bred. . . . The oligarchy of Lichfield, in fine, was held together with in-
numerable small bonds of mutual silence."[9]

But why, the author asks the characters of his books, must the place of
residence where all that does go on among them be cited as taking place
in a made-up city known as Lichfield, rather than in a more publicly re-
nowned city "familiar to everybody, and to me too, so that I might record
your doings against an at once recognizable background of local facts and
civic traditions and customs and foibles and general polity?" The response is to cite the fate of George Washington Cable of New Orleans,
whose identifiably Louisiana romances "brought about his exile from the
South," and of various other authors, who, by failing to chronicle their
communities in altogether laudable terms, likewise incurred civic wrath
of a very unpleasant sort.[10] By transporting the citizenry of Richmond to
Lichfield, therefore, and from Lichfield to Poictesme, James Branch Cabell was enabled to remain a resident of Richmond-in-Virginia in good
standing.

So much is reasonably well known to those who have read Cabell's books.

9. James Branch Cabell, *Preface to the Past* (New York: Robert M. McBride, 1936),
295.
10. *Ibid.*, 277, 278.

What interests me, however, is the highly ultimate manner in which it is set forth. Numerous other authors, one remembers, have faced a similar division as between civic residence and artistic conscience. William Faulkner, after all, managed to live in Oxford, Mississippi, for most of his adult lifetime even though, as one of his fellow townsfolk once expressed it, some of his books were locally quite as popular as a skunk in a sleeping bag. Eudora Welty has felt it unnecessary to abandon Jackson, Mississippi, and—one hesitates to invoke the name—even Ellen Glasgow was to be found during her adult years comfortably at home at One West Main Street in that Virginia city which she denominated fictionally and not always admiringly as Queenborough.

With James Branch Cabell, however, it was not merely a matter of living in Richmond and also writing about it; the sense of a public role would seem to have been involved. For he was, as he often noted, a Cabell, with ancestral roots that went back well into colonial Virginia. However ironically he might depict the foibles and even the outright unpleasantries of Richmond social and civic attitudes, he was not about to dismiss them as mere vanity and snobbery. His lifetime interest in Virginia genealogy is not unimportant to an understanding of the man. The author-compiler of *Branchiana* and *Branch of Abingdon* was doubtless aware that on a cosmic plane, the question of Virginia ancestry is one of the lesser laws of planetary thermodynamics, and that on Mother Sereda's washday the vestiture of what was then called the Richmond German is unlikely to retain much of its temporal splendor. But Cabell was, for all his philosophical detachment, interested in the short run as well as the long. What went on in Richmond *mattered*.

I know almost nothing about Cabell biography other than what I have read, but it is my distinct impression that the young manhood of James Branch Cabell was marked by an extraordinary amount of disturbance and outright scandal, including even an unsolved murder, some of which did indeed "get into the papers," and that Cabell, who from all accounts including his own was an extremely shy and not very pecunious young man, was greatly mortified at such happenings. Moreover, though his position of descent as from the Cabells and the Pattesons was impeccably respectable, the money that the family had, which for a time was considerable, derived from the Branches, who were Methodists and, besides, came from Petersburg. Indeed, the impulse behind his Branch genealogical research, and the money to do it with, arose from the wish to establish more formidable ancestral quarterings than presently existed. The concern for genealogy, therefore, was not the product of purely anti-quarian zeal.

In any event, I note the cumulative impact of such social and civic pressures as would tend toward the development of a somewhat self-anxious sense of social identity and role. And I note, too, what is obvious: that when to James Branch Cabell at the age of thirty-three came, finally, a wife and domesticity, he set out at once to make that marriage into as genealogically impeccable and as socially prestigious an affair as could exist in Richmond, with—as he relates in *As I Remember It*—quite notable success. Thus, whatever might have happened in earlier years in the way of divorce, murder, alleged perversion, and other occasion for gossip, there was surely no social flaw in it thereafter.

Meanwhile, one sees, coexisting with that young Cabell of Cayford, a fiercely creative young writer who set out early in life to pursue a career and to seek distinction, quite in defiance of the Richmond social and business community's view of what constituted a sensible vocation, in, to choose a phrase that delighted him, "the mere beauties of the *belles lettres*."[11] And this socially shy but artistically forward young man possessed, or was possessed by, a daemon far too intense ever to remain satisfied by what in Richmond-in-Virginia circles was held to be appropriate and decorous performance in literary matters.

I adopt the word *daemon* deliberately—Cabell also used it—because it seems to me that this young artist viewed the urge to tell stories and write poems as something not merely compulsive, but actually sinful and diabolical in its urgency. It appeared to involve a deliberate willingness to flout the public morality, to scoff at the lares and penates of Richmond-in-Virginia, to satirize and strike back covertly at all those who had given social offense to himself and his immediate family, and to relish doing so. In the ferocity of its impulse it seemed, especially to one who had, after all, inherited the Presbyterian affiliation of the Cabells, to emanate as from the devil himself. Thus throughout Cabell's writing appears the red-headed Horvendile—the devil's own dear son, in anagram "horned evil"—who pointedly reminds all the inhabitants of far-off Poictesme that it is he alone who does the dreaming by which all of them are enabled to exist in words and thus survive their mortality. This same Cabell remarks that "the hypothesis does appear at least tenable that it is Satan who foists upon the 'born' creative writer the ability and the need to be about a vocation thus doomed to be more or less gravely blasphemous." And, "I

11. James Branch Cabell, *Let Me Lie* (New York: Farrar, Straus, 1947), 123.

elect to think of each and every valid romantic novelist as a skilled sorcerer."[12] I believe he meant what he said.

In short, what we have here is just that tension between art and community identity that characterizes other southern writers of the twentieth century—between the requirements of membership in a ritualized and fairly traditional social community with its own very compelling civic legendry and heroic myth (as it must have seemed to the son of one of the Virginia Military Institute cadets who charged so gloriously at New Market, and the grandson of Col. James Read Branch, C.S.A.), and the need to pursue forms and meanings, to get beneath the surface assumptions, to re-create reality in its true lineaments through language, that marks the vocation of literature and which was termed by Cabell "the desire to write perfectly of beautiful happenings." There was that too and in the time and the place which served to distance the imagination of this particular Virginian from his community, in a fashion that had not been importantly present for an older writer such as, for example, Thomas Nelson Page. What resulted was a modernist living in Richmond-in-Virginia.

Let me here assert at once, and clamorously, that I am not merely rehearsing the tired motif of the Alienated Modern Artist. The latter are available at the price of a dime a dozen, and so-called alienation has produced of itself precious little noteworthy art. It is fairly easy to be alienated; and it is another and altogether more creative thing to be estranged. It was because of the presence, side by side within the one sensibility, of the Cabell who took his social role and his membership in the Virginia oligarchy with ironic seriousness, and the Cabell who was possessed by the "daemon" and who did not see his role as that of edifying the self-esteem of his community—it was because of the tension wrought by the twin roles, and the creative impulse toward an artistic resolution of the contradictions involved therein, that the Cabell books got written.

The discovery, along about the time of *The Cream of the Jest*, of the covert uses of the symbolic Sigil of Scoteia—that is, of the way of transmitting Lichfield to Poictesme so as to write about what he knew and was—constituted the maturation of the literary art of James Branch Cabell of Richmond-in-Virginia. Thereafter he knew the way, just as, a decade later, a young Mississippi writer discovered, while writing a novel entitled *Flags in the Dust*, the possibilities of a place called Yoknapatawpha County.

William Faulkner had a role, too: to be a Falkner of Mississippi, after

12. James Branch Cabell, *As I Remember It* (New York: Robert M. McBride, 1955), 200.

the model of the swashbuckling, railroad-building old colonel whose statue might be seen in Ripley, Mississippi, and whose novels, travel books and epic poems were to be found in the family library. The pursuit of that role, through the province of writing books, clashed with the community pieties and social assumptions of the town of Oxford, Mississippi, to the citizens of whom he was, by virtue of his dandyish airs and his Byronic posturing, known locally as Count No-Count. If the lineaments of Lichfield-Poictesme and of Yoknapatawpha County are greatly different, so were those of Richmond and of LaFayette County, Mississippi. For Cabell the distancing was comically ironic; for Faulkner it took on proportions that made possible the tragic vision. In any event, it seems undeniable that James Branch Cabell's muse was deeply and intricately concerned with· his somewhat oblique identity as a citizen of Richmond, and in Edgar E. MacDonald's summation, "in his cosmic comedies, Cabell appears to stand outside of time and place, but it would be difficult to find an American writer whose environment played a larger role in creating those stresses which result in literature."[13]

In *Figures of Earth* a stranger accosts the young swineherd Manuel at the pool of Haranton and asks him about a nearby objet d'art; "what is that thing?" he inquires.

> "It is the figure of a man, which I have modeled and re-modeled, sir, but cannot seem to get exactly to my liking. So it is necessary that I keep laboring at it until the figure is to my thinking and my desire."
> "But, Manuel, what need is there for you to model it at all?"
> "Because my mother, sir, was always very anxious for me to make a figure in the world, and when she lay a-dying I promised her that I would do so, and then she put a geas upon me to do it."
> "Ah, to be sure! but are you certain it was this kind of figure she meant?"
> "Yes, for I have often heard her say that, when I grew up, she wanted me to make myself a splendid and admirable young man in every respect."[14]

Annie Branch Cabell, we are told, was not one for reading imaginative literature (any more than was her daughter-in-law, Priscilla Bradley Cabell). Of all Cabell's closer relatives, he tells us, only his maternal grand-

13. Edgar E. MacDonald, "Cabell's Richmond Trial," *Southern Literary Journal*, III (Fall, 1970), 71.

14. James Branch Cabell, *Figures of Earth: A Comedy of Appearances* (New York: Robert M. McBride, 1921), 4–5.

mother, Martha Louise Patteson Branch, was a reader, and she liked far-fetched romances about dukes and the like. That she would have approved of Count Manuel of Poictesme seems as unlikely as that Annie Branch Cabell, whatever her firsthand knowledge of such doings as beget scandal and gossip, would have approved of a model of literature that utilized any such sordid material. If it was absolutely necessary that one pursue literature as a career, then doubtless something along the Thomas Nelson Page model was what was desirable. So that it is quite likely that the figure that James Branch Cabell made in the world was not exactly what had been expected of him, and certainly not in accordance with the role that a Cabell was traditionally supposed to play in his community. Yet the ultimate result, one assumes, would have been to their satisfaction, and to that of almost everyone else concerned, since the author in question turns out to have achieved a public distinction such as perhaps only one other of his Richmond contemporaries can be said remotely to have approached.

A difference between Jurgen the Pawnbroker and Manuel the Redeemer is that Jurgen stuck mainly to his trade and wrote his poems, while Manuel repeatedly put aside the imperfectly modeled work of art in order to do high things in Poictesme and become the public hero. Surely we would agree to put Cabell's own course of action on the Jurgenish side of the equation, insofar as his career went. But if Cabell did indeed stick to the writing trade, the figure of a man that he modeled and remodeled was James Branch Cabell himself, so that his collected works constitute, more than anything else, an extended essay in variously disguised autobiography. "And if your book is ultimately to count, however transiently, you will in your book have managed to expose that person," which indeed he did.[15] His never-failing interest was in what James Branch Cabell was thinking and feeling. His life and his career are as consummately an egotistical performance as exists in our letters. He told stories, made allusions, discovered life and letters, anatomized his community and his literary peers, played pranks, struck back at his critics, nursed grudges, took sides, struck poses and assumed attitudes, chronicled his adventures and explicated his books, allegorized, fantasized, criticized, praised. He is, from first to last, the overt Author—a personage, a character, a creation, a role.

His favorite key on his typewriter, one might say, was the capital *I*. And so intent was he upon re-creating himself, with improvements, in lan-

---

15. Cabell, *Straws and Prayer-Books*, 244.

guage that he has left us, I think, one of the more revealing, honest, and largely attractive depictions of a man in his time and place as exists in all literature. Freely I admit that I do not go for all of it. Nevertheless the man, the author, the James Branch Cabell of Richmond-in-Virginia who writes about being himself, I continue to find irresistible. And this being so, I have no wish to compare him with other authors, whether Virginian, southern, American, or otherwise, to rank him, to "place" him. How, after all, can one consider him in relation to other authors when there is, in all the reaches of literature, no other like him?

# CABELL IN LOVE

## Edgar E. MacDonald

Hers was the child's face that peered into his inner life from his earliest memories. Grave, laughing, concerned, illusive, she was an intimate part of his dreaming, yet she led a mysterious life in a twilight world apart.

For his fifth birthday party, James Branch Cabell's fairy godmother and his real grandmother, Martha Louise Patteson Branch, summoned the small creatures of 1884 Richmond society to come dressed as characters in the Mother Goose rhymes. Young Master Cabell was dressed as Jack, Mother Goose's very own son, "in a lovely costume of pink and green satin, perfectly gotten up, even to the golden egg in his hand. By his side walked Mother Goose herself—viz., Miss Ella Moncure. The quaint figure performed her part to the life, watching over her son Jack and his precious egg with a vigilant eye."[1]

Gabriella Brooke Moncure was the second child of Capt. James Dunlop Moncure, M.D., C.S.A., and Anne Patterson McCaw, herself the daughter of a long line of distinguished physicians. Miss Ella Moncure was four years older than young Master Cabell, having been born March 7, 1875. Her father had studied in Germany and France before the war but had returned to play his gallant role in the southern drama. That obligation over, he studied medicine at Virginia and Maryland and returned to Paris in 1868 to become a specialist in mental and nervous diseases. He came to the Pinel (Pinnell) Hospital near Richmond in 1876, and in 1884 he

1. Richmond *State*, April 16, 1884, p. 4.

was elected head of the Eastern Lunatic Asylum in Williamsburg. His wife having died in 1882, Captain Moncure remarried in 1889 when Gabriella was fourteen, and her stepmother was only five years older than she. They lived in the superintendent's house on the hospital grounds, then located on Francis Street, one of the three thoroughfares which constituted Williamsburg.

In 1894, Cabell was prepared to enter college at the relatively early age of fifteen. His secondary education had received its finishing flourishes under the expert supervision of the legendary John Peyton McGuire, whose school at Belvedere and Main prepared the scions of Richmond's leading families to take their places in the professional life of the commonwealth. Just why Cabell matriculated at William and Mary in Williamsburg is a point for speculation. Only recently reopened, it was a struggling, private institution dedicated to preparing middle-class males for public school positions. He knew few if any members of the student body when he arrived there in the fall of that year. Younger, more scholarly, less athletically inclined, essentially a shy youngster, he doubtless applied himself to his studies as much from a sense of alienation as from his natural aptitude for intellectual pursuits. The rurally oriented students found Cabell's city manners a cause for raillery and dubbed him "sister." In a sense barred from a close relationship with most of his peers, he turned to two older persons whom he found sympathetic and who encouraged his scholarly endeavors. Charles Washington Coleman, college librarian and son of Cabell's landlady, took an increasing interest in the awakening adolescent. Then there was Mother Goose, now in the guise of a dark-haired, brown-eyed, young lady of nineteen. She lived only a street away, and a younger sister remembered Cabell as a frequent guest on Francis Street. By the end of his first year, Cabell had established himself as a scholar, and he had made his social adjustment in an environment he found increasingly congenial. He returned to Williamsburg in the fall of 1895 a confident young man of sixteen.

In his French studies Cabell read in the courtly romances of the medieval pages who were allowed to serve as youthful courtiers to noble ladies, ladies who tempered ardor into chivalrous expressions of love, so that the lover learned to extract from the transitory moment an enduring poem to immortalize his lady. Gabriella Moncure had been bred in the tradition of the game. She was nobly born, and the boy had been entrusted to her care as a child. Cabell proved adept as a troubadour. In the background was the older poet, the whimsical, suggestive, decadent (poetically) Charles

Coleman. In the garden was the lady, alternately defensive and receptive, increasingly aware of the ironies of the relationship.

Cabell dedicated his second "novel," *The Cords of Vanity* (1909), to Gabrielle Brooke Moncure with the cryptic dedication in Latin, "The crowd knows much, so far as it knows anything, so much greater is its need to know," perhaps implying that only the youthful lovers could know the truth seeded in the work. He acknowledged that the character Bettie Hamlyn in that work was modeled on that of Gabriella Moncure during his three-and-a-half-year association with her in Williamsburg, his fictional Fairhaven. While *Cords* is a weakly structured work, an episodic reworking of six previously published short stories and some thinly disguised biography, the character Bettie Hamlyn gives it a semblance of unity, a unity that doubtless reflects the central position Gabriella Moncure held in Cabell's thought at that time. The cad-hero is named Townsend, Cabell's punning alias for his youthful persona. After referring to his frivolous mother, Townsend observes, "It was not until my career at King's College that I may be said to have pretended to intimacy with anybody . . . and at my graduation I carried little of moment from the place save many memories of Bettie Hamlyn." In the passage following this observation, Townsend-Cabell then gives a portrait of Gabriella Moncure that accords with that of those who remember her. She was not reputed a beauty in the fashion of her day, but she is remembered for her wit. "Her enemies deny that she is good-looking, but even her friends concede her picturesqueness and her knowledge of it. Her penetration, indeed, is not to be despised; she has even grasped the fact that all men are not necessarily fools in spite of the fashion in which they talk to women." Townsend comments on her critical nature and adds that "when driven by impertinences into a corner she conceals her real opinion by voicing it quite honestly, as if she were joking. Thereupon you credit her with the employment of irony and even with being open to reason." At the end of the passage, the author observes: "Four years, in fine, we spent to every purpose together, and they were wholly happy years. To record them would be desecration."

But Cabell does record them. Townsend-Cabell assigns a number of pseudonyms to his various loves in the novel and tells us that Heart o' My Heart was his favored appellation for Elizabeth Hamlyn. Here Cabell plays with the French origin of the name *Moncure, mon coeur* or "my heart." Townsend is presented as a youthful poet, one who writes solely for the pleasure of reading his poems aloud to Bettie Hamlyn. Keeping in mind

the four-year difference in ages between Gabriella and Cabell, the following scene from *Cords* gives us an insight into their relationship at
that time.

> "Dear boy," said Bettie, when I had made an end of reading, "and
> are you very miserable?"
>
> Her fingers were interlocked behind her small black head; and the
> sympathy with which she regarded me was tenderly flavored with
> amusement.
>
> This much I noticed as I glanced upward from my manuscript, and
> mustered a Spartan smile. "If misery loves company, then I am the least
> unhappy soul alive. For I don't want anybody but just you, and I believe
> I never will."
>
> "Oh—? But I don't count. Or, rather, I have always counted your
> affairs, so that I know precisely what it all amounts to."
>
> "Sum total?"
>
> "A lot of imitation emotions." She added hastily: "Oh, quite a good
> imitation, dear; you are smooth enough to see to that. Why, I remem-
> ber once—when you read me that first sonnet, sitting all hunched up
> on the little stool, and pretending you didn't know I knew who you
> meant me to know it was for, and ending with a really very effective,
> breathless sob,—and caught my hand and pressed it to your forehead
> for a moment—Why, that time I was thoroughly rattled and almost
> believed I was falling for you."
>
> She shrugged. "And if I had been younger—!" she said, half regret-
> fully, for at this time Bettie was very nearly twenty-two.

And Cabell was eighteen. The novel ends with Townsend ambiguously
engaged to Bettie Hamlyn, fiction here compensating for the painful
parting between Gabriella Moncure and Cabell which really took place.
The refrain in the last pages is, "I must tell Bettie everything." *Cords*, as
will be seen, was an attempt to convey to Gabriella, across time and space,
Cabell's conception of the irrational forces which separated them.

Cabell's last months at William and Mary, in contrast to the first three
and a half years, were a time of intense emotional stress owing to the
homosexual rumors which linked his name with that of Charles Coleman
and others. His withdrawal from college in April, 1898, appeared to the
gossip-prone as an admission of guilt, and his almost immediate readmis-
sion did not reestablish him in the former easy social relationships which
had drawn him out of his innate shyness. In particular, his shame and his
fear of further linking Gabriella Moncure's name with his own discred-
ited standing in Williamsburg effectively ended their relationship. Gabriella Moncure's life was soon to be drastically altered, and what might

have been a brief separation with a happy reconciliation was denied by other complicating circumstances in both their lives. Some months after he was graduated from college, Cabell sent Gabriella two notebooks of poems, which he had read to her in happier days, with a passionate avowal of his love for her.

As well as recording Cabell's despairing and serious attachment for Gabriella Moncure, these notebooks constitute a record of his intellectual growth. They are, in effect, a diary of Cabell's inner life during the three-year period of 1895–1898, and they reveal that Cabell's themes, as they were to be developed in his major work, are stated here in embryo form, awaiting a mature craftsman to give them voice. Considering Cabell's youth, one can compare the swiftness of his intellectual development with that of Keats, from the insouciance of the adolescent, through the despair of love unconsummated, to an acceptance of art as man's timeless record of all emotion.

In these notebooks Cabell copied poems which had been written earlier, but with very few exceptions he carefully recorded the date of composition of each poem. Thus while the poems follow a chronological sequence, occasionally a poem written in one month will precede a poem written the previous month. The poem on page 1 of the earlier notebook is "The Pagan to his Mistress," dated October, 1895. Its opening quatrain was prophetic for the years to follow.

> Love, heed we not the future with its Din
>     Of coming Joy and Sorrow. Can it win
> Us aught to ravel out Obscurity,
>     And raise the Curtain ere the Play begin?

The earliest poem recorded, however, is dated April, 1895, and is in the predictable vein of a youth just turned sixteen.

> *On Meter*
>
> There's a meter for poetry, a meter for gas,
>     And a meter for measure of stone;
> But O how much sweeter, than each other meter,
>     To meet her by moonlight alone.

The next poem in time, September, is equally sophomoric. Entitled "A Ballad of Ye Hungrye Maydde," it recounts the rivalry of two suitors for the favor of a maydenne "Clad in a sad sweet smile— / Also a necklace." Upon the rival males killing each other, she thriftily cooks and eats them. The facetious tone of these poems is soon abandoned, however, and while the succeeding poems retain their youthful ardor, they develop into serious expressions of growing love. The direct influence of Swinburne, Browning, and Keats becomes increasingly evident.

Interspersed among the earlier poems are several short prose passages of a poetic nature. One dated December, 1895, and entitled "Cleopatra" refers to the Egyptian's warm lips, to her thirsting, panting body, to her unfathomed passion, and ends with the exhortation, "Kiss me Cleopatra." The lad needed a gentle reproof. Above the poem written in another hand is this quatrain:

*Love*

One sweet grave thought my heart would ne'r forget
　　Lest gall'd shame should life's white trust eclipse—
A fresh fair morning and a violet
　　Amid the grass, with dew upon its lips.
　　　2 February, 1896
　　　　　　　　　　　　G.

The following poem, dated December, 1895, "The Castle of Content," was the first in date of composition to be included in *From The Hidden Way*, the collection of Cabell's poetry first published in 1916 and incorporated later in the Storisende Edition. In the preface to the latter edition, Cabell comments on its early composition, recalling its date as October or November of 1895.

"Hymn to Aphrodite," January, 1896, shows Cabell's close study of Algernon Charles Swinburne's rhythmic patterns and shimmering surfaces; its refrain, "Hear us, Aphrodite,—hear us, mother of mine," echoes Swinburne's repetitive devices in much of his poetry. This poem is Cabell's earliest reference to the love goddess, the woman of pleasure, in his theme of triune woman as a reflection of man's three basic attitudes towards life, the chivalric, the gallant, the artistic. One can see Cabell working toward this concept in a poem entitled "Sonnet—January 1896," in which the lover sees all these conceptual loves embodied in one real woman and ends with the plea:

Bend, O beloved, to my waiting breast
And whisper, "Love, I know you love me best."

Upon his reading this poem to her, Gabriella Moncure's evasion was to ask for another proof, a poem that was specifically about her. Cabell's response was a poem entitled "Gabrielle," January, 1896, in which the first verse states his obligation to write to order. The poem continues:

Which shall it be—ye villanelle,
Ye epigram, rondeau, rondelle,
   Ballade, or sonnette—each is highte
    Ye lyttle rhyme?

Yet none will aid my hapless plighte;
Ye lyttle rhymes are shorte and slighte;
   Ye Epic's length alone can telle
    Ye manie charms of Gabrielle.
It is in vaine—I cannot write
    Ye lyttle rhyme.

Cabell later included this poem in *From the Hidden Way*, changing *Gabrielle* to *Florimel* in the tradition of pastoral poetry. While this effort was slight, the poem was pleasing, and above all it safely made love a game in which the lady maintained control of the poet's ardor. An approving note to the young lover resulted in another poem, spontaneous and charmingly free of the affectations Cabell found so irresistible in his courtly models.

        *Your Letter Came*

Your letter came—before me lay
An Exercise with long array
   Of foreign words, whose verbs despise
   The proper tense and wax in size
As Nouns with Prepositions play.

The Grammar spread its dreary sway
Till all the world seemed old and gray,
   And while I cursed that Exercise
    Your letter came.

And then—the book was cast away,
For skies were bright, and life was gay;
   I saw again your laughing eyes,
   I heard your musical replies,—
It was a very pleasant day
    Your letter came.

The form of this poem was one of the young writer's favored, a variation of the rondel. At first glance, it appears to be a sonnet, but then one notes the extra line, occasioned by repeating the first line as a refrain in the middle and the end. Thus this device underscores "Your letter came." Another example of this poetic form written at this time, entitled "My Lady's Eyes," February, 1896, is included in *From the Hidden Way*, but there Cabell's "thirty years of repolishment" rob the poem of its youthful freshness.

In *The Cords of Vanity*, Cabell makes Bettie Hamlyn's dislike of Charteris obvious, and one can see it as reflecting the distrust that Gabriella Moncure felt for the influence that Charles Coleman had on Cabell's poetic endeavors. Cabell's penchant for the rondeau and rondel with their structures limited to two rhymes gave his poetry a tinkling effect; it lacked a sonority which bespoke seriousness. Much of Coleman's poetry reflected the influence of Swinburne. Gabriella could not approve of Swinburne's "paganism," nor could she warm to the superficial feeling engendered by some of his affected diction and veiled archness. In an effort to win his lady over to an admiration for Swinburne, Cabell gave her a treasured volume from his collection, *Laus Veneris*, "In Praise of Love." It bears Cabell's autograph and address, 113 East Franklin Street. Whatever her reservations may have been, this volume remained with her until her death. One of her graduation presents given to her four years earlier had been a volume of Browning's poetry; in it were recorded the names of friends who had graduated with her from Miss Gussie Daniel's school in Richmond. In exchange for the Swinburne, she gave this volume to the young poet. In it Cabell wrote his name and the year and treasured it the rest of his life. The influence of Browning becomes apparent in certain of Cabell's poems along with a deeper probing into human relationships. In a poem entitled "After Thoughts," April, 1896, Cabell debates the implications of a kiss Gabriella gave him upon his seventeenth birthday, the fourteenth of April, a kiss which had flamed into passion so that "the sun above / Reeled in the sky—for I found you human." Ideal love and earthly desire had trembled in the balance; the latter had triumphed and the former

> Fled with the shadows in bitter fear.
>
> And now—well, I love you—and yet suppose
>   I had never kissed you, had never rifled
>   Your heart of love—with our passion stifled
> Were we more happy? Ah, Love, who knows?

The struggle within the young poet to effect a reconciliation between his chivalrous and gallant natures resulted in his longest poetic endeavor to date, a poem in four parts covering eight manuscript pages, a total of 142 lines. The hero with whom the poet identified was the Roman who relinquished the world for love. Oddly though, "Antony," April, 1896, has as its hero a Christian tortured by his passion for a pagan Cleopatra. The psychological implications here are obvious; not having great worldly honor to lose, the young Cabell's "honor" was his inbred Victorian concept of purity. Cabell will make significant revisions in this poem two years later, altering its affirmation of God's power to a serious questioning of his justice. But in April, 1896, the young poet, in his struggle with the precepts of the church, soon relinquishes an ascetic Christ and returns to his more satisfying *carpe diem* verses. Significantly the next poem is entitled "The Poete Tunes Hys Lyre." The following month, in "Ballade, Irregular," he is Arnold's forsaken Merman singing the refrain

> Heart of my heart, dost thou not hear
>     The poet calling from far a-part
> With other voices—"*I love you dear*—
>     Heart of my heart?"

He was again punning on the French *Moncure*. He will later include this poem in *From the Hidden Way* with some poignant revisions. In that same May, Cabell further revealed his growing respect for literature as a serious voice rather than as an outlet for youthful effusions. In "To My Verses" he wrote:

> Ah, had we but the power—then you and I
> Should sing together notes so pure and high
> That no man but must listen nor pass by.

This verse is quoted in part in the introductory poem, "At Outset," in *From the Hidden Way*, a hidden acknowledgment to the "co-author" of all these rhymes.

As the school year drew to a close with a summer's separation from Gabriella in prospect, he wrote "A Rondeau," May, 1896, with the refrain "Will you forget?" In June he confessed that all his fantasy loves were centered in her.

> Should she devine that I in all my lays
> But feebly fashioned forth some varied phase
>     Of love for her beneath a fabled name
>     Have written every word to win her fame
> And found no strength to sing save in her praise—
>
> Ah, then the glance of pity that repays
> The years of waiting—and—perchance she says,
>     *For thy reward what guerdon wilt thou claim*—
>         Should she devine.

When Cabell revised this poem for publication years later, he changed the refrain to "Had she devined," carrying the implication that their lives would have resulted in union rather than separation.

That same June of 1896 Cabell read Shakespeare's *As You Like It* and responded with "A Ballade of Arden." Another gift volume of Swinburne's poetry from his mother in London reawakened his admiration for the seductive rhythms and imagery of that poet; he saluted the "master" with a sonnet, "Vale (To A. C. S.)." A picture of his mother as a girl elicited "A Miniature," July, 1896, wherein he praises the mature woman as more beautiful.

That same summer he wrote "A Ballade of the Celestial Kingdom," a poem he later included in *The Cords of Vanity* and in the second edition of *From the Hidden Way.* This tinkling bit of chinoiserie with its overtones of a child's verse probably reflects the influence of Charles Coleman. Bettie Hamlyn's outburst against Charteris in *Cords* comes to mind here: "'I hate that wizened man,' she presently volunteered, 'more bitterly than I do any person on earth. For it was he who taught you to adopt infancy as a profession. He robbed me. And Setebos permitted it.'" Such an observation strikes through the guise of fiction; too many critics have commented on Cabell's allowing a sophomoric whimsy to intrude in passages where it seemed inappropriate.

Three poems written in July contain sea imagery, one entitled "Sea Scapes" appearing later in *The Hidden Way.* A sonnet apostrophizing the painter Sargent's *The Israelites Led in Captivity* gives evidence that Cabell may have spent the summer abroad in 1896. A sonnet to Molière follows. That fall, poems addressed to Alpha Zeta Fraternity, to shadows, to Ares God of War, to Solitude alternate with love lyrics. In a truncated villanelle he offers an apology "Toe Hys Mystresse" for "ye Villainous Verses" he has written wherein he has addressed her under multiple pseudonyms "inn Lover's guise." December finds him writing "A Ballad of My Lady's Service," a poem of four pages highly autobiographical in nature. Cabell has sought love through poetry. His lady says, "Serve me with deeds." A personification of Disbelief witnesses their discussion, but the poet swears that "none shall love thee in so pure a wise" until his death. In the final line she asks, "Who is this woman that he worships thus?" The year closes with "A Christmas Message" to Gabrielle. He sends her

> The simple words of my heart's repeating,
>     The old, old words that I still must tell,
> *I love you dear*—'tis my only greeting
>     To Gabrielle.

The year 1897 was perhaps the happiest of Cabell's life, and he filled a hundred manuscript pages with verses. Almost every fleeting thought flowered into a poem. He addressed the months, Theocritus, Congreve, Beowulf, ballplayers, Thanatos, Horace, the game of poker, Keats. In February, the poet writes "Ballads of Burdens" bewailing the rigors of mathematics and Greek, advising his professors that they are trying to fill another Williamsburg institution, the asylum. April has him again singing, "Heart of my heart, I am thine alway." He imagines himself Shelley: "Has she / Forgotten I lie at the heart of the sea?" He addresses Gabriella as Sylvia, Stella, Ettarre, Chloris, Phyllis, Heart's Desire, all names he will apply to the fantasy women in his later work. As the year drew to a close, however, overtones of melancholy intrude, engendered one gathers by Cabell's jealousy of Gabriella Moncure's other friends. Twenty-two and eighteen were not so far apart as twenty and sixteen had been. Poems entitled "The Passing of Chloris," "Twilight," and "The Dream Mistress" speak of parting. The closing lines of the latter poem, written in December, 1897, would prove an ironic prophecy.

> I shall not lose my hold on Chloris' heart
> So long as I keep friends with Jack o' Dreams.

In the new year four poems are dated January, 1898, including an effective paraphrase of Verlaine's "Chanson d'Automne."

> The long low sobbing of the violin,
>    Sad as the stillness of an Autumn day
>    When wistful Summer lingers on her way
> A little while, speaks of the Might-have-been.

Another, "A Ma Maîtresse," is in French. "Ye Ballade of Enquirie" repeats the question, "Doe I love thee, Dorothy?" The answer has a significance which will be made clear later:

> As Man loves God—why, even soe
> Do I love thee, Dorothy.

The last of the four poems, and indeed the last of Cabell's happy poetry, is addressed:

> *For Mystresse Phyllida.*
>   *Care of Dan Cupid*
>     *Arcadie.*

Then the event occurred which altered Cabell's perceptions of life profoundly. On the evening of January 18, Cabell was host at a fraternity party, a party so lavish with liquid spirits that it created legends. Among the exaggerated rumors concerning its festivities, the term *homosexual* surfaced in the talk. The trial of Oscar Wilde, a scant three years before, doubtless gave this aspect of the rumors its impetus. Charles Coleman was implicated in the gossip; his poetry was considered daringly pagan in Williamsburg, and young Mr. Cabell was too much under the older man's influence.

Only one poem is dated February, entitled "The Last Lover," a poem of twelve stanzas covering three manuscript pages. The Lady Alice receives a lover risen from the grave. She speaks:

> "For I, besought by many a knight
>     And many a lusty squire,
> Turning from all in sick dispite,
>     Not having my desire,
>
> Finding nought good to sight nor touch,
>     Weary of words man saith,
> I that have loved life over-much,
>     Take for my lover, Death."

In his shame Cabell did not see Gabriella, and in separation he became her aching alter ego. As the dead lover, he turned to Poe for his model, a poet he had read as a child and whom he would later declare the first American literary genius.

March records no poems that year. On the thirty-first, the faculty of William and Mary considered the rumors of "certain practices alleged . . . tending to the detriment of the college."[2] After several meetings devoted to the issue, the faculty adduced on April 12 that no evidence supported findings against anyone, but the withdrawal of three students was accepted. At the same meeting, the resignation of Charles Coleman was submitted; he had fallen from a ladder in the library and broken a leg. The withdrawals and the resignation were construed by the gossipmongers as admissions of guilt. When Cabell's family learned he had withdrawn, they effected his almost immediate reinstatement, but Cabell did not return to the congenial Coleman home for his last weeks in Williamsburg, nor did he visit the Moncure family with whom he had spent so many happy hours. He lived a lonely exile at an inn. One poem dated April appears in the verse diary, entitled "Sonnet, à Rebours," a title which suggests his looking backward as well as a sense of regret for the turn of events.

---

2. For a more detailed account of this episode see William Leigh Godshalk, "James Branch Cabell at William and Mary: The Education of a Novelist," *William and Mary Review*, V (Spring, 1967), 1–10.

> The shadows of the shameful time
> Around all last year's memories climb;
>   And all old things that were to me
>   More dear than life, take wing and flee.

In May Cabell transcribed a poem entitled "Une Nuit Blanche" wherein he recorded his sleepless nights, lying in "the shadow of an unknown shame." Abandoned by friends, he cries out, "Ah God, thou knowest what I am." While the young poet admits that "thirsting lips were set to kiss, / My throat made lax as one that sings," he obviously feels that his transgressions have not deserved the ostracism he suffers. But God too, like human friends, is mute: "He answers not! He hath not heard."

Cabell's last month in college inspired four poems, all touching on his separation from Gabriella Moncure. A rondel is built on the contrast of joyful nature and unhappy lover.

> Over the grave where our youth lies dead,
> With sudden tears to our eye-lids springing
> Spring comes back to us laughing and singing.

The second, a longer poem of three ten-line verses, is addressed to Dorothy, who will reappear much later in *Jurgen* as Dorothy-the-Desired. In this poem he laments that she sees him dishonored so that

> My love is her shame
> And I stain what I strive for and praise.

If she could only know him truly, rather than turn away she would love him. It concludes:

> Though all men have trust in me, still
> My heart hath its fill
>   Of all bitterness, seeing I know
>   That you never will.

The next poem, a sonnet, starts with the cry "Could I but come!—Sweete, I am bound in *Hell*." The fourth, also a sonnet, is entitled "A Leavetaking" and is again addressed to Dorothy.[3]

---

3. Chapter 28 of *Cords* presents ironical details concerning this period. In *Quiet, Please* (Gainesville: University of Florida Press, 1952), 90–91, Cabell reminisces on his inclusion in *Cords* of "the final letter from her whom we may with discretion continue to term your Dorothy la Désiree. It in the way of unhappiness had meant a great deal to you at the time of its receipt." The letter, as utilized in *Cords*, opens: "Thank you very much for returning my letters and for the beautiful letter you wrote me. No I believe it better you should not come over to see me now and talk the matter over as you

> I shall not e'er repeat
> My rhymes to her, nor e'er bend to meet
> Her lips this side of Eternity;
> Farewell, my sweet.

This is the last poem addressed directly to Gabriella Moncure in the manuscript notebook although two fragments and a long poem of twelve pages follow. Cabell was graduated with a B.A. on June 23, 1898, a happy occasion for others but for Cabell a time of intense despair.

The first fragment of two manuscript pages which continues the verse diary starts, "What should I hold thee—a god?" The nature of Christ's divinity is debated, and a disillusioned Cabell appears to reject the Godhead of Christ in exalting his humanity—his rage, his pride, his fear. For a reader in 1898 the poem may have approached blasphemy in its fusion of spiritual and physical love.

> We have but love for the man;
> The man that Magdalen loved.

Gabriella Moncure too suffered as we shall see, but when she read this poem she was not prepared to follow Cabell into the anguish of religious doubt—at that moment. Two leaves constituting four manuscript pages are torn from the notebook. The emotions which led Gabriella to this act can only be speculated on, but from the tone of the poem and the ideas advanced in the remaining pages, she may have reacted to an implication that she had not responded with humanity to the poet's human weakness. With the ending missing, we cannot know the date of this poem, but the following fragment, a poem in French, is dated July. In the style of Ronsard, it has as its refrain "Le Temps Jadis," translated "Yesteryear." While the cruel mistress is a convention of this type of poetry, Cabell's sense of time passing, never to be recaptured, is underlined.

> Other men have lived as I live,
> Will live when I am in the tomb,
> And today will be yesteryear.
>
> When you think of me (and you will)
> My vows and half-forgotten rimes

---

suggest because it would probably only make you unhappy. And then too I am sure some day you will be friends with me and a very good and true one. I return the last letter you sent me in a seperate envelope, and I hope it will reach you alright, but as I destroy all my mail as soon as I have read it I cannot send you the others." Cabell had made a point of including Gabriella Moncure's misspelled words, the word *separation* being misspelled in her hand in the Swinburne volume.

And the happy time when you were cruel—
    Yesteryear.

In not completing the thought in the last quatrain, the young poet does not presume to predict precisely what the cruel mistress' emotions will be.

At this bitter time, Cabell returned to an earlier poem. It should be rewritten, God was not just. The long, tortured poem entitled "Antony" that was Cabell's last offering in the notebooks is perhaps more properly a study for the clinical psychologist, with its mixed metaphors, images, and symbolism. One can readily understand that the bereft lover empathized with Antony; his world too had been lost with love. The poem is in four parts, the first consisting of four eleven-line verses. In this part, Antony, a Christian doing penance for an unholy love, awakens just before dawn and is visited by the ghost, a very sensual ghost, of the dead lover. If she can force her tongue between his clenched teeth, his soul will be lost. Part II, consisting of six six-line verses, is an impassioned plea to God to save him from this vision brought back to test his will anew. Part III, a passage in iambic pentameter of fifty-six lines in rhyming couplets, starts in praise of the beloved's beauty and in her pride of her dominion over the lover whose soul slept during the supremacy of passion. But Cabell-lover remembers he serves "the great pale Christ"; he scourges himself and is pardoned. Assured of Heaven, he awaits death tranquilly. Then a fatal question: "It is well with me; / O woman that I loved, how is it with thee?" He can envision her in no other place but Hell, and then a new blasphemy enters his thinking.

      When I am sped
To the fair courts of Heaven and art among
The blessed saints, how shall I bend my tongue
To worship him that damn'd thee? Shall I be
Happy in Heaven, and through eternity
Hear thy voice call in agony to God
And he not hearken, dear?

The fourth section of the poem contains even more ambivalence. Its sixty-nine lines, most of which continue the rhymed couplets in iambic pentameter, encapsules a lyric of twelve lines. The first thirty lines apostrophize Lust, "masker of all temporal things," a god in whose service the poet has made his poems. Then comes the lyric with its implications that the poet's service had its rewards despite the cost.

    Grieve not for memory of past delight,
    My sweet, and take no sorrow for the night,
      Now we have garner'd all the joy thereof.

And whosoever made us—be his name
Jove or Jehovah—shall we blame
    Our Maker that he also hath made Love?

For He that made the faltering soul of man,
That fashion'd all things after His own plan,
    Disclosing nothing of the ends there-of,

Made Love; and if Love prove victorious,
Who made Love strong? And if Love conquer us,
    How shall he dare to blame us, that made Love?

Back in the persona of Antony-Cabell, the poet rejects the lyric's premise that because God does not disclose his own nature (his ends) he may not be in a tenable position to judge man's. But again the voice in the poem shifts, and again the youthful lover questions the purpose of Lust. "I know not. Yet I trust / God sees the meaning clearly." *Trust* is used ironically here, for the poem further narrows the distinction between God who created the world and the god of Lust. The poem concludes with a statement and a question. "God is God. Can God do wrong?"

The import of this poem carries a number of implications. First an observation concerning the form. Cabell's essential communication with Gabriella Moncure during their three-and-a-half-year intimacy had been through poetry, not the verbal superficialities of most courting couples. Thus when he wished to convey to her his tortured state engendered by their separation, only the rhetoric of poetry could serve, expressing what an outwardly shy youth could never say in person. Its length, with its shifting voices, is indicative of a new effort to call into service a poetry capable of sustaining a deeper thought, a deeper passion than the light lyrics of happier days. If it does not succeed as poetry, it does as a record of a psychological state and marks a growth in artistic ambition. The interior conflict in the poem, a youth divided by love of the ideal and physical passion, conveys with sensitivity the direction Cabell's feeling for Gabriella Moncure had taken from 1895 to 1898, from chivalry to gallantry, from the desire to worship to the desire to possess. Other seminal ideas in the poem, observable in his later work, are apparent. First, lust as the procreator of life is thereby also the creator of art, leading to his third attitude toward life (after the chivalrous and the gallant), the artistic: life or experience is merely the raw material of art. Second, any act of creation can be construed as sin as it invades the domain of God, who claims universal copyrights. Third, if man is imperfect, his nature divided, the cause may lie with God, who gives and withholds at the same time; at best, such seeming irrationality appears unjust, at worst, inartistic. These ideas reach their fruition in *The High Place* (1923). The hero of that work observes: "Gods and devils are poor creatures when compared to man. They live with knowledge. But man finds heart to live without any knowledge or surety anywhere, and yet not go mad. And I wonder now could any god endure the testing which all men endure?"

"Antony" is dated December, 1898, five months after the previous poem. It marks the conclusion of an important stage of Cabell's development and fixed, when he was not yet twenty, the direction his major work would take—its philosophy, its forms, its themes. When Cabell determined to send these two manuscript books of poems to Gabriella Moncure, it was more than an acknowledgment of what she meant to him; a new man spoke, in part her creation. It told her he acknowledged his fate, and it announced his resolution, like Romeo's, to defy the stars. The following letter accompanied the poems:

> Dear, since I love you above all women on earth, it is not fitting that my gifts to you should be of little value. And so I send you these two books. It seems a gift of little worth, these books of halting rhymes, pilfered from Swinburne and Austin Dobson. But you, who have seen these verses in the making, you know better. There is nothing of my life for the past three years that is not set down there-in. All of me is there.
>
> And so it is fitting that you should have the books. For my life in this time has been yours—yours, yours, all yours. We are no longer two persons. You will remember in reading not only, *The boy who has written this is mine, but This boy is I*. And the verses? Ah, there is no one of them, good, bad, or indifferent, that would ever have been written save for you. Take them, dear. For the verses are yours not mine.

At this unhappy time, other events were conspiring to effect a permanent parting of the two friends. Cabell's parents had separated, an act not lightly considered in 1898. It is highly unlikely that a Victorian gentleman such as Dr. Cabell would have discussed his marital problems with his son, and James was doubtless aware of his mother's awkward position in Richmond society. He was also aware that his middle name was Branch. Both sides of Gabriella Moncure's family were distinguished by ancestry of impeccable public service. If Cabell's Branch ancestry was known primarily for its wealth in a time of general poverty, at least his Cabell lines were socially acceptable. That had recently been attested to by the monumental *The Cabells and Their Kin* in 1895. The first twenty pages of the second manuscript notebook that Cabell sent Gabriella Moncure are filled with genealogical charts copied from this work. His own later family research would be on the Branch lines in an effort to prove that even if they were undistinguished they were respectable. The murder of his mother's first cousin, John Scott, in 1901, with the resultant gossip associating their names, was a further deterrent in his making any open avowal of his love for Gabriella Moncure.[4]

In November of 1898, Gabriella's father died, leaving a young widow with children. Gabriella, twenty-three, had to make a life for herself. She turned to art. Her father had studied medicine in Paris; she would go there to study painting. But the winter in Paris brought on pneumonia; she was warned that continued residence might lead to tuberculosis. She returned to the United States to be watched over by her physician uncle, Walter D. McCaw, a bachelor serving in the Army Medical Corps. Recovering, she kept house for her uncle, moving with him to various army posts, and she continued her art studies. A clue to her feelings for Cabell is a notation in the volume of Swinburne he had given her in Williamsburg; over the poem "Rococo" she wrote the word *seperation*.

> Take hands and part with laughter;
>   Touch lips and part with tears;
> Once more and no more after,
>   Whatever comes with years.
> We twain shall not remeasure
>   The ways that left us twain;
> Nor crush the lees of pleasure
>   From sanguine grapes of pain.

After grauation from college, Cabell held various jobs. He was a reporter for the Richmond *Times*, the New York *Herald*, and the Richmond *News*; he also worked for his uncle John Patteson Branch, sometimes as a genealogist and at one time in the West Virginia office of that gentleman's coal-mining interests, giving rise to the repeated myth that Cabell had labored in the mines. In 1901 Cabell launched his literary career with the publication of three short stories, and some of his short stories became "novels." While the physical separation of the lovers lengthened into years, the years did not diminish Gabriella Moncure's influence on the maturing writer. What if one day when they were old the lovers again came face to face, Gabriella having come to return the poems she has cherished through the years? In "Love-Letters of Falstaff," *Harper's Monthly* (March, 1902), the aged knight burns "Toe Hys Mistresse" (November, 1896) and "Cupid

---

4. For a fuller account of this period in Cabell's life see Edgar E. MacDonald, "Cabell's Richmond Trial," *Southern Literary Journal*, III (Fall, 1970), 47–71.

Invaded Hell" (February, 1897), two of the poems in the notebooks. "When You Are Very Old," Cabell's paraphrase of Ronsard dated July, 1898, in the manuscript, becomes the theme of "The Conspiracy of Arnaye," *Harper's* (June, 1903). The August issue of that year contains "The Castle of Content," grown out of the poem of the same title dated December, 1895. "Rustling Leaves of the Willow-Tree" dated October, 1897, appears in "The Story of Adhelmar," *Harper's* (April, 1904). The following year all these stories reappear in *The Line of Love*. At the end of *The Cords of Vanity* (1909), dedicated to Gabrielle, the hero determines to return to Bettie Hamlyn, for she is in a sense the collaborator who will make him the writer he aspires to be. Knowing friends still predicted that Cabell and Gabriella Moncure would be reunited. In *The Soul of Melicent* (1913), the chivalrous Perion wins his way back to his lady after multiple foes and events separate them. At their moment of reunion, no longer young, Perion falls to his knees: "Their love had flouted Time and Fate." But in the same year, aged thirty-four, Cabell proposed to Mrs. Shepherd, a widow with five children and a healthy inheritance from her husband. She had dark hair and eyes; she was four and a half years older than Cabell. When Gabriella Moncure learned of the impending nuptials, she took out Cabell's avowal of love for her and wrote across it: "Oh Absalom my son my son! September 1913." Like King David she had gone up to the chamber and wept, "O my son Absalom, would I had died instead of you."

But Cabell tells us in his loving account of his marriage to Priscilla Bradley Cabell in *As I Remember It* that they never mentioned the word *love*. In 1916, he published many of the poems he had written for Gabriella Moncure under the title *From the Hidden Way*. The following year saw the publication of his first critical success, *The Cream of the Jest*, wherein the writer Kennaston leads a dual life; during the day he lives in a real world with his pedestrian wife, but nightly he escapes into a dreamworld, lured there by Ettarre, the eternal witch-woman. But when Kennaston touches Ettarre, the dream vanishes, and he awakens again in his mundane surroundings. Cabell had become his wife's seventh physical child, but he remained under Gabriella Moncure's enchantment.

In *Jurgen* (1919), Cabell again plays with the idea of having a second chance to alter the course of his life. In passing through his chivalrous stage, Jurgen composes a "sirvente" for Guenevere. It takes the form of a sonnet, its fourteen lines falling into an octave and sestet, but every line ends with the word *love*. Presented as prose, some readers are unaware they are reading poetry, but Cabell scholars have debated its form and marveled sweetly. This poem appears in the notebooks as "A Word With

Cupid," dated September, 1897. While *Jurgen* brought notoriety to Cabell, it brought a hidden message to Gabriella Moncure. In his next work, *Figures of Earth* (1921), Cabell carried the game farther. Alerted by the preface in the Storisende Edition, Warren A. McNeill analyzed in his *Cabellian Harmonics* (1929) the "fifteen passages of contrapuntal prose to be found in *Figures of Earth*." The first passage considered by McNeill (occurring on page 19 in the Kalki Edition, page 17 in the Storiesende) is that beginning, "Oh, out of the void and darkness." The first stage of this poem is found in the notebooks entitled "The Swimmer," dated July, 1897. Cabell was then eighteen. McNeill suspected quite rightly that Cabell had transcribed actual poems in many cases, but concerning a passage beginning, "I cry the elegy" (Kalki 110, Storisende 90), he makes the mistake of opining, "It seems improbable that Mr. Cabell had any verse form in mind when he wrote this and the two succeeding paragraphs, but that they were carefully planned according to his idea of prose counterpoint seems equally evident." Cabell had in truth incorporated another poem written in July of 1897. McNeill terms the passage beginning, "Yes but the long low sobbing of the Violin" (Kalki 295, Storisende 242) one of "the most interestingly planned passages in the book." He analyzes its skillful blending of verse and prose. Three other observations should be made: the poem is a paraphrase of Verlaine's "Chanson d'Automne," Cabell wrote it in January of 1898, and its reworking in *Figures of Earth* is intensely autobiographical. Only Gabriella Moncure could know the import of what Cabell said in this passage.

Almost all the female characters in Cabell's work are modeled on two women: Priscilla Bradley Cabell was the prototype for all the real, the domestic, women (with minor reservations for Cabell's mother); Gabriella Moncure was the genesis of all the fantasy women.[5] In *Figures of Earth* the former is embodied in Manuel's wife, Niafer. Cabell tells us in the preface that the germ of this work came to him in his study when he saw his wife and child through the window. What if he were to open the window to find that wife and child were but images in the glass and that the window really looked into the twilight world of the sweet-scented past? Gabriella Moncure plays multiple roles in this work, but most significant in psychological terms is Suskind, an anagram for *unkiss'd*. At the end of this autobiographical allegory, Manuel invades the twilight world of Suskind to kill her. "She is my heart's delight," Manuel says, "my heart" echoing once

5. The character of Dorothy la Désiree in *Jurgen*, being neither domestic nor elusive, may have had another model. In *Quiet, Please*, Cabell equivocates on these matters but makes it clear that the name belongs to Gabriella Moncure.

again *Moncure*. But Manuel cannot survive the death of Suskind; they are one heart. In a far-off May, a boy had written, "Heart of my heart, dost thou not hear?" Did she hear now? The work ended, as numerous Cabell students have observed, where it began. Most of his works are circular, a quest that returns to its starting point. In the writing of *Figures of Earth*, Cabell made a profound discovery: all his work was biographical. It was really a Biography with a capital *B*.

The year after the publication of *Figures of Earth*, Cabell started writing *The High Place*, in many respects his best work. He at last understood fully the psychological and artistic implications of his love for Gabriella Moncure, and his firmness of purpose shines through this autobiographical allegory. Significantly it incorporated no previously published short stories, nor did Cabell indulge in his usual deception of attributing this work to another author. The hero's father advises his son that the great law of life is, "Thou shalt not offend against the notions of thy neighbor," doubtless echoing the advice of Dr. Cabell, a Presbyterian, to his sons. Melior is modeled on "Mr. Townsend's mother," a pseudonym for Anne Branch Cabell. Priscilla Bradley Cabell plays no significant role in this comedy of disenchantment, but Gabriella Moncure enters the drama in two significant guises. She is the fairy Mélusine who guides all the dreaming of the young hero and who determines all the conditions for the operation of the machinery. She is also the clear-seeing half sister, Marie-Claire, an adept at necromancy; "In their shared youth these two had not been strangers." Cabell gives Marie-Claire the physical attributes of Gabriella Moncure, in particular her intensely dark eyes with extraordinarily thick lashes, her gaze giving him "the illogical feeling that, where he was, Marie-Claire saw some one else, or, to be exact, saw some one a slight distance behind him." Another of her features, apparent in old photographs, is described: "Her neck remained wonderful: it was still the only woman's neck familiar to Florian that really justified comparison with a swan's neck by its unusual length and roundness and flexibility. But her head was too small for that superb neck." Chapter 24 of this work contained many messages for the woman in Cabell's youth. "Marie-Claire alone knew that this fourth Duke of Puysange was still the boy who had loved her; and her blind gazing seemed always to penetrate the disguise." Upon its completion, Cabell was more pleased with *The High Place* than with any of his other works. It had a well-defined plot, it had symmetry, it was really the type of work he had intended writing all along.

Cabell was ever ready to tell his readers what they should see in his work; it was time to tell them that he really was an epic romancer of no small order. He made the announcement in *Straws and Prayer Books*; he assured the 1924 reader that the Biography was really begun in 1901 with his first story. Then, unfortunately, he would realize too late that he had to rewrite all his earlier work to make it conform to its projected perfection. *The Silver Stallion* (1926) continued the high level of Cabell's best writing, but *Something About Eve* (1927) displays a lack of control about which Cabell temporizes in the preface. Its failure ironically exemplifies its theme: the failure of the poet to attain that perfection which he envisions in Antan. Then Cabell devoted three years to the crushing task of trying to make all his literary output conform to the outline of a truly unified epic. The Storisende Edition (1927–1930) proved the reverse.[6] His prefaces spoke bravely of its planned order, but Cabell knew better. He had been bound to a dream impossible to attain. At the end of *Figures of Earth*, Manuel had symbolically killed Suskind (Gabriella). Now he would have to kill the author of the Storisende Edition. He announced the demise of James Branch Cabell and wrote under the name of Branch Cabell for the next sixteen years. But having killed the lover of Gabriella Moncure, he appeared to have lost his direction. Branch Cabell was a bitter, ironic commentator.

For Gabriella Moncure too the years spent in Williamsburg with young James Cabell were doubtless a sweet-scented April twilight. Time was an irreversible distance. She had a bush social life on the army bases where her uncle was stationed. She was called Gabrielle, rhyming with *villanelle*, rather than by her schoolgirl Gabriella. With World War I, General McCaw, then Assistant-Surgeon A.M.C., acquired a house on Nineteenth Street in Washington, and Gabrielle began to spend her summers in Woodstock, New York, congenial for its mountain freshness and its artists' colony. She bought a house there, and when General McCaw retired, they made it their permanent home. Her brother William, also a career army officer, brought his family to live close by. She was fond of her nephews, she liked cats. Her young sister-in-law found her generous-natured and a sparkling conversationalist. With age, Gabrielle's wit became a little sharper, but her words were softened with a wry smile and an understanding gaze. When she died on June 6, 1955, she was buried according to her wishes in the Artist's Cemetery in Woodstock.

In *Let Me Lie* (1947) James Cabell accepted his Virginia heritage and returned from his self-imposed exile, exchanging places with Branch

6. See Edgar E. MacDonald, "The Storisende Edition: Some Liabilities," *Cabellian*, I (1969), 64–67.

Cabell. The following year saw three previously published stories appear as *The Witch-Woman: A Trilogy About Her*. Ettarre the elusive continued to trouble an aging Cabell with her haunting music. Widowed and remarried to a competent, no-nonsense second wife, Cabell wrote an affectionate appreciation of Priscilla Bradley Cabell, his first wife. "She meant more to me than did all the books in the world," he concluded in *As I Remember It* (1955). A grieving and remorseful husband wrote those lines. Bettie Hamlyn, Mélusine, Marie-Claire, Ettarre smiled with compassion, but when these lines appeared in print, Gabrielle was dead, and Cabell had written his last book.

# CABELL AND HOLT
## *The Literary Connection*

### Dorothy McInnis Scura

James Branch Cabell's most important literary relationship—both personal and professional—was with Guy Holt, his editor at Robert M. McBride and Company from 1915 to 1926. Cabell generously acknowledged his affection and his debt to Holt, privately calling Holt "the pearl of my collaborators." In print he characterized Holt as "the most staunch and most beneficent of all my literary friendships" and termed his indebtedness to Holt "paramount." When Holt left McBride to join the John Day Company, Cabell wrote him that "After eleven years, I felt so utterly at sea as to be almost seasick." Seven years later Cabell still missed Holt's aid, and he wrote his former editor, "I lament the old ideal arrangement of sensible criticism during the progress of writing." And Cabell continued to miss Holt. Early in his working relationship with his editor John Farrar, Cabell wrote Farrar (in 1938) that after working with Guy Holt, "I cannot possibly be wounded by any editorial suggestions, howsoever acerb, toward a book's betterment. . . . I want an unmealy editor."[1]

The public record of the Cabell-Holt relationship is found in many places. Cabell dedicated *Beyond Life* and *Preface to the Past* to Holt, wrote about him in the prefaces to *The Cream of the Jest* and *Beyond Life*, and

1. Cabell to Guy Holt, December 3, 1917, in Barrett Collection, Alderman Library, University of Virginia, Charlottesville; James Branch Cabell, "Author's Note," *The Cream of the Jest: The Lineage of Lichfield*, Storisende Edition, XVI (New York: Robert M. McBride, 1930), xiv; James Branch Cabell, *Preface to the Past* (New York: Robert M. McBride, 1936), 15; Cabell to Holt, April 3, 1926, April 12, 1933, Cabell to John Farrar, May 22, 1938, all in Edward Wagenknecht (ed.), *The Letters of James Branch Cabell* (Norman: University of Oklahoma Press, 1975), 181.

included in his last book, *As I Remember It*, a warm tribute to his former editor. Holt wrote an introduction to *Beyond Life* and *Jurgen and the Law* (1923) and edited *A Bibliography of the Writings of James Branch Cabell* (1924). If the public record establishes the fact of Holt's relationship with Cabell, the private record left in their letters reveals the quality and content of that relationship.

Cabell was thirty-six years old in April of 1915 when he visited the editorial offices of Robert M. McBride and Company on Sixteenth Street in New York City. He brought with him four manuscripts: *The Rivet in Grandfather's Neck, The Certain Hour, From the Hidden Way,* and *In the Flesh* (early title of *The Cream of the Jest*). The editor Cabell met was twenty-three-year-old Guy Holt. Born in Boston, Holt had attended public schools in New York City and then Columbia College. He entered the publishing business at seventeen with Doubleday, Page and Company. After five years with that house, he edited two magazines, first *Lippincott's* and then *McBride's*. He was in charge of the book, editorial, and sales departments at McBride's from 1917 to 1926.

Cabell later explained that at first meeting he and Holt "took to each other at once."[2] Separated by geography and age, each of the men had been a wunderkind—Cabell teaching undergraduate Greek and French at age seventeen at William and Mary, Holt entering the publishing business at the same age. Yet their temperaments were contrasting. Cabell led a quiet life of authorship and contemplation in Richmond, while Holt was a pragmatic, active man who understood "the whole Art of the Book" from composition to manufacture, promotion, and distribution. Too, Holt possessed an instinctive sensitivity to literature as well as editorial talent, critical and creative. He was described in a high tribute as having the faculty for never "mistaking literature for merchandise, or the even more common publisher's error of mistaking merchandise for literature."[3] The intelligent, sensitive, and energetic Holt was just the editor the obscure Virginia writer needed. Their mutual love of writing gave them common ground for a profound relationship, but their differences made them a compatible team.

When Cabell and Holt met, Cabell was the author of six published, but little-noticed, books: *The Eagle's Shadow* (1904), *The Line of Love* (1905), *Gallantry* (1907), *The Cords of Vanity* (1909), *Chivalry* (1909), and *The Soul*

---

2. James Branch Cabell, *As I Remember It* (New York: Robert M. McBride, 1955), 184.

3. B. R. R., "Guy Holt: January 18, 1892–April 21, 1934," *Saturday Review of Literature*, XIX (May 5, 1934), 676.

*of Melicent* (1913). During the next eleven years of their professional relationship, Cabell experienced the most creative and productive period
of his literary life—publishing eleven books, rewriting the six earlier ones,
shaping his work into the eighteen-volume Storisende Edition, becoming
internationally known with the publication and suppression and vindica-
tion of *Jurgen*, and making literary friends with the best-known writers of
the period. The more than 275 surviving letters of the Holt-Cabell correspondence document the story of those eleven years.[4]

The supremely hardworking, efficient, and conscientious Holt did all
those things an editor is supposed to do. He responded to manuscripts,
made suggestions for revision, worked out contracts, wrote advertising
copy for Cabell's books, helped design the layout, marketed the books,
traveled over the United States selling Cabell to booksellers, worried over
dealings with foreign publishers, sent royalty statements, and tried to sell
movie rights to *Jurgen*. The list of his services is long and the kinds of
services various. He soothed the author when he was irritable, buoyed
him when he needed support, and, in general, dealt with him with all the
polished skills of a diplomat while working like a tiger to promote him.

But it is not really these palpable chores Holt performed for Cabell
that make the relationship so interesting and significant to Cabell's career; it is rather the impact Holt had on Cabell's writing, an impact that
shaped the work itself for over a decade. Holt read Cabell's material,
understood it, absorbed it, and debated with him about it, responding
critically and specifically to the form and content of the writing. Thus he
became Cabell's most sensitive and perceptive reader and critic. The great
increase in the quantity and quality of Cabell's work along with the mak-

4. Part of the Holt-Cabell correspondence between 1916 and 1922 was published in
Padraic Colum and Margaret Freeman Cabell (eds.), *Between Friends: Letters of James
Branch Cabell and Others* (New York: Harcourt, Brace & World, 1962). Seventy-one of
Cabell's letters to Holt were included in Wagenknecht (ed.), *The Letters of James Branch
Cabell*. Letters used for this essay are cited by date and unless noted otherwise are found
in the Barrett Collection, Alderman Library, University of Virginia, Charlottesville. These
letters from the Holt estate include 192 originals of Cabell's letters to Holt and 78
carbons of Holt's letters to Cabell. In addition, there are 8 original Holt letters to Cabell
in Special Collections, James Branch Cabell Library, Virginia Commonwealth University, Richmond. These letters were found folded into books in Cabell's personal library.
Although I have located approximately 278 letters exchanged between Holt and
Cabell, there are two problems. First, many Holt letters are obviously missing. Most
important, I have worked from Holt carbons since I have not been able to locate the
originals of most of Holt's correspondence with Cabell.
Cabell routinely used ellipses in his letters. Unless otherwise noted, Cabell's ellipses
have been removed so that ellipsis points indicate that material has been left out.

ing of his reputation as a writer happened concurrently with his close relationship with Holt and was indeed caused, to a great extent, by that relationship.

Although the Holt-Cabell correspondence extends from 1915 to 1933, the letters exchanged in the first four years reveal the nature of the relationship. Cabell is briefly introduced to working with Holt during the revision of a book of poetry, *From the Hidden Way*, in 1916. The full pattern of the working relationship is set with *The Cream of the Jest* (1917), but it is in the making of *Beyond Life* (1919) that Holt and Cabell develop their most intimate connection. Holt inspired Cabell to write a book of essays delineating his "aesthetic creed," worked with Cabell on the manuscript, and contributed part of the text of the last chapter. After *Beyond Life*, Holt continued to work with Cabell, their connection becoming a public matter during the *Jurgen* controversy, and the editor-author relationship survived until 1926 when Holt left McBride to join the John Day Company. Cabell stayed with McBride but did contribute *The Music from Behind the Moon* (1926) to Day's first season's list. Their professional connection ended in 1926, but their friendship continued until Holt's sudden death on April 21, 1934, at age forty-two, of a heart attack. Their last surviving contact is the inscription Cabell wrote in a copy of *Smirt*: "For Guy Holt—inasmuch as we cannot think of a new sentiment, with all the old ones unaltered. Branch Cabell and James Branch Cabell. 26 February 1934."

Their letters show that the collaboration between author and editor began with *From the Hidden Way*. In a letter dated April 19, 1916, Cabell expresses his pleasure that McBride has accepted "the verses" for publication, and he responds agreeably to Holt's suggestions. He will limit "the number of the ostensibly translated [verses]," revise "the Introduction along the lines suggested," English the Latin titles ("to avoid the possibility of yet again offending the over-susceptible illiterate by betraying our superiority"), "look into the matter" of the meters, and remove "a few unnecessary archaisms—such as 'of yore' and 'anon.'" Cabell praises Holt's criticisms calling them "sensible" and asks the editor to send any others that occur to him. Later Cabell would describe *From the Hidden Way* as the favorite among his books "for reasons utterly unliterary." Perhaps part of this lasting affection is due to its having initiated his editorial relationship with Holt.[5]

5. James Branch Cabell, preface to Guy Holt (ed.), *A Bibliography of the Writings of James Branch Cabell* (Philadelphia: Centaur Book Shop, 1924). See Edgar E. Mac-

Although *From the Hidden Way* received attention from Holt, this book of verse as well as the novel and collection of tales published by McBride, *The Rivet in Grandfather's Neck* (1915) and *The Certain Hour* (1916), were not literary successes. Cabell explained later that all three books "failed forthwith and utterly."[6] Pleasantly (but not profitably) introduced to Holt's editorial response to *From the Hidden Way*, Cabell would with his next book, *The Cream of the Jest*, begin the full-scale relationship that prevailed for the next decade in his dealings with Holt.

The Cabell-Holt letters on the subject of *The Cream of the Jest* reveal the outline of the activity. Cabell submits a manuscript with his own positive opinion ("I think it far and away my best work." December 20, 1916) and asks for Holt's response ("I would appreciate and heed any and all admonition short of advice to burn the manuscript"). Holt then details his criticism of the work ("Now, pray, permit me to carp." January 3, 1917). Cabell makes revisions based on some suggestions and argues about others ("For I approve of almost all your fault finding." January 7, 1917). During the publishing process Cabell is writing a new book which he frequently mentions to Holt ("The essays [of *Beyond Life*] go on nicely." June 9, 1917). After the manuscript is completed, Cabell makes suggestions on format ("We must see to it, though, that the Cream comes to some three hundred pages or more, in a neat chocolate binding." April 16, 1917), reviews ("And the number of reviews thus far received has been appallingly small and featureless." November 3, 1917), publicity ("I distinctly did not like the Vanity Fair advertisement." November 10, 1917), sales ("The accounts, however, do not after all tell the main thing I wanted to know, which is how many copies of the Jest, approximately, have been sold thus far." January 5, 1918), and royalties ("I shall look with renewed interest for a royalty statement." April 27, 1918).

Many years later Cabell wrote about the period of his literary life when he was seeing *The Cream of the Jest* through publication.[7] He explained that the novel, at one time entitled *In the Flesh*, had been rejected by more than thirteen publishers when he submitted it for the second time to McBride. Finally accepted in April of 1917, this book according to Cabell, "became the most potent of all my books in its influence upon my career as a writer." He explained that "as a marketable product" *The Cream of the*

---

Donald's "Cabell in Love" in this volume for another reason for Cabell's affection for *From the Hidden Way*.

6. Cabell, "Author's Note," *The Cream of the Jest*, xvi.

7. *Ibid.*, xvi, xx.

*Jest* "fell wholly flat." But the book attracted the attention of Burton Rascoe, Sinclair Lewis, Joseph Hergesheimer, and H. L. Mencken. Thus, because of this book Cabell made the "warm friends" who would play an important part in his literary life. So, not only did this book set the pattern for Holt-Cabell "collaboration," it also marked a significant turning point in Cabell's career.

Holt's criticism of the manuscript of *The Cream of the Jest* is detailed in two letters written in January of 1917. These letters reveal Holt's careful reading as well as the kinds of revision he thought would improve Cabell's work. Although he liked the book, Holt wanted Cabell to remove some of the Cabellian cuteness from the manuscript. His comments are frank:

January 3, 1917

My dear Cabell,—

You pay me a poor compliment when you assume that I do not like the "Cream of the Jest," nor do you encourage me in the occasional fits of reticence to which I like to believe I am prone. I know, indeed, that it is impossible for you to conceive me as hesitating to give an opinion about a subject for the mere reason that I am ill informed on it, but such happens to be the case in this instance at least.

When I wrote you I had merely skimmed through the manuscript, reading the first two books and the last three or four chapters and dipping into the rest. I had omitted entirely the philosophical parts, not intentionally, however.

Now I can say I have read it all. And I like it. Greatly! You are right, I believe, in saying that it is the best thing you have done—at least in part—and you will pardon me if I venture to accuse you of being "vital," despite yourself. For this book, however tricked out with fantasticality, is of the very blood and bones of life. It states your problem—and mine, and everyone's—and that it proposes no answer can never be cause for criticism by sensible people. Anyway, Euclid is the only literary man who solved the problems he propounded—and he exhausted his subject.

Kennaston's nocturnal adventures I think are very beautiful. They have the teasing incompleteness of dreams themselves. I think I like them better because they do not satisfy.

But it is the depiction of Kennaston himself that you have outstripped (and stripped, perhaps) yourself. He is finely done and he has blood in him!

So much in rebuttal. Now, pray, permit me to carp in my turn. First then, a minor criticism or two: I am a bit afraid of the composite authorship. Harrowby does not, as I see it, need your intervention—and could easily be made the purely fictional character he seems, despite you, to be. This is, in a lesser sense, true of Kennaston. Those references to Froser's biography, and the occasional footnotes—I wonder if they are worth the loss of interest they might occasion. To me the book is too big to need them, and although I fancy that I see why you might wish to make him seem an actual character, I do not see how you can do it. He is—to paraphrase an idea of your own—too true to be real.

There are minor matters, as I say. Chapter II. The first paragraph is somewhat obscure, I think. If Harrowby were to preface it with more than an apology for "beginning it in his own way"—even if he offered the hackneyed invitation to "picture" or "imagine" the setting for the scene—the transition from today to the time that never was might well seem less abrupt and be less confusing.

Then, again, on page forty-five, at the end of the first paragraph, Harrowby speaks as a detractor of literature. He writes too well to do that, nor does it necessarily harmonize with his character of amateur occultist.

My principal quarrel with you, however, is occasioned by Chapter V [Chapter XII of the Storisende Edition]. Your parodies of publishers' names, and worse still, of the best-sellers of yesterday, as well as of their authors! I cannot believe that you intended them for other than the amusement of publishers' readers. And yet I must run the risk of assuming that they are an integral part of the book, and suggest that you rewrite the chapter identifying—if you wish—publishers, authors and books by their characteristics, and using for them whatever names you must, such as do not partake of the qualities either of spoonerisms or rather abortive echoes. And perhaps one letter of rejection would be enough to quote.

I think, too, that the conversation of Messrs. [Theodore] Roosevelt, et al. might well be reduced to a mere suggestion, somewhat after the manner of the banquet scene in "La Peau de Chagrin" (I believe that is the book, but it is one of Balzac's), where by fragmentary bursts of talk the reader may deduce babel. You may remember it, and probably know what I mean. As it stands, the chapter reads not unlike an excerpt from Don Marquis' "Hermione" to which I commend your disapproving attention.

This, I believe, is all I have to make in the way of criticism. I should be tempted to apologize for the heat of my comments were it not that I really detest those two chapters [Chapters XII and XIV of the Storisende Edition] heartily, and I fear they might prove excellent obstacles to other folks' admiration. And besides—you gave me this box of matches and might reasonably expect a blaze of some sort. . . .

I have emptied my bag now. I shall in due course and after securing your permission offer the book to McBride's. I spoke of it yesterday to one of the editors of the CENTURY, but their custom is to consider no serial without book rights. Perhaps the ATLANTIC MONTHLY—what do you think? . . .

Faithfully yours,
Guy Holt

On January 7, Cabell responds cheerfully to Holt's suggestions. He is willing to make some changes—get rid of the composite authorship and of the footnotes—but he balks at omitting Froser's biography. He will rewrite the White House luncheon scene, but he does not understand Holt's objections to the publishing chapter:

My dear Holt:—

It is rarely I get a more interesting letter than your last, nor, upon the whole, one that gives me greater pleasure. I am—and, indeed, have long known myself to be—very deeply your debtor.

My main end in the complete revision I gave the book last summer was to make Kennaston an individual and real person. Previously the tale was all dreamland. So I tried, leaving his head in the clouds, to get his feet firm set on earth. If I have done that, I am content. He is, of course, rather loathsome. Some reviewer will probably be discovering some day that he lacks the tonic uplift of Pollyanna and Mrs. Wiggs et als.

Meanwhile—do you think there is any real chance of getting the book serialized? Nothing would more delight me. Other matters apart, it would mean getting some actual money for writing a book, and I have always had a liking for novel experiences.

And if, as I understand it, things are fairly safe in Union Square for another year, you may regard the book as formally submitted to McBride's for publication in the spring. And at all events, make Mr. Anderson free of its contents with my heartiest compliments. And if he finds time beg him also to criticize and suggest.

For I approve of almost all your fault finding. The composite authorship is bungling, though far from purposeless. Suppose, though, the introductory note by me were omitted, and the present first chapter just as it stands put in place thereof, and the book proper begun with "The tale tells how Duke Florestan, &c." That would, roughly, enable me still to begin on the modern key—as I quite surely ought to—and spare us the trouble of getting to Storisende, by the simple process of beginning there. To the transition from Storisende to Lichfield, at the start of Book Second, I would vaingloriously call your attention, as being in my opinion not at all badly managed. And we will remove all the foot notes at one sweep, some to oblivion and others to the text proper. Mr. Froser's Biography, I think, may remain without arousing undue worriment—or, at a pinch, the reader can be referred to a little-known masterpiece entitled The Eagle's Shadow. And Harrowby's assertion that fiddling with pen and ink is no fit employment for a grown man, can—and should—be softened to just that dreary suspicion common to all writers once in a while that such may be the case. In fine, it should not be advanced as a belief, but as a doubt which occasionally arises.

I understand your objection to the White House Luncheon—though it comes ill from you, who warned me against making my dialogue unnaturally clever. Secure in the knowledge of that chapter's existence, I smiled, sir, as you talked. Now, the table-talk is, almost, a transcript from what they actually said, but, just as my friend Kennaston suspected, it displays no startling originality of thought. My notion, then, would be to remove most of it, and break the remainder into very short paragraphs, to cover not over two book pages at most, and to allure the eye onward by the light look of it. Is that not what you mean? You see, this platitudinous talk has a quite definite place in the book's scheme, echoed in the dream at Vaux-le-Vicomte and in the call the Kennastons pay the Harrowbys, and duly summed up in the book's peroration. It must be indicated, and indicated as the dull twaddle it is.

Now, as to the publishing chapter, I do not understand. The publishers' letters, if they make too tedious reading, can be summed up in a paragraph to the effect that they all praised the novel as literature and as, therefore, of no conceivable appeal to the public that buys books. The publishers could with equal point be called Brown, Jones & Smith, of course—but what is the objection to the present jumble, which suggests all publishers indefinitely? I don't follow you at all. And the puns on the best sellers and their authors likewise can be altered: the point is, to suggest what sort of books were being avidly seized on at this exact time, and this the puns do actually indicate. These puns, I must modestly point out, are themselves a species of literary criticism. Or do you mean that they sound vicious? or that this material would not interest persons outside of the bookmaking business? In fine, suppose you alter that chapter yourself, and let me see specifically what you do mean. I am agreeable to any arrangement which preserves the essential points of the chapter. And—well, I believe that is about all.

So, as I said before, let us consider first the chance, if any, of serializing the book. In this matter I would like to have you act as my agent, on the customary ten per cent basis. And also you can duly submit the book to McBride. And so soon as I hear from you a bit more definitely I can rewrite the two offending chapters. . . .

Yours faithfully,
James Branch Cabell

Holt responds to Cabell on January 12, 1917, and outlines his criticism of the two chapters which he finds too topical and vicious:

My dear Cabell:—

This letter must in a large way be a recapitulation of my note to you of the other day of which unfortunately I have no copy. I am assuming that you are more careful in these matters than I and that you have a copy of your letter of the 7th inst. So pardon me if I refer to paragraphs one and two, etc. of that letter and let me know if you have not a copy of it, so that I may be more definite.

I do think that there is a limited chance of serializing "The Cream of the Jest" and as I wrote you, I shall at once set about trying the Atlantic Monthly with it. Or rather I shall tell them about the story, trusting to have a revision of the offending chapters in a sufficiently short time for me to submit a comparatively final manuscript to them. And in due course the book will be submitted to those of us here who have not yet read it, i.e., Mr. Allen and Mr. McBride. Mr. Anderson has read it and admires it immensely. As to criticism—he feels that excepting chapters five and seven of Book II and such trifling matters as you and I have already discussed, the book needs no changes.

Now as to those proposed changes. I believe that your suggestions as to the omission of your introductory note and the substitution of chapter one for it, leaving chapter two to begin the book proper, would solve all preliminary difficulties and would enable you to begin the book as you wish. The deftness of your transition from Storisende to Lichfield had not escaped my attention or my admiration. Your other suggestions in that paragraph of your letter will, I think, admirably dispel whatever small objections the over-captious reader might offer.

Paragraph six of your letter: I must defend myself against your accusations. My warning against unnaturally clever dialogue was directed toward those extremely ingenious circumlocutions which many of your characters have indulged themselves in in times past. I did indeed urge a slight dulling of the wit in some instances but as to twaddle—no. I may speak and write it but I cannot stomach it. Note also that there is a vast difference between the twaddle talked at the White House and the unalluring commonplaces of the Harrowby-Kennaston visit or the chatter of Vaux-le-Vicomte. The White House conversation is the only one of the three which needs the eraser. As to improving it, your suggestion shows that you have caught my idea exactly. It would be advisable, however, to soften the portraits of these gentlemen a trifle. Morgan's nose, for instance, could be trimmed down to normal size and perhaps the entire scene would gain, if the characters were made a little less definitely recognizable.

You see I feel that in both this chapter and the publishing one you have approached what is known in vaudeville as "the topical" too closely.

In a sense you limit your interest to conditions that are temporary and of no permanent importance. And by so doing you run the risk of seriously hurting the rest of the book, one of whose merits is that it is in no sense momentary. I don't know whether I make myself clear or not. I have an idea but it is very difficult to express.

Now let me see if I can explain my exact objections to the publishing chapter. First, then, the publishers' letters. I think they could be summed up in the paragraph you suggest, although it might do no harm to quote one or two letters. The publishers' names are unsatisfactory again chiefly because of their purely contemporary interest. I have a notion that too great a particularity in non-essentials is likely to seem out of place very shortly. For instance, if you ever happen to read in a novel of ten or fifteen years ago a reference to some old song which was never dignified and has long been forgotten, you are likely to become confused and perhaps a little irritated. I know that I am. And I suppose that my objection to the parodies of publishers' names as well as those of authors and novels is rooted in this same unreasoning distaste. I do know that distaste exists and both Anderson and Allen, who read that particular chapter, have expressed the same feeling about it. And perhaps, too, these parodies do sound a bit vicious.

At any rate since you do not object to changing them why not revise the chapter this way:

Change the names of the publishers to something not so colorless as Brown, Jones and Smith are, nor quite so recognizable as they exist at present and without any suggestion of the comic in them. In a word name them as you would any of your characters. "Dappley," for instance, might be a happy medium between "Dappleton" and "Jones." The Centennial Company would perhaps not be impermissible, although the Contemporary Company might be better, and so on.

As to the names of the novels can you not paraphrase them in some other way? "The Inside of the Cup" could be suggested better by an association of ideas than an association of sound, particularly when the latter association has a farcical quality that is not at all consistent with the dignity of the rest of your book. In other words, can you not make these titles just exactly the same sort of thing that every publisher advertises every year, allowing them, however, sufficient resemblance to the original so that they could be recognized by the initiated. Your description of their contents could, of course, stand, particularly that of our friend, Thomas Dixon. The conduct of the "Holton-Harpury Company" in regard to "Kennaston's" book could be left practically untouched, changing only Fluffily Formal's "The Highbrow Way" and the other books mentioned in that particular section.

On page 60 The New York Times need hardly be indicated definitely and on page 61 the reference to the Castles and to the Mutt and Jeff series could be either omitted or considerably changed. I should prefer the former course, because I believe that the kind of success which a book like "The Man Who Loved Alison" would achieve would be very unlikely to occasion this particular evidence of popularity. And, since you are praising him, why not call Booth Tarkington by his right name and mention his books? There I think the description of affairs beginning "But presently Mrs. Gelatine Gin" could be omitted or altered to a mere reference to the changes in public taste, leading up to the conclusion that Kennaston's romance was forgotten, etc. And so we are at the end of the chapter.

I would remind you, however, in answer to your statement that you wish to indicate what sort of books were being avidly seized upon at this exact time, that the books you mention were published over a period of twenty-five years which give the parodies, especially in the paragraph which I have just commented upon, less occasion for existence. And the Castles and Monsieur Beaucaire were not contemporary.

All these comments are obiter dicta and you are under no compulsion to take them for more than they are worth. They represent, however, the opinion of Anderson as well as myself and are thus entitled to your double consideration. I fear I have badly bungled my suggestions and can only hope that your ready discernment will find in them something worthy of your attention at least and that I shall soon receive revisions of those two chapters. At any rate let me know whether I have made myself clear.

> Faithfully yours,
> [Guy Holt]

Cabell agrees to rewrite the "two offending chapters" (January 15, 1917) and returns the manuscript to Holt (April 16, 1917) with a request: "Let me know if anything still impresses you as unsatisfactory." Cabell explains that he has "'linked'" *The Cream of the Jest* with his other books with "Balzacian thoroughness." Then, on June 23, Cabell mails Holt the "final revision of the Jest." As the novel moves through the publishing process, Cabell continues to write Holt about the book—urging him to promote and advertise it (October 3, 1917), complaining about the lack of reviews (November 10, 1917), and finally expressing pleasure at the good reviews by Lewis Galantiere, Hans Hertzberg, and H. L. Mencken (December 3, 1917). In this last letter Cabell explains that his joy over the reviews is tempered by the lateness of his royalty statement: "Still, our pecuniary parsnips remain unbuttered, and the whole thing is infernally disheartening."

But Cabell was more than heartened by the reception of *The Cream of the Jest*. Not only was he getting good reviews, but Sinclair Lewis, who had turned the book down as an editor at George H. Doran Company, wrote him a letter praising the book. And he was exhilarated by the experience of working with his indefatigable editor who took an interest in all stages of the book publication. While discussing the promotion for *The Cream of the Jest*, Cabell had written Holt, "Yesterday in cleaning out my desk I ran across the first notes for the Cream, which rather startled me by their divergence from the finished product" (June 9, 1917). Part of that "divergence" was due to Holt's criticism. Indeed, Cabell's discussions with Holt had precipitated the text of *Beyond Life*, on which he had been working for some time. In announcing the book for which he had "invented a new essay-form," Cabell told Holt that he would "elucidate my aesthetic creed—being persuaded by you and Mr. Follett et als that I have one" (May 26, 1917). Two decades later in *Preface to the Past* Cabell explained Holt's part in generating the ideas for *Beyond Life*: "A large deal of this book was stumbled upon in talk with him, during the first four years or so that this the most cordial and efficient of friends, and the most helpful of literary editors whom any author has ever had, was quite fruitlessly attempting to sell my books."[8]

While Holt is attempting to sell *The Cream of the Jest*, Cabell is writing to him about the new book. Two weeks after his first announcement of *Beyond Life* Cabell writes about his progress:

> The essays go on nicely. . . . You see, I was in Fairhaven recently, and of course called on John Charteris. I spoke to him of your rebuttal, in fact, read it to him, and he replied at considerable length. He is better qualified than I to speak on literary topics, because he has access to all the books of Bookland,—such as all the novels of Arthur Pendennis, a library set of David Copperfield's works, a copy of Beltraffio, and any number of other such masterpieces. And of course he has all the books that were never written—the complete Weir of Hermiston, and Denis Duval, and so on,—as well as the dream-version of every published book, including all the books I meant to write. . . . So he replied from the dream-versions of my books—these being my real masterpieces—and spoke for, precisely, ten hours. . . . I enjoyed it not a little, for he proved my theories were entirely correct. So far we have reached two A.M., but he is to talk until dawn. . . . So in this too we are to collaborate, at your convenience, I hope.[9]

Six weeks later Cabell is "polishing off my Dizain des Ecritures," and he has finished everything but the first chapter in this "interpretative criti-

---

8. Cabell, *Preface to the Past*, 23–24.
9. Cabell to Holt, June 9, 1917. Ellipses are Cabell's.

cism of my own books" (July 25, 1917). Then, on September 20, 1917, Cabell announces that he is sending Holt "a remarkable production." He confirms how much Holt has had to do with the making of this book: "I found, as I think you too will find, that the entire discourse is written at you, in a quite personal way, so that I in particular want your opinion thereupon."

For the next three months Cabell continues to mention *Beyond Life* to Holt. He suggests that the manuscript has "probably irritated you" (October 3, 1917), offers to revise it and asks if it is publishable (November 3, 1917), and then proposes that Holt "refute the whole thing" for "an ante-penultimate chapter" (December 3, 1917). With this last suggestion Cabell offers to "dedicate the book" to Holt and send his name "thundering down the ages."

Holt's responses to *Beyond Life* are found in three documents—an outline made after his first reading and two letters. Important because they depict the critical debate engaged in with Cabell, they reveal the substance of Holt's advice to Cabell. Too, material from the letters was incorporated into the text of the published book.

The outline response drafted just after Holt read *Beyond Life* for the first time was written on hotel stationery from Springfield, Massachusetts. Holt mailed this outline some months later to Cabell, on April 13, 1918, with a note explaining that "It may amuse you." It shows Holt attempting to respond to the book in a parody of the book itself:

*Beyond Words*
Dizain des Impertinences
by
Guy Holt

|       |                                                              |
|-------|--------------------------------------------------------------|
| I.    | Introducing the Ageless Fallacy                              |
| II.   | Upon the advantages of ignorance                             |
| III.  | Life at twenty-five—and some of its literary "reactions"     |
| IV.   | Decline of the demi-urge                                     |
| V.    | The Moderns (What they are doing.)                           |
| VI.   | The Romantic Principle in Realism                            |
| VII.  | "The Discovery of the Commonplace"                           |
| VIII. | The Case against James Branch Cabell                         |
| IX.   | The Case for James Branch Cabell                             |
| X.    | Epilogue[10]                                                 |

10. Holt began to fill in the outline, but abandoned the plan very soon. Here are his notes:

   I. i.e.: That it is worth while dividing Romance from realism and imputing to either the sole possession of the virtues.

In a rambling letter (undated, but probably late December, 1917), Holt develops some of the ideas suggested in his early notes. He argues that Cabell himself has explained that the purpose of the romance is "cheerfully to misrepresent life." And since Cabell "cannot keep up the romantic pretense with any convincing show of sincerity, why not openly join us of the other side." Holt argues that Dreiser does not write "badly because he is a meticulous chronicler of facts," but because he has "an untidy mind and no sense of beauty of any degree, save that most primitive form which recognizes the awful virtue of bigness." He argues that "all of us are living exemplifications of a compromise between the romantic dream and the realistic facts" and that "this compromise is truth and humanity." Holt is arguing against the "ageless fallacy" that true art is exclusively romantic or realistic; he urges Cabell "to pay this much lip-service to commerce and write of ageless men who live nowadays." He reminds Cabell "that treacle served in a silver goblet is treacle, for a' that. Give us wine, sir. God knows we need it—and you have some heady stuff in your bottle."[11] After this general discussion of art, Holt focuses on the text of *Beyond Life*.

He rejects Cabell's idea of incorporating Holt's comments in the book; the idea "dismays" him for "it destroys a pet scheme of my own for making *Beyond Life* more publishable and possibly more saleable." Holt wants "to eliminate James Branch Cabell from the text entirely," as well as references to Cabell's other books. "And, on the whole," Holt explains, "you lose only the pleasure of writing more openly about yourself than otherwise you could, a chapter-heading, and acquire a somewhat altered introduction." Holt proposes "complete anonymity for you—even upon the covers; certainly between them." He offers strong motivation for Cabell to do this, for Cabell may lose the "approximation of your Intended Edition," but he will "gain a publisher," "a public," and "a more unified book."

---

  b. That any author really knows his own characters.
  c. That there is any real conflict between form and content.
  d. That a good writer is always unpopular.
 II. ?
III. What the twenty-eth century reads & thinks. What it believes it knows. Skepticism and the pragmatic trend of literature. The art for art's sake doctrine—and what people really think of it.
   Pessimism must turn to falsehood—bravery may face truth with a high heart. What we desiderate in literature.

11. In a letter dated January 9, 1918, Cabell seems to be responding to this suggestion: "Romance, sir, furnishes the proper service; its silver was mined in the moon (by lunatics, of course) and its napery is woven of dreamstuff."

Another practical suggestion offered to Cabell is to make the chapters separate essays so they can be published in a magazine prior to book publication.

Then, Holt closes this letter with a passage that—slightly rewritten—would find permanent life in the tenth chapter of *Beyond Life*: "Do you let me know how these suggestions seem to you; and bear with me while I commiserate with you upon your monstrous pessimism. I had thought this was the province of youth, to view God and man with a doleful eye. But here am I upon the verge of twenty-six and with the wisdom of my generation quick within me, looking sadly down upon you from the rosy heights. You are all of a dozen years older than I and should of right be putting Pollyanna to blush, by this."[12] This letter was followed on January 5, 1918, by a formal rebuttal to Cabell's ideas as expressed in the manuscript of *Beyond Life*. This rebuttal was preserved by Cabell in the pages of a copy of *Beyond Life* in his library. Written in Cabell's hand on top of the letter is a note: "This letter from Guy Holt was thriftily incorporated into the tenth chapter of Beyond Life." Cabell, ever the ironist, cannibalized Holt's views and put them in the mouth of Cabell himself in the last chapter of the book. Since much of the material is incorporated into Cabell's argument with John Charteris, the letter is interesting to study in full:

My Dear Cabell:

Almost my last official act of the year just past was to send you with more apologies than were evident a statement and a check. My first essay with pencil and paper this year was an attempt finally to set forth the celebrated rebuttal of your artistic creed—and performances. That it does not go to you until today is due partly to my own occupation elsewhere and partly to a natural hesitancy to inflict the tortures of boredom upon you with my ineffectual comments—even though the subject be interesting to you.

However, you asked for it and so here goes. I shall say in my own defense merely that you have so successfully used your own inconsistency that any remark of mine will come as a feeble repetition of something already better stated in this book by you. I realize this and it has

12. Here is the passage in the opening of Part 4 of Chapter 10 of *Beyond Life*: "— My dear Charteris, I really must in passing congratulate you upon your retention of youth. I had thought it the peculiar privilege of immaturity to view mankind and God with doleful eyes. But here am I, quick with the wisdom of my generation, compelled to shout denial of your doctrines from comparatively roseate heights, for all that you are by some twenty-two years my senior, and your opinions ought in consequence to be already gilded by a setting sun. Instead, you appraise earth in the dumps."

made me the more timid when I read over what I wrote on Tuesday. Yet it is consoling to recognize one's inadequacies, and I therefore leave what follows very much as it was first written, knowing that, even did time permit, I could not much mitigate its awkwardness or dullness.

So much by way of apology. As for you, sir, I shall say at the outset that not in a long time have I read so fascinating, so ingenious and withal so sincere a book as "Beyond Life." It is an apology for romance by a man who believes that romance is dead beyond resurrection, and who knows therefor that it is perfectly safe to lament it. It is a tissue of delightful misconceptions—the more delightful because intentional—and has so blandly honest an air that I protest, upon my first reading I was entirely taken in by it and really fancied its author sitting in honest grief over the lost youth of the world. And the style of it! Greek sentences or no, here is limpid clearness, where often before has been a whirlpool of subtleties and circumlocutions. I have often got pictures from your sentences before this; but too frequently they were not of what the words described, but of the careful lapidary who shaped and polished those phrases, and who, I think, too frequently sacrificed transparency for lustre. But in this book you wear simplicity with an astounding grace. (Here, by the way, is a tangle of metaphors.)

But, that aside, let me consider soberly this conceit of yours. At the outset, of course, I must protest that you have been shamefully unfair with realism throughout; for however pleasingly you have defined Romance—by implication, at least—Realism remains indeterminate to the very end of the book. Indeed, your method seems to be thus: Romance in literature is that method, governed by that viewpoint, in which all virtue lies; Realism is precisely the reverse. To your reader you leave the completion of this imperfect syllogism. Now that is an excellent way to convince the unwary; it is, on the other hand a poor method of discovering truth. Yet, I confess, you do it so plausibly that you almost convinced me that what you spoke was sober verity; and even now you have an alibi—for you have said that your spokesman, John Charteris, was sometimes inconsistent and sometimes ironical. Pardon me if hereinafter I ignore your subterfuge and adopt the attitude that your contentions are presented in all seriousness. And permit me to restate for my guidance your principal thesis.

Romance, I infer, is the expression of an attitude which views life with a profound distrust as a business of exceeding dullness and of very little worth, and which, therefor, seeks beauty by an abandonment of the facts of living. Living is a drab thing, a concatenation of unimportant events; man is impotent and aimless; and beauty, indeed all the fine things you desiderate in literature and life, are non-existent and impossible. To the problem of living, Romance propounds the only possible answer, which is not understanding, but escape. And the method of that escape is, you imply, the creation of a pleasing dream which shall somehow engender a reality as lovely. So Romance in literature invents its dynamic illusions (Ibsen called them vital lies, did he not?) of brave men and lovely women, of living as a "uniformly noble transaction," and hopes that in the end mankind will play Peter Ibbetson upon a cosmic scale.

Now, I shall avoid the obvious comment that this viewpoint outdoes in pessimism the ugliest vision of the realist, and that it has its root in cowardice, and finally that it presents the difficulty which Chesterton once voiced: That what is wrong with the world is that no man can say what would be right with it. This applies to Sophocles equally with John Charteris. But I must insist that what you have so often regarded as beautiful, I with equal justice have deemed merely pretty.

But let me defer this matter for a moment and point out in entire seriousness one quality you have overlooked in your catalogue of desirable ingredients of literature: You have said that these are the auctorial virtues *par excellence*: distinction and clarity, beauty and symmetry, tenderness and truth and urbanity. These are good, I grant; and it may be upon a mere matter of words that we differ. Yet it seems to me that all books have been made re-readable through the possession not of these qualities alone, but of one other, which is salt to them all—namely, gusto. To me it appears that all enduring books, of however delicate a texture, have possessed a heartiness akin to the smacking of lips over a good dish. It is not joy, for many joyless writers have displayed it, and it is inherent in the blackest of tragedies. It is not ecstacy, although this it may approach. I think it is almost a physical thing, an unconscious recognition of life, and an abandonment of self in the very act of being. It is a drunkenness of the soul, perhaps, and blood sister to the fierce pain and joy which we call ecstatic living and which the creative artist must always seek to reproduce in his work, just as the fully living man does in his life—and whether through sin or holy fervor is immaterial. Gusto, I should say, is the very life-blood of art; and in the measure of its possession does the artist overtop life, for he is by so much enabled to produce the image, constant and enduring, of that which is in reality only of the moment.

It is in this, both in its larger and smaller aspects, that your own dream has so often faltered. Nowhere in your writings do I find either that earthiness which makes all men Falstaffs for the moment, or that madness which makes them monsters or saints. They are weak, they are melancholy, they are mildly regretful; but always, even though you say otherwise, are they restrained and calm voiced—always, because their author is seeking beauty in the phrase and not in the thing which the phrase clothes. And so people admire your books in restraint. They know a mild wonder at the beauty of phrasing, at the keenness of insight, at all the delicate tinsel and lace in which you have costumed your thought. But the thought itself escapes them, and they may contemplate a soul's tragedy and say, "Pretty" over it. It is not their fault, entirely, either. They come to you for a story, and you give lovely sentences and a graceful gesture. But never do you—despite your theories— give them even that romance that you seem to promise. For underneath you are all realist, as you well know.

It comes to me that you have always deceived your readers, either by preying upon their ignorance with invented celebrities, or by imposing upon their tendency to take you at your face value, by pretending to be what you are not—what seemed expected. And with whatever pleasing glamour you have tinted the surfaces of the people of whom you wrote you looked with the realist's eye in viewing their inadequate souls.

And in doing so you have missed not only popularity but truth. You have offered us a sugar pill and those who wished realism fought shy of it; but the homeopathic reader, once he tasted the bitter dose you have hidden in your wares, suspected the chemist for all time. And you have missed truth, I say, because the inadequacy and contentment with half measures which you so unceasingly picture in your more "romantic" books, are, I believe, consonant rather with the facts than with the truth itself. In a word, is not your position of romanticism more true than your application of it in your books, and than the thesis upon which, paradoxically enough, your conception of romanticism is based? Why, the presence of the dream gives the lie to the hopeless facts. And you, in seeming to do bitter justice to the human soul perpetrate more enduring falsehoods than ever did realism in portraying some dull round of existence.

It may be that I am writing arrant nonsense. I am not sure, and am perfectly content to leave that matter to your own decision. Yet I cannot rid myself of an uneasy conviction that in all of your "romantic" books you have shown man not only as he is not but as he ought not to be.

But let that pass. I do agree with you when you say that all enduring literature in the past has been of the romantic quality you describe, from whatever different standpoint it has been conceived. And it is true that surface faithfulness alone, such as many modern novelists seek to achieve, is the emptiest of artistic aims. Far better to lie pleasingly. . . . Indeed, despite your silence as to the true value of realism, your comments upon the best way to produce realistic art form the best recipe that I have yet seen. It is merely because I believe you have ignored some essentials that I venture to be banal upon this subject as well. Bear with me while I recite a modest credo of my own.

I believe, then, that it is more important that literature should seem true to life, than that it should be faithful to appearances. I believe that we can never love a man or woman in a book if we do not—at least while the spell is upon us—believe heartily in that person's existence, and share in the emotional atmosphere of the scene. And finally, I believe that the illusion of reality can be produced by the romantic or realistic method—either one, provided that the artist, given insight, is sincerely striving to show fundamental things as he sees them and thereby, perhaps, to hint at their true and unknowable nature.

All platitudes! And yet, consider where you would lead us with your doctrine of original dullness. Grant that man is as inadequate as you please, and living as uneventful; still we have our flashes struck from midnights (to pervert Browning to my own uses) still, even the humblest of us, our glorious moments, either good or bad. And these, I contend, it is the business of the artist, Romanticist and realist alike, to interpret for us and, if he can, to evaluate in terms of approximate eternity.

For art is a branch of pedagogy, as it is a branch of the priesthood. To only a few of us is it given or desirable to see within. The rest must for practical purposes separate the dream from the existence; and since it is our nature to learn by parable, we turn to the artist, the seer, seeking entertainment, and hoping more or less consciously to acquire understanding.

What does it matter then, the method? Whether truth be placed in a mass of carefully considered facts about John Jones or lie in the exquisite tissue of falsehoods that enmesh the personalities of Felix Kennaston or the Sieur d'Aigremont, is a matter of conspicuous unimportance. We ask only that our story treat of such a man as captures our attention, and that in this man and his fortunes lies somewhat of an answer to the great question you once worded as: "What's it all up to?"

You see, I say nothing of style and make no caustic remarks about the taste of my fellow citizens. For I know that what is one man's inspiration is another man's soporific, that to the fellow-craftsman only is the craftsman's skill apparent,—and that, for all that, if you but capture a splendid truth (or lie—these are truths) within a phrase, it will in time become what is more and less than literature, common speech, and so live when all masterpieces and their makers are forgotten.

Think, indeed, of what splendid oblivion has overtaken him who first invented God or Cinderella! Remember how all the creators of religion are become forgotten dust and how only the anthologists—Christ, Buddha, Mohammed and the like—remain. This is the artist's reward that he shall be forgotten and so no longer be inadequate. But his words and the words of many other men will be gathered together until time

will discover a new and single maker for them all. And so these men·
will have become a legendary whole and their work will live on as simple
fragments of song or high-hearted thought. They will not be pondered
over; but they will be the stuff of which many little dreams are woven.
In this they will become witnesses of your own truth; for they shall
shape many dynamic illusions and so in time create reality.

Here, I think, ends my attack. I have said nothing that you did not
know or have not said better. I have expressed merely the "reaction" of
one who, by a perfectly natural association of ideas, prefers Thackeray
to Dickens, who realizes without bitterness that it is the business of the
author and not of the public to see that the distinction between literature and reading matter be rendered less invidious, by proving that
literature may be both, and who, finally, is assured that James Branch
Cabell is a realist who, if he would, could tell a story, more simply, more
humanly, and more appealingly than he has yet done, without sacrifice
of beauty or of truth. But as a romanticist this Cabell appears the drill
sergeant of a pretty troop of marionettes, who revolve endlessly in a
graceful series of manouevres which lead to no enduring whither.

EXPLIQUAT.<br>G. H.

On January 9, 1918, Cabell responds to Holt's criticism by explaining
that he is "tranquilly annexing your rebuttal as the penultimate chapter
of *Beyond Life*." Cabell is delighted with "the book's scheme, whereby I am
enabled to air my naked opinions without incurring any responsibility
therefor; since nominally I stay always on the other side!" Holt's suggestion that gusto "is the very life-blood" of art prompts Cabell to complain
that he does not find gusto in his favorite pages. And for Holt to recom-
mend that Cabell "acquire an eager and multifarious and sympathetic
disposition," Cabell writes, "is precisely as though you suggested I could
improve my appearance by having brown eyes."

Then, on January 17, Cabell writes Holt, "You are evidently determined to have your book precisely what you want it." Cabell tells his editor that "you are peculiarly, if not entirely, responsible" for the volume.
And he attacks Holt's argument for removing references to Cabell's works:

> You inveigle me into believing that I am the possessor of an exact aes-
> thetic creed, which incidentally you believe to be pernicious, and that
> my Collected Works proclaim this creed. I am thus led to compose this
> dizain as an Apologia for my dizain of creative books. That is what it is,·
> a premeditated defence of these ten volumes. And now you propose
> that the lawyer for the defence say what he has to say upon condition

that he make no reference whatever to the defendant. To do this would lend just the crowning touch to my exemplification of human unreason, so that I think your plan is admirable.

The author goes on to detail the use he is making of Holt's ideas, which he has "pilfered with avidity." Holt's remarks will suffer a "sea-change" in being added to the text of the book, but Cabell compliments Holt on his "fine cadences" and "excellent prose."

Cabell rejects complete anonymity and insists that the "deliverer" of the observations in the book remain one of his "book characters," because he wants this work "to join to the body of my work explicitly." But Cabell agrees to remove the "creator" from the book and let the "I" remain anonymous. He also agrees to publish *Beyond Life* anonymously observing that "the book may be attributed to any number of people."

On April 5, 1918, Cabell responds to Holt's suggestion that he rewrite the "collaborated chapter." "As it stands," writes Cabell, "it is quite good, has sufficient glitter—I am very clever at repartee if you give me a week or two—and is speciously fair-minded." He explains that he has written the last paragraph of Chapter 9, adding "a 700-word eulogy of human dullness" which "makes a running resume of the whole book."

On April 10, 1918, Holt refers to Cabell's recalcitrance in making revisions by indicating slyly that the book may not sell. He tells Cabell that he hopes *Beyond Life* will be published in September and adds, "another brown volume will grace your and my shelves, if no others." He insists that Cabell set the scene and provide background for the speakers in Chapter 10. He argues that this will make the text more readable and less monotonous in appearance. "Descriptive phrases," argues Holt, will make it "resemble less closely a Socratic dialogue."

The manuscript of *Beyond Life* shows that initially the tenth chapter consisted of dialogue with two participants identified before each speech as *Myself* or *Charteris*. Cabell has corrected the manuscript by setting the scene in the beginning—describing Charteris as "not at all fatigued" and a clock in the background as "asthmatically" clearing its throat. Then, the speakers are identified in the text by the dialogue itself: "But, my dear Charteris, consider soberly this conceit of yours." The effect is to change formal speeches into casual conversation with both setting and speaker described.[13]

Cabell and Holt continue to debate changes in *Beyond Life*. On April

13. The manuscript of *Beyond Life* is in the Barrett Collection, Alderman Library, University of Virginia.

13, Cabell tells Holt to send the last chapter back for its "one-hundred-and-tenth-revision," and when he returns the chapter on April 27, he calls it "another instalment in the serial of revision." He concludes the letter by insisting that Holt continue to "send me your snarls and fleers and cavils" along with suggestions for the "next revision." On May 9, Cabell writes Holt that he wants the book to satisfy Holt: "For it is—in any event, is meant to be—peculiarly your book."[14] Beginning in April while Cabell was still revising the text, Burton Rascoe had been publishing *Beyond Life* serially in the Chicago *Tribune* where it was attracting interest.

All the while Cabell was revising *Beyond Life*, he was also hard at work "amid a host of familiary distractions" (June 5, 1918) on a new work, *Jurgen*. By the end of June he had completed the rough outline of the book except for the last chapter. In December of 1918, Cabell delivers the manuscript of *Jurgen* to Holt, and he prophetically promises, on January 6, 1919, that *Jurgen* will be a best seller.

The story of the making of *Jurgen* is outlined in the letters printed in *Between Friends*. The Cabell-Holt connection becomes a public matter, so connecting the editor's name with the author's that Holt's obituaries in 1934 mention Cabell and the *Jurgen* controversy. As a result of this controversy, Holt edited *Jurgen and the Law*, thus producing the first of two books about Cabell that would bear Holt's name. It is not in the public *Jurgen* story, however, that the true story of the Holt-Cabell relationship is told, but in the private making of *Beyond Life*.[15]

By 1926 the Holt-Cabell relationship was comfortably established. Holt was an editor, friend, supporter, and fan of Cabell's. During the eleven years of their relationship Cabell published *The Rivet in Grandfather's Neck* (1915), *The Certain Hour* (1916), *From the Hidden Way* (1916), *The Cream of the Jest* (1917), *Beyond Life* (1919), *Jurgen* (1919), *Figures of Earth* (1921), *The High Place* (1923), *Straws and Prayer-Books* (1924), and *The Silver Stallion* (1926). He also rewrote the six books published before 1915 in order to make them conform to his planned "Intended Edition." So when Holt decided to leave McBride to found (along with three others) the John Day

14. Cabell to Holt, May 9, 1918, in Special Collections, James Branch Cabell Library, Virginia Commonwealth University.

15. On January 6, 1919, Cabell writes Holt that he is sending Holt the manuscript of *Beyond Life*. Cabell's practice had been to destroy the manuscript once the book was printed, but Holt persuaded him not to destroy this one. Holt's copy of the manuscript is in the Barrett Collection at the University of Virginia and has the following inscription: "The original manuscript of *Beyond Life* as regretfully preserved and presented (under protest) to Guy Holt, in grateful acknowledgment of his collaboration, and in frank applause of his contributions thereto."

Company, he would have liked to have taken Cabell with him. Cabell, however, was faced with a dilemma: he had to choose between his editor and his precious Intended Edition which McBride was planning to publish. Holt's new company could not afford to buy all of Cabell's books and finance the eighteen-volume Storisende Edition. Cabell made the predictable choice, his Intended Edition—all uniform, tied together, complete. Cabell himself described the agony of this decision in a passage written for *As I Remember It* but not included in the published book:

> So did I then face the sorry choice either to stay on with McBride's, and thus have my Biography of the Life of Manuel published as a unit, at the price of losing my invaluable collaborator, or else, through being marketed henceforward by the John Day Company, to retain his so omnipresent aid and continual stimulus, at the cost of disrupting the Biography.
>
> The choice was difficult. It in fact seemed agonizing, because I abhorred either solution. In the end, however, selfishness won its usual triumph in dealing with the auctorial. I decided that to complete the Biography as a visible unit was, for me as a writer, the more urgent need . . . and after *The Music from Behind the Moon*, I gave up Guy Holt's co-operancy in exchange for fond but no longer shared labors of revising and of writing more firmly all the innumerous sections of the Storisende edition of it.[16]

The reader can only speculate as to what would have happened to Cabell's writing had he followed Holt's advice more closely—removed himself from the texts of his books, resisted games with the reader, endowed his characters with more flesh and blood, eschewed the topical, abandoned the compulsive need to tie all the books together, and, perhaps most important, been willing to aim his work at a larger audience. To have done all this, of course, would have been just as Cabell had explained to Holt in 1917—to have made his blue eyes brown.

What most impresses the reader of the Holt correspondence to Cabell is the quality of Holt's criticism. He saw immediately that Cabell's "romanticism" was a pose; it took years for others to perceive only gradually that Cabell was an unhappy realist. Too, Holt saw clearly that Cabell would always be writing about himself and that he should make his intrusions a part of the artistic fabric and not obtrusively self-indulgent.

In assessing Holt's considerable impact on Cabell during his most cre-

---

16. First draft of *As I Remember It*, in Barrett Collection, Alderman Library, University of Virginia.

ative period, one cannot ignore the attenuation of Cabell's powers during those years following the Holt relationship, from 1927 to 1934, for example, when the quality of Cabell's published work declined. The Holt connection "made" Cabell as a national writer. It did not change him measurably as an artist, but it stimulated his creativity and resulted in his becoming marketable and famous for a while. Although Cabell repeatedly called Holt his "collaborator," Holt's impact on Cabell was inspirational and perhaps psychological rather than material. It was, above all, Cabell's closest, most important, and most pleasurable literary connection with another person.

# AFTER THE JAMES BRANCH CABELL PERIOD

## Joseph M. Flora

For James Branch Cabell the Norns had decreed a spectacular rise to literary fame and notoriety. After its suppression and the obscenity trial over *Jurgen*, Cabell was a hero of the Smart Set that came to dominate the national scene following World War I; furthermore, he was not a one-book author. New romances, often with shock value equal to or greater than that of *Jurgen*, continued to appear. Young sophisticates delighted in Cabell's satire of their elders and of their nation much as they were delighting in the satiric exposures by H. L. Mencken and Sinclair Lewis.

But just as assuredly as the Norns had decreed a major role for Cabell as a figure in the Jazz Age, they had decreed a dramatic fall from the dizzying heights. Only, the gentleman from Richmond was hardly surprised by the tricks of the Norns. He was, after all, himself not a youngster in the 1920s. By the time of the suppression of *Jurgen* he was on the safer side of forty. Besides, Cabell the writer was essentially born to controversy; he had experienced something of a warm-up for the *Jurgen* embroglio when *The Eagle's Shadow*, his first novel, had been published in 1904. That romance aroused a significant number of opponents (one suspects that Cabell masterminded this campaign; there are advantages to notoriety) who waged battle for the honor of American Womanhood in the pages of the New York *Times*: if young women were talking as Cabell's heroine did, they surely ought not to. But the controversy, manufactured or otherwise, had not kept *The Eagle's Shadow* from making its way to the remainders table. Hence, Cabell was able later to observe the to-do over

*Jurgen* with a certain amount of detachment, with a certain *déjà vu*. He could anticipate its ending.

As the 1920s neared an end, Cabell was busily revising many of his books to prepare the definitive editions of the Biography of the Life of Manuel, the eighteen volumes published from 1927 through 1930 as the Storisende edition of *The Works of James Branch Cabell*. He knew well what the Norns were up to. Much of his fame was for reasons not to his liking; he could see that the demands of the reading public in the coming years and his own interests would no longer suit each other so nicely. There were also newer writers on the scene, writers eager to give the public a different kind of fare. So it was that even before the stock market crash of 1929, Cabell wrote his own tribute to the 1920s, foreseeing that the 1930s would not be paying much attention to him and others of his contemporaries; hence the revealing subtitle to *Some of Us—An Essay in Epitaphs*. Cabell knew that young collegians would not any longer be eagerly awaiting the latest word from himself, Mencken, or others of the doomed dizain for whom he had written epitaphs.

Almost in defiance of the Norns to do their worst, Cabell further marked the end of the James Branch Cabell period by truncating his authorial name after *Some of Us* to Branch Cabell. However, the Norns were being rather thorough about *their* business, too. For the Cabell of *Some of Us* could not foresee the economic crisis of the Great Depression that would make readers of the 1930s unlikely to appreciate the resolute frivolity of his irony. It does not overstate the case much when we say that by the time of Pearl Harbor no one was reading Cabell.

Still, neglect did not dissuade Cabell from writing. Posterity might be an ass, but at least there was posterity. In the 1920s Cabell knew that he had been fortunate in his gallant champions, men like Mencken, Burton Rascoe, Sinclair Lewis. He acknowledged, in fact, that no writer had been more fortunate in his defenders. Nevertheless, the influence of Cabell's most famous advocates held sway in the James Branch Cabell period rather than in the Branch Cabell period.

Some new champions did, of course, ride forth after 1929. One of these was the novelist Vardis Fisher, an angry young man in the early 1930s who struck many as a new Dreiser or Dostoievski. Fisher often wrote in a tough naturalistic vein; he was intent on exposing sham and dishonesty—and his voice was often strident. He seemed right for the 1930s, and in that decade he found his greatest fame. Curiously—or perversely, many thought—Fisher in his autobiographical novels insisted on praising James Branch Cabell, finding the neglect of Cabell as symptomatic of his nation's ills. When Fisher wrote essays, it was much the same. Clearly, he admired Cabell's irony and satire. (It is probably worth pointing out here that almost the only other twentieth-century writer Fisher bothered to praise, although not as extensively as he did Cabell, was Ellen Glasgow. I suspect that it was the vein of irony that again pleased him.) Fisher's defense of Cabell culminated in *God or Caesar?*, his 1953 handbook for the writing of fiction, really Fisher's statement of critical principles. In that book Fisher honors Cabell more than any other writer. It is certain, however, that Fisher never brought to Cabell the numbers of readers that a champion like Mencken did; Fisher never wielded so extensive an influence.

Nor did another champion of the Branch Cabell period—Fred T. Marsh of the New York *Times*. Although no Mencken, Marsh was nevertheless a significant spokesman for Cabell. It had been Marsh's review of *In Tragic Life* (1932) that prepared the way for Vardis Fisher's fame in the 1930s, and Marsh was unquestionably Fisher's most influential advocate in the 1930s. When Marsh came to review Cabell's *Smirt* in 1934 he also was reviewing a "new" author in the first published novel of Branch Cabell.

But first a context in which to place Marsh's review. T. S. Matthews in his review of *Smirt* for the *New Republic* asserted: "Mr. Cabell is a snob, and an American snob is almost a traitor to his country"; and George Stevens in the *Saturday Review of Literature* could find nothing very new in Branch Cabell, declaring, "The principal new development revealed in 'Smirt' is the abandonment of the sexual symbolism of 'Jurgen' in favor of a more direct terminology . . . we can only conclude that Branch Cabell has been plagiarizing from James Branch Cabell."[1] The New York *Times* accorded Cabell more respectful treatment, and the choice of Marsh for the reviews was a happy one. Marsh knew and admired the earlier Cabell; moreover, he would be assigned each of the volumes of Cabell's trilogy for review. Although Marsh's review of *Smirt* appeared on Page 8, it was full-length and carried a picture of Cabell—a fitting format for a writer whose national fame had been so great. While Marsh could not provide all of the answers to the question of what Cabell was doing in this new book, he ended by recommending *Smirt* as "first-rate" Cabell. About *Smith* (1935) Marsh was less affirmative; he ended his review by concluding: "Mr. Cabell is a rare and gifted ironist in whom we miss a certain balance.

---

1. T. S. Matthews, "Truth and Some New Fictions," *New Republic*, LXXVIII (April 18, 1934), 284; George Stevens, "The Two Cabells," *Saturday Review of Literature*, X (March 10, 1934), 537.

Even of a good thing there can be too much." And when Marsh came to consider the trilogy as a whole after *Smire* appeared in 1937 he found the urbanity "a little thin at times" and the irony "a little shrill."[2] He nevertheless called for more of Cabell's fantasy and went on record as enjoying and valuing Cabell's work.

Marsh did not review each of the volumes of Branch Cabell's next trilogy, *Heirs and Assigns*, but he did write an appreciative view of the last book of the trilogy, *The First Gentleman of America* (1942), that unquestionably places him among Cabell's champions. Marsh found *The First Gentleman* one of Cabell's best books: "The familiar Cabell ironic verbal playfulness is better kept in hand . . . than in some of his histories; and there is less fustian in the brocade than in others. In addition, because of its origin, theme and setting, it has a certain charm and pertinence independently its own." Marsh was not evangelizing for Cabell as Mencken earlier had, but those methods would not have worked in the 1930s and 1940s, nor finally have served Cabell well. There were plenty of reviewers who treated Cabell glibly during these years—although not, of course, all. Ellen Glasgow found *Smith* the most ably written of Branch Cabell's books, but since it was the second novel to be published under that name we may merely chuckle at the joke of Cabell's friend. In reviewing *Smith* William Rose Benét touted Cabell's achievement: "As well as absorbing all the mythologies of the world he has succeeded in elaborating one of his own in a fashion that will remain a remarkable feat in American letters."[3] The majority of Branch Cabell's reviewers emphasized or implied that his achievement was in the past, but in the time of his greatest neglect, Marsh probably did more than any of Cabell's reviewers to encourage serious and ongoing attention for Cabell. He seemed willing to read the work before him and not to go endlessly seeking for another *Jurgen*.

After World War II several academic critics provided needful reassessments of Cabell, but it is appropriate that we give special recognition to one later champion not from the academy. I refer, of course, to Edmund Wilson: Wilson's 1956 essay "The James Branch Cabell Case Reopened"

---

2. Fred T. Marsh, "Mr. Cabell in His New Incarnation," *New York Times Book Review*, March 11, 1934, p. 8; Fred T. Marsh, "Branch Cabell's 'Smith' and Other Recent Works of Fiction," *New York Times Book Review*, October 13, 1935, p. 6; Fred T. Marsh, "Branch Cabell Closes a Trilogy," *New York Times Book Review*, March 28, 1937, p. 2.

3. Fred T. Marsh, "Mr. Cabell's 'Comedy of Conquest,'" *New York Times Book Review*, February 1, 1942, p. 6; Ellen Glasgow, "Branch Cabell Still Clings to His Unbelief," *New York Herald Tribune Books*, October 6, 1935, p. 7; William Rose Benét, "Lord of the Forest," *Saturday Review of Literature*, XII (October 12, 1935), 12.

(originally published in the *New Yorker*) makes salutary rereading today.[4] The very title of Wilson's essay speaks pointedly to the devaluation of Cabell that Cabell foresaw with *Some of Us*. What is most interesting about Wilson's defense is that during the Cabell boom Wilson himself was not very taken with the Cabell books that he took up and he had ceased to read him. But twenty years later, encouraged by a friend to give Cabell another chance, Wilson found Cabell very much worth his time. He viewed Cabell's fictions as "poems" rather than as "novels" and invited his readers to view Cabell in a southern context. For Wilson, Cabell was clearly not a one-book author; Wilson especially praised *The High Place* and *Something About Eve*. One suspects that across the land at least some others upon reading Wilson's essay must have thought reassessment of Cabell was in order.

Cabell died two years after Wilson so humanly (confessing his own shortcomings) and effectively "reopened" the Cabell case; Wilson marked Cabell's passing in the *Nation* with a brief further tribute. A couple of features from the memorial tribute strike me as of particular interest. Since writing the earlier essay, Wilson in considering Cabell's work thought that he had not enough praised *Figures of Earth* and *The Silver Stallion*. The more Wilson thought of those books, the more remarkable they seemed. Wilson now thought of *Figures of Earth* as "on a plane, perhaps, with Flaubert and Swift."[5]

At the time of the earlier essay, Wilson had not read the fictions of Branch Cabell beyond the *Smirt-Smith-Smire* trilogy, although he found that trilogy admirable. He had since read the later fictional trilogies, and the memorial tribute includes his assessment of the last trilogies. While Wilson granted amusing magical moments to *There Were Two Pirates* and *The Devil's Own Dear Son*, he was disturbed by the *Heirs and Assigns* trilogy. He found Cabell's late work marked by a disagreeable development of "misanthropic sadism"—a feature already apparent in the earlier work. Wilson judged *Hamlet Had an Uncle* as "not merely inferior Cabell" but "deliberately atrocious, the ugliest of all Cabell's works," and the atrocity seemed to Wilson rather pointless.

Wilson's displeasure with the *Heirs and Assigns* trilogy brings him into noticeable confrontation with one of Branch Cabell's champions—namely

4. Edmund Wilson, "The James Branch Cabell Case Reopened," *New Yorker*, XXXII (April 21, 1956), 140–68. The essay was reprinted in Wilson's *The Bit Between My Teeth: A Literary Chronicle of 1950–1965* (New York: Farrar, Straus, 1965), 291–321.

5. Edmund Wilson, "James Branch Cabell: 1879–1958," *Nation*, CLXXXVI (June 7, 1958), 519–20. The essay was reprinted in *The Bit Between My Teeth*, 322–25.

Fred Marsh, who ranked the final volume of that trilogy as among Cabell's best books. Wilson's assessment is also at odds with that of a later academic critic. In his 1967 book on Cabell, Desmond Tarrant was to judge the *Heirs* trilogy as likely "the best of the later fiction" and "the backbone of the writings after the Biography." My point here is not to attempt to settle the absolute ranking of Cabell's books, nor even to expose a weakness in Wilson's last and important defense of Cabell. Indeed, there *is* something very different about this late trilogy that Wilson seeks to identify. Perhaps "misanthropic sadism" does not adequately define it. Since the topic of this essay is Branch Cabell, I propose to attempt to seek further for an answer to Wilson's own question: "What, one wonders, at the time he was writing these books, had made Cabell's imagination so black?"[6]

Wilson posits that Cabell's late peevishness came from his isolation in Richmond, from a lack of communication with others, and from Cabell's declining health. It is possible to account for Cabell's late dark mood in terms of the material which he was researching—for in *Heirs and Assigns* Cabell is not rooted in Poictesme. Joe Lee Davis emphasizes Cabell's changed fictional techniques and new models: he points out that in *Hamlet Had an Uncle* Cabell was working in the manner of the Norse sagas; that in *The King Was in His Counting House* Cabell's models were the Jacobean dramatists; that in *The First Gentleman of America* he was using the devices of folklore. Davis was also aware that Cabell's late trilogy had roots in the power politics then so frighteningly unleashed in the world.[7] Surprisingly, this was the element that Edmund Wilson had overlooked.

Cabell's ordering of the *Heirs and Assigns* trilogy, defensibly enough, called for the reader to pursue them in the order of the historical periods they treat rather than in the order of their composition and publication. But there is also value in considering the books in the order of their composition so that the increasing blackness of Cabell's work becomes even more pronounced. For in the trilogy Cabell was studying the dynamics of raw political power in ways and to a degree that he had not done before. While the stereotyped view of the 1930s was to label Cabell "an exquisite" who avoided the real world, he was deeply disturbed by the real world, and the fiction that he was writing dealt with the grim nature of the real

---

6. Desmond Tarrant, *James Branch Cabell: The Dream and the Reality* (Norman: University of Oklahoma Press, 1967), 251; Wilson, "James Branch Cabell: 1879–1958," in *The Bit Between My Teeth*, 324.

7. Joe Lee Davis, *James Branch Cabell* (New York: Twayne, 1962), 135–41.

world.[8] It is certain that Cabell's "escapist" fictions dealt more penetratingly with the world of the 1930s and 1940s than did the more direct work of many of his contemporaries, who—in retrospect—more deserve the label "romantic." Who can now read *Heirs and Assigns* and not see how far from the mark Alfred Kazin was in 1942 (the very year Cabell completed the trilogy) when he declared that it was apparent that Cabell and Hitler did not occupy the same universe?

The title of the first novel of the *Heirs* trilogy, *The King Was in His Counting House*, comes from the childhood rhyme "Sing-a-Song of Sixpence." It was appropriate to Cabell's subtitle, "A Comedy of Common-Sense," but it also identified a new emphasis for Cabell's fiction. Cabell was concentrating on the king *in* his counting house. I need hardly remind you of what the king was doing there; he was counting out his money—that is, attending to the business of this world, to the business of governing. The king of Cabell's comedy would not be any romantic Prospero.

In the Biography of the Life of Manuel, Cabell focused on three approaches or attitudes to life, the chivalric, the gallant, and the poetic. The various volumes usually emphasize one or the other of these attitudes, but any attitude implied or was played off against the others. These attitudes are found in *Heirs and Assigns*, but the trilogy cannot be defined adequately in their terms. In fact, as each volume of the trilogy appeared, these traditional Cabellian attitudes occupied less and less of Cabell's attention until, finally, they almost disappear from *The First Gentleman of America*. I suggest that Cabell was concerning himself with the attitude of political power in these dark comedies written during the years when totalitarian states were bullying their way into greater power and had begun to plunge the world into new warfare.

In his earlier work Cabell had also treated the theme of power. Indeed, he had always portrayed the artist (a favorite topic) as related to the power-oriented. As far back as 1917 in *The Cream of the Jest* Horvendile was arranging and destroying kingdoms, but—of course—as a part of a pretty romance that he was inditing for poetic ends. Horvendile is a notorious double-dealer. In Kennaston's dream life, he and Ettarre often visit or view the powerful of history: Napoleon, Oliver Cromwell, Tiberius Caesar—but never in moments of battle. Kennaston is always careful to end his dreams before anything unpleasant happens to him or to Ettarre. But

8. For a typical 1930s view of Cabell, see Alfred Kazin, *On Native Grounds: An Interpretation of Modern American Prose Literature* (New York: Harcourt, Brace, 1942), 227–35.

it is worth remembering that in the last of Felix Kennaston's remarkable dreams he appears as an aged king, "the strongest of kings. People dreaded him, he knew; and he wondered why anyone should esteem a frail weakling such as he to be formidable. The hand of this great king—his own hand, that held aside the curtain before him,—was shriveled and colorless as lamb's wool. It was a horrible bird-claw."[9]

In the books that Cabell wrote after *The Cream of the Jest* this old man took shape as Manuel of Poictesme, in whom there was much of the bully and simultaneously much of the frail weakling. But we do not view Manuel in *Figures of Earth* primarily in the process of obtaining political power; nor is it the clash of human warfare that is to the fore in *The Silver Stallion*, the romance that recounts the adventures of Manuel's knights. We do, however, get that kind of focus on political machinations in *Heirs and Assigns*. Cabell was greatly interested in the theme and reality of good government—however dimly he might view the possibility for achieving it. The first two volumes of his political trilogy are more affirmative than the third, for at their end the state is—at least momentarily—in the capable hands of a leader who has defeated the forces who are motivated by unreason and greed.

The king in his counting house in Branch Cabell's 1938 comedy was Ferdinand dei Vetori, who was brought to power in Melphé through the bloody work of one Carneschi, who becomes Ferdinand's prime minister. Ferdinand, for a long time, had seemed everyone's fool. He was assuredly a cuckold; only the maternity of his four sons was certain. But like Robert Graves's Claudius, Ferdinand is not the fool he seems. He learns all about politics, and, in his own best interest and in Melphé's, he has Carneschi executed. He determines to rule and to rule well, to rule for Melphé's good rather than for gratification of his own enjoyment of power. And he does so.

Like other kings, Ferdinand is concerned with what will happen to Melphé after his death. It does not really matter to him that the next ruler of Melphé be his biological son; what does matter is that Melphé be well-governed. Two of his technical sons are quickly removed from consideration: one murders a brother and is consequently himself executed. The possibilities come down to Cesario and Lorenzo, neither of whom seems destined for greatness. Cesario is too much the poet; an idealist in

9. James Branch Cabell, *The Cream of the Jest* and *The Lineage of Lichfield*, Storisende Edition, XVI (New York: Robert M. McBride, 1930), 195. *The Cream of the Jest* first appeared alone in 1917 (New York: Robert M. McBride) and was later revised for the Biography of the Life of Manuel.

love, he finds his beloved Hypolita as corrupt as Messalina, and so he retreats to the Forest of Branlon, the dwelling place for minor poets. Lorenzo remains and anticipates. Meanwhile, Ferdinand counts the costs; he wants to test Lorenzo before he dies. He decides to share power with Lorenzo. Alas, Lorenzo has no vision of Melphé's best interests, and he is soon exploiting the kingdom shamelessly. He murders his wife in order to marry Hypolita, and it is that lady who effectively controls the kingdom. Ferdinand sees all and so realizes that he must turn to Cesario— and he causes Cesario to replace his life in Branlon with a commitment to the real world. Ferdinand explains: "The men and women of Melphé, the mere run of mankind . . . it is they whom we have to consider, first, and their poor human needs. It takes so very little to content them. They need only a home and food, a little work, their mates and their children. Out of these simple things, in the ever-present black shadow of chance and of death, they create, very incredibly, their contentment. So for their sake Cesario, you must put aside Branlon, and the fine dreams of your youth, and your rights as a private person to any special happiness, or indeed to any particular virtue." Thus, Cabell's comedy becomes the story of Cesario's conversion from domnei to an attitude of poetry to an acceptance of the attitude of political responsibility. Late in the comedy Cesario explains to Hypolita, "My passions, nowadays, incline equably to accept the muck and sunshine of this world just as Heaven mixed them."[10]

Reviewers of *The King Was in His Counting House* made the inevitable comparisons with *Jurgen* and, in general, either damned with faint praise or outrightly damned the book. Basil Davenport in the *Saturday Review of Literature* found Cabell smuttier than ever.[11] Admittedly there is a great deal of sexual adventure in the book in addition to a great deal of bloodshed. But Cabell was not using his sexual theme irresponsibly. While he would usually find human sexuality not without its humorous aspects, he was portraying the sexual realities behind power politics, and today we surely know better than to doubt the appropriateness of the theme in a political novel. What Basil Davenport did not see is that Cabell portrays the sexually unwise as politically unwise; more, the evaluation that the characters put on sexuality is symptomatic of their worth as people. Cabell's sympathies are clearly with Ferdinand and Cesario and Hermia and not with Ferdinand's wife, Lorenzo, and Hypolita.

10. Branch Cabell, *The King Was in His Counting House: A Comedy of Common-Sense* (New York and Toronto: Farrar & Rinehart, 1938), 222, 273.
11. Basil Davenport, "Not Magic After All," *Saturday Review of Literature*, XVIII (October 22, 1938), 11–12.

Two years after the publication of *The King*, Cabell published *Hamlet Had an Uncle*. The year was 1940; although Cabell had completed the book in 1939, at the time of publication virtually all of Europe was involved in a war whose coming had been all too evident.

Cabell begins the preface to his Hamlet story playfully enough: "The story of Hamlet, in a perverted form, is not unfamiliar to the more highly cultured of our literati, even in America. As has been said in another place, his fame is world-wide—and completely mendacious."[12] It is amusing to have the American romancer advocate presenting the true adventures of Hamlet—to seem, anyway, to argue for fact over imagination.

But why Hamlet in 1939 or 1940? Shakespeare's drama we have always considered as among the most universal of all works. What of the universality of the Hamlet Cabell found in Shakespeare's sources? And in the Hamlet of Cabell's book? To be sure, Cabell was amused to play off his Hamlet against Shakespeare's. It is a delightful irony that the Hamlet of Shakespeare's sources knew little of the pale cast of thought, but Cabell was up to more. It was precisely because Cabell's Hamlet is so universal that he was so abhorrent and relevant to 1939; while Edmund Wilson found Cabell's detailed portrayal of Hamlet's brutalities very distasteful, Cabell's theme demanded such treatment.

Cabell's Hamlet is unquestionably the man of action. He is a vulgar ruffian whose language is often coarse. When Hamlet's alleged father, Horvendile, is murdered by his brother Fengon, Hamlet need await no revelation from any ghost to set him to the task of revenge. Cabell replaces the ghost with Orton, really an incarnation of the Horvendile of Cabell's earlier romances, and Hamlet is all eagerness to get the job done. To this end, Orton is of greater help than ever the ghost of the dead king of Shakespeare. Thus, by the middle of Cabell's book, Hamlet has swept to his revenge and killed Fengon. Ironically, in so doing he has killed his father and avenged the death of his uncle.

Shakespeare's commentators frequently observe the amount of death in *Hamlet*. How bloody is that final scene! How many die because Hamlet delays: Polonius, Rosencrantz, Guildenstern, Ophelia, Laertes, Gertrude, and finally Claudius and Hamlet. Yet the count is modest when we consider what happens in Cabell's "comedy." The following description of Hamlet's methods in Cabell's version makes clear the great gulf between his and Shakespeare's Hamlet. Here is that young man in action after his return from England:

12. Branch Cabell, *Hamlet Had an Uncle: A Comedy of Honor* (New York: Farrar & Rinehart, 1940), preface.

The noblemen of Jutland, being thus stuffed with meat and stupefied with drugs, began by-and-by to sleep in the same place where they had dined. They one and all reposed snortingly upon the rushes, like gorged hogs, when Prince Hamlet ripped away the upper part of the new red-and-gold tapestries which adorned the banquet hall, leaving the bottom of these tapestries nailed fast to the wall. He pulled down these tapestries over the snoring earls of Jutland, like coverlets. He fastened each tapestry to the ground, very tightly, with his sharp wooden sticks. He locked up the doors of the hall, with bolts, from without. He set fire to the four corners of the building of pine-wood and maple-wood.

No victim escaped alive from that great burning.[13]

Cabell's emphasis on the completeness of Hamlet's work reveals that he, indeed, had the twentieth century in mind. Cabell meant the reader to see parallels between Hamlet and the likes of Hitler and Mussolini. But, cunningly, Cabell broadens the comparison and invites his reader to compare Hamlet also to Franklin D. Roosevelt. With the revenge of Fengon accomplished, Hamlet becomes a political figure. The American overtones are obvious in Orton's report of Hamlet's triumph:

In brief, he bamboozled the improvident gross-witted proletariat, after an ancient and time-approved fashion, beside the yet smoking ruins of the banquet hall, in what he described, rather humorously, as a fireside chat. He promised them a reduction in all government expenditures at once; and a balancing of the budget next year through the use of counterfeit money; and a more abundant living for everybody, now that pensions would replace taxes; and a renewal of indefinite prosperity; and no more war, or disease, or bad weather; and every other handsome sort of insanity. . . . They believed him of course, very uproariously, because in all known lands it is the quaint trait of popular sentiment to dislike any sort of rationality and to find truth unpatriotic. So all passed smoothly; and the accession of King Hamlet was received with delight by his loyal subjects.[14]

Although Hamlet is skilled in delivering fireside chats, he is not a wise leader in foreign policy any more than in domestic policy. Cabell's Hamlet is a creature who is easily maneuvered into unwise action. King Edric of the Deiri allows Hamlet to talk himself into going to Pictland, ostensibly to serve as Edric's representative in a suit for Queen Hermetrude—who has killed all previous suitors. The world would have been spared much grief if Hermetrude had continued as the "virgin" queen and slain Ham-

13. *Ibid.*, 112–13.
14. *Ibid.*, 117–18.

let. But Edric's plan thus to dispose of Hamlet backfires: Hermetrude is·
attracted to the vigorous beast, and she easily talks Hamlet into abandon-
ing his wife, Edric's daughter, for her. Later, Hamlet, unwisely for him,
allows the one man who can do him in to escape his clutches. And eventually Hamlet pays for his unwisdom with his head—cut off by that Hermetrude whose bed Hamlet loved sharing. Thus, Hamlet richly deserves
his uncle Wiglerus' designation "as a mere synonym for unreflectiveness
and too hasty action."[15] Because of the essential unwisdom of Hamlet,
Orton deserts him—proving himself a double-dealer, much as the Horvendile of *The Cream of the Jest* deserted Maugis d'Aigremont for Sir Gui-
ron des Rocques, husband of La Belle Ettarre. While Cabell's story is not
a slavish allegory, Cabell clearly saw FDR in a Hamletian mold.

Hamlet is not, however, the protagonist of Cabell's tale; nor is the uncle
of Cabell's title the uncle whom Hamlet avenges. The uncle celebrated in
the title and the hero of the book is Wiglerus, Hamlet's maternal uncle,
Prince of Denmark and later Denmark's king. Cabell's title emphasizes
the essential contrast between character types on which his tale is structured. Wiglerus does not like war and bloodshed; he is something of a
poet: he would rather make love than war. His nephew Hamlet prefers
love and war. And because Hamlet is so easily maneuvered by others, he
gets ample opportunity to demonstrate his skills at warfare. His personal
goals prove unsettling to the whole Northern world.

In *Hamlet Had an Uncle* Cabell portrays warfare with a thoroughness
he had previously eschewed. War was much on Cabell's mind as the 1930s
continued to darken, as his fiction shows. At first the battles go Hamlet's
way, but after Wiglerus learns "modern" (the designation is Cabell's) warfare, he proves to be highly efficient. Let one example of a Danish *blitz-
krieg* here suffice:

> He ordered his Danes to kill the Jutlanders, men, women and chil-
> dren alike, but always, when this was possible, to hang or to strangle
> them, so that none might hope to enter Valhalla. He forbade any dal-
> liance with living women, permitting his soldiers to violate only the dead
> bodies of the women of Jutland. He instructed his army to burn each
> town just as Hermetrude had burned Aalborg; to plough the tilled fields
> with salt; to cut down the woods and the fruit-trees. His passing left the
> land bare. His oppressions terrified all Jutland. There was no resisting
> the malignity of time-tutored Wiglerus, now that he went about leaving
> in every place destruction. Behind Wiglerus, no windmill turned nor

15. *Ibid.*, 260.

did any chimney smoke; wherever he had been, the cocks ceased their crowing, and the dogs their barking, so complete was the ruin behind Wiglerus. Grass grew in what remained of the houses; briars and white-flowering thorns alone showed where villages had once stood.[16]

Wiglerus is in the mold of Cesario of *The King Was in His Counting House*, the primary difference being that when we first meet Cesario he is young and in the power of the domnei that characterizes the attitude of chivalry. Wiglerus is beyond chivalry in *Hamlet*—he is middle-aged and a practicing gallant. But the remnants of his earlier ideas color his life, and he does not seek political power. But it eventually comes to him; like Cesario, he has no choice but to accept the challenge. While his methods are for the moment bloody in the extreme, he works for a time when the absurd feuding will end. Denmark is fortunate in having him on its throne, for he is one of those rare creatures who knows what human nature is.

Whereas Cabell's readers might feel removed from the Italy of Jacobean drama or the feuds of the lands of the North where Odin was still worshiped, they could hardly feel as distanced from *The First Gentleman of America*, Cabell's "Comedy of Conquest," a book that appeared only months before Pearl Harbor. While in that concluding volume of his trilogy Cabell was treating the history of the Northern Neck of Virginia between the Potomac River and the Rappahannock River in the sixteenth century and the history of Spanish conquests in what came to be the United States of America, he was careful to play off that distant time with the present, to remind his readers constantly of twentieth-century America. The epigraph of Cabell's comedy is "My Country 'tis of thee." Cabell's work reflected his horror with the European scene even as it indicated his apprehension about the future of his own country.

The gentleman of Cabell's title is Nemattanon, the son of a Spanish noble who set himself up as the god Quetzal in Virginia. Quetzal was in retreat from the ways of Europe, and he knew that civilization would not be a boon to the native Americans. The key to Quetzal's success in Virginia is his antiwar stance. When he first took charge of the affairs in the land of the Ajacans, he declared: "My chief law . . . is for you to avoid fighting with other tribes, because there is no special sense in it."[17] From the start, Cabell's book is a protest against war.

A large portion of *The First Gentleman of America* is concerned precisely

16. *Ibid.*, 203–204.
17. Branch Cabell, *The First Gentleman of America: A Comedy of Conquest* (New York and Toronto: Farrar & Rinehart, 1942), 7.

with demonstration of the stupidity of war. And there are again several scenes that depict mass violence. Cabell makes unmistakable the contemporary edge he is giving the events he describes; having recounted the massacre of a troop of Frenchmen by the Spaniards, he says: "This was not, of course, an impressive massacre, as go our modern standards, which incline to esteem the more forthright exercises of patriotism in a strict ratio to the number of dead bodies produced. Yet in its tact and restraint and ease, and in its polite consideration for the persons being murdered—and in brief, for its complete if slender adroitness—this massacre, to the attentive judgment of Don Luis de Velasco, appeared to excel."[18]

Appropriate for a novel that Cabell also intended to be a lesson in early American history, its shape is controlled by the career of Nemattanon. The peace of Ajacan is disrupted one day when Señor Pedro Menéndez de Avilés, captain of Spain's West Indian fleet, arrives in Ajacan as a part of his exploration for King Philip. Don Pedro warms to Nemattanon as to a lost son, and Nemattanon, who knows Spanish, desires to go with Don Pedro to learn about the rest of the world. He does so, enabling Cabell to recount the Spanish exploitation of Mexico and the conflict between Spain and France in the New World. Don Pedro is not, of course, an evil man. He is merely serious about his dynamic illusion—a fervent nationalism. Indeed, the Spaniards and Frenchmen both claim the goal of the spiritual well-being of the people that they are exploiting. But since the demands of efficient conquest sometimes are at odds with Christian teachings, Don Pedro often has to consider his conscience; usually he ably salves it.

Mark Twain would have been amused at Don Pedro's wrestling with his conscience—a wrestling that at one time enables him to justify his taking a wife polygamously. I think, in fact, that Mark Twain would heartily approve *The First Gentleman of America*; for Cabell's satire is often bitter and pointed, and his themes are much like the themes of the later works of Mark Twain. Cabell's "Comedy of Conquest" bears many resemblances to *The Mysterious Stranger*, "To the Person Sitting in Darkness," and "The War Prayer."

Since Nemattanon is a bright young man, he, too, increasingly comes to a position similar to that of Mark Twain. The Christianity of Europe has not inevitably worked for the betterment of the Europeans (they do what the worshipers of Odin did, but with more style), nor certainly for

18. *Ibid.*, 178.

the well-being of the peoples that they conquer. Thus, Nemattanon denounces the ways of civilization—he will work to save Ajacan from Spanish conquest; he cannot be a party to Don Pedro's program when his godfather prepares to do in Virginia what he had accomplished in Florida. Like Cesario of *The King Was in His Counting House* and Wiglerus of *Hamlet Had an Uncle*, Nemattanon must face his destiny and seize political power. Hear him accept that destiny as he renounces Europe: "You conceive, sir, each one of these gentlemen, in his dealing with the people of America, has held to his sense of duty; and in dealing with the East-people, I too shall hold to my sense of duty. I have observed, with my own eyes, how these Europeans treat us Americans, as well as how they treat one another. Their motives are, no doubt, excellent; but when once they obey the ideals of patriotism, then their actions become pernicious. They compel me also, in brief, to become a patriot, by ridding our own dear land of their enormities." [19]

The ending of the American comedy of Cabell's trilogy takes a particularly American slant. It is true that Nemattanon does take some effective measures of war against the Spanish, but he cannot achieve that larger sense of kingdom possible to Cesario and Wiglerus. For the invasion by the Europeans in the lands of northern Virginia is inevitable. However, no Spaniards or—later—Englishmen ever find or conquer Nemattanon and the Ajacans. The Ajacans go—in their quest for freedom—where Americans have traditionally gone: to the forest, to the mountains. Mark Twain knew something about that ending, too.

No doubt during the Branch Cabell period—and up to his death— Cabell must have felt himself something of an exiled Philoctetes with an odorous wound that separated him from his countrymen. However, even the brief survey undertaken in this essay reveals that there was a base of support for Cabell even during the years of his greatest neglect, suggesting that this Philoctetes would yet be given a secure place of honor by his countrymen, that his countrymen would yet find his bow a desirable weapon. It is pleasant to think that Edmund Wilson's essay on Cabell two years before Cabell's death gave assurance to Cabell that both the Branch Cabell case and the James Branch Cabell case had been reopened, that he had indeed written some books that would have a life beyond life.

Most assuredly, Cabell could take pleasure in the achievement of the Branch Cabell period—a period that found him writing ably and wittily

19. *Ibid.*, 240.

of his own life and past, and of his present neglect. Furthermore, in his fictions he was *not* endlessly plagiarizing James Branch Cabell but expressing himself in new modes. To his mind, anyway, he was laying bare realities of human nature at a time when human nature was behaving most appallingly. If the world wished to be deceived, Cabell was not a party to the deception.

# JAMES BRANCH CABELL
## *A Photographic Essay*

Edgar E. MacDonald

83     <small>CABELL'S BIRTHPLACE</small>

101 East Franklin Street, Richmond, Virginia, the house in which Cabell was born April 14, 1879. He was named for his grandfather James Read Branch, whose widow, the dynamic Martha Louise Patteson Branch, lived here. She is apostrophized in *As I Remember It* and was metamorphosed into Jurgen's grandmother. At the time of Cabell's birth his parents were living on the third floor of this house, following a Richmond custom of newlyweds living with a parent until the children arrived. This house was later razed to make way for the Richmond Public Library at First and Franklin streets, and Cabell liked to observe that he had been born on the second floor, approximately, of the public library. An Italian white marble mantel from this house is now in the Cabell Room of the James Branch Cabell Library, Virginia Commonwealth University.

ROBERT GAMBLE CABELL, JR.

Cabell's father, Dr. Robert Gamble Cabell, Jr., was himself the son of another physician of the same name who had lived at 709 East Franklin Street, next door to Robert E. Lee. In his youth, this first Robert Cabell had been a schoolmate of Poe's and had swum in the James River with him. At the age of sixteen, Robert Cabell, Jr., fought at the famous battle of New Market where the cadets of the Virginia Military Institute had been called out; his brother William, aged eighteen, fell on the field of battle. While trained as a physician, Cabell's father gave up the practice of medicine to run a drugstore. For the last fifteen years of his life he was the superintendent of the Richmond city home for the indigent. When he died May 7, 1922, newspaper headlines mourned the passing of a legendary hero. The Cabells were Presbyterian, and portraits of these fearless Calvinists enter into the Cabell opus. Hell in *Jurgen* is the creation of Coth of the Rocks, a sinner who demands punishment for his earthly crimes.

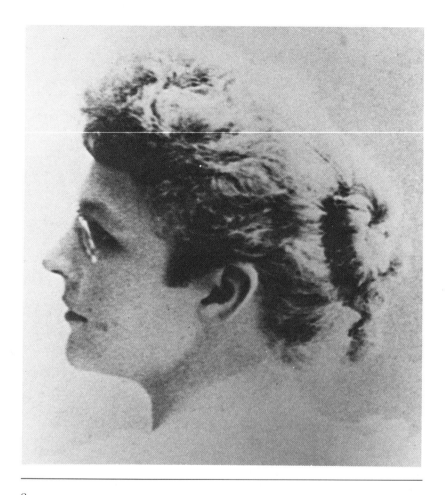

ANNE HARRIS BRANCH CABELL

Annie Cabell, Cabell's mother, was some twelve years younger than her husband. Young Mrs. Cabell, freed from Branch Methodism by her mother's Patteson Episcopalianism, would dare to smoke and drink cocktails before other Richmond ladies confessed to these pleasures. In Cabell's earlier work she appers as "Mr. Townsend's mother," and she is the model for the charming Melior in *The High Place*. If "this bright light creature's very diverting chat" does not savor of the intellect, the hero reasons that after all "he had not married her in order to discuss philosophy." The divorce of Cabell's parents in 1907 colored his subsequent work with a darker irony. Anne Branch Cabell died in 1915 at the age of fifty-four in the home of a sister. Her brief obituary did not mention her husband's name and she was buried with her parents in Hollywood Cemetery. Ugly gossip had saddened her last years, and in Cabell's thinking a happy child-spirit had been slain by a lie; his bitterness toward certain cousins flawed his attempts to write "contemporary" works such as *The Rivet in Grandfather's Neck*.

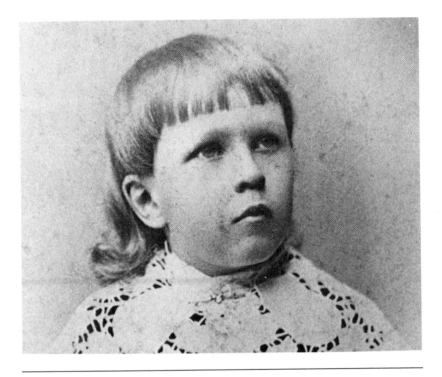

86                    JAMES BRANCH CABELL, AGE FOUR YEARS AND FIVE MONTHS, SEPTEMBER 28, 1883

For his next birthday, his fifth, April 14, 1884, Cabell's grandmother Branch gave a splendid party at 101 East Franklin Street, inviting a host of young Richmonders to come dressed as characters from the Mother Goose rhymes. James was Jack, the son of Mother Goose, and led a grand parade through the rooms decorated for Easter. Mother Goose was Gabriella Brooke Moncure, some four years his senior. This event, chronicled in a local paper, remained vivid in Cabell's memory and is referred to obliquely in a number of his works. In Chapter 17 of *Figures of Earth*, "Magic of the Image-Makers," the Rune of the Blackbirds consists of four metrical, double parodies, each paraphrasing a Mother Goose rhyme in the manner of a well-known poet. Freydis assures Manuel that when the rune is perfected that it will outlive "all those rhymes that are infected with thought and intelligent meanings such as are repugnant to human nature."

87   GABRIELLA MONCURE (TOP CENTER, IN PINAFORE AND WITH RIBBON IN
     HAIR) WITH A GROUP OF HER CLASSMATES
     Gabriella Moncure was nine when she played Mother Goose to Cab-
ell's Jack at his fifth birthday party. She appears here a few years older as a student at
Miss Gussie Daniel's School for Girls, Adams and Main streets, Richmond. She colored
all Cabell's subsequent dreaming. When he left college at nineteen, with Gabriella twenty-
three, Cabell had experienced the passion of "being in love," a passion he professed
never to have felt again. Up until the time he was thirty-four when he married Mrs.
Shepherd, friends expected his youthful romance with Gabriella to result in marriage.
Instead, she became "The Witch-Woman" who directed all his efforts to recapture the
lost magic of their time together. *Courtesy of Valentine Museum, Richmond.*

CABELL AS A SCHOOLBOY

A shy child, immersed in reading, Cabell was protected from the vicissitudes of the outer world by his mammy, Louisa Nelson, memorialized in *Let Me Lie*. When she died, a long obituary penned by Cabell appeared in a local paper. Cabell's first schooling was received from a very young Virginia Randolph Ellett, later to become the legendary Miss Jennie Ellett who could get Richmond girls admitted to prestigious northern colleges. Her school grew into present-day St. Catherine's. Cabell later attended the preparatory school for boys at Belvedere and Main run by another local legend, the elder John Peyton McGuire.

89      CABELL AT FOURTEEN

Cabell in 1893, photographed in Chicago where he had gone to the World Columbian Exposition. Among the souvenirs he brought back for his family, a ruby glass goblet survives; the name of Louisa Nelson is painted on it. This is the youth who would enter William and Mary, then a provincial college for teachers, at the age of fifteen. There he would meet again Gabriella Brooke Moncure, then nineteen. For three years she would inspire a poetic outpouring later incorporated into his saga of Manuel the Redeemer, termed the Biography.

90        GABRIELLA BROOKE MONCURE (SECOND FROM RIGHT, SEATED) WITH A GROUP OF HER CLASSMATES AT MISS GUSSIE DANIEL'S SCHOOL, ABOUT 1891.

When Cabell went to college in Williamsburg, he met again Gabriella Moncure, whose father had become head of the psychiatric hospital there. Although she was four years older, their friendship intensified, and the youthful author would refer to her under a variety of pseudonyms, most often as "Heart o' my heart," a punning translation of the French origin of her name, Moncure (*mon coeur*). In *The High Place* (1923), Cabell gives the character Marie-Claire, an adept at necromancy, the physical attributes of Gabriella Moncure: "Her neck remained wonderful; it was still the only woman's neck familiar to Florian that really justified comparison with a swan's neck by its unusual length and roundness and flexibility. But her head was too small for the superb neck." Swan-women appear in other Cabell works. *Courtesy of Valentine Museum, Richmond*

91      THE AUTHOR OF *The Eagle's Shadow*

Cabell in 1906. Ellen Glasgow was likewise photographed in this chair in 1906, by the Richmond photographers Homeir and Clark. In 1924 Cabell satirized himself in a sketch entitled "The Author of *The Eagle's Shadow*" (1904), wherein the youthful author seeks the advice of the author of *Jurgen*. "He was fat, remarkably fat for a lad of twenty-two or thereabouts; and he had, as I noticed first of all, most enviably thick hair, sleeked down, and parted 'on the side' with some fanfaronade in the way of capillary flourishes. He was rather curiously dressed, too, I considered. . . . It must have been, in fine, a good bit over twenty years since I had seen anybody apparaled quite as he was."

THE AUTHOR OF *The Soul of Melicent*

A copy of this photograph is so inscribed in the hand of Cabell. He is here thirty-four, at Rockbridge Alum Springs, in 1913. As an eligible bachelor Cabell earned his bed and board at summer resorts by writing of social events and enumerating their guests for Richmond papers. The tone of this "society reporting" is reflected in his earlier work. The year before, Cabell had met Mrs. Emmett A. Shepherd at the springs, a vivacious widow who became the subject of "A Brown Woman," a story published in *Lippincott's Magazine* and later incorporated in the Biography. Cabell and Mrs. Shepherd, who had inherited a comfortable estate from her husband, married November 8 the year this photograph was made.

93             PRISCILLA BRADLEY SHEPHERD CABELL

Priscilla Bradley Shepherd was four and a half years older than Cabell when they married in 1913. Nearly forty, she was the mother of five children, one an invalid from a childhood illness. Cabell's affectionate portrait of his wife of thirty-six years is detailed in "Another Book About Her," the first half of *As I Remember It*. She was the prototype of all the "real," the domestic, women in Cabell's work, most notably Dame Lisa in *Jurgen* and Niafer in *Figures of Earth*. They had one child, Ballard Hartwell Cabell, born when Priscilla was forty. Dr. Cabell, grandfather of Ballard, knew that his grandchild was born defective but refrained from telling the happy parents for some time. Priscilla Cabell came to cherish her sixth child as she did all her other children and rather treated her husband as a seventh child to be protected from the vicissitudes of life.

DUMBARTON

When Cabell married Priscilla Bradley Shepherd in 1913, he moved into her commodious country house a few miles north of Richmond. She assigned him the triple-windowed room on the second floor over the front door for his study. It is termed the Room of Ageus (anagram for *usage*) in the last part of *Figures of Earth*, and the triple windows figure significantly in Manuel's rejection of the dreamworld beyond the glass and his acceptance of such reality as domesticity held: "It was only in the old glass of Ageus that his wife and child appeared to live and move." The aged Manuel returns through this window having killed Suskind (*unkissed*, read Gabriella Moncure), "for it was she alone who knew the secret of preserving the dissatisfaction which is divine where all else falls away with age into acquiescence." After the Cabells moved from this house in 1925, it was used for a while as a nightclub. Its burning in 1937 "both depressed and pleased" Cabell.

95      CABELL AT THE ROCKBRIDGE ALUM SPRINGS

Cabell wrote in his preface to *Figures of Earth*, "So I began 'the book about Manuel' that summer,—in 1919, upon the back porch of our cottage at the Rockbridge Alum Springs, whence, as I recall it, one could always, just as Manuel did upon Upper Morven . . . observe that the things one observed were all gigantic and lovely. . . . Upon that same porch, as it happened, this book was finished in the summer of 1920." In 1922, the Cabells chose Mountain Lake as their summer abode, and the scenery there became the location of Brunbelois in *The High Place*. "For the corresponding high place of holiness I drew upon my memories of the now deserted and fallen Rockbridge Alum Springs, to which, if it at all matters, the curious may discover that Upper Morven bears a remarkable resemblance: and while I was about this scene shifting, I lifted from the ruined Alum lawns the boulder beside which Florian builds his little fire."

96        CABELL CIRCA 1915–1916

Ballard Hartwell Cabell, Cabell's only son, was born August 25, 1915, and snapshots of Cabell with Ballard as an infant would appear to date this portrait around that time. Cabell would be thirty-six or thirty-seven, the author of *The Rivet in Grandfather's Neck*, dedicated to his wife, and *From the Hidden Way*, the collection of poetry written primarily in college for Gabriella Moncure.

97      THE JAMES BRANCH CABELL SCHOOL

    The notoriety of *Jurgen*'s suppression catapulted Cabell into international fame, and he became the leader of a group of writers in the early 1920s known as "The James Branch Cabell School," later castigated by socialist critics as "The Sophisticated School" or "The Aesthetes." Cabell's chapter on this period in *As I Remember It* is entitled "Remarks upon a Once Glorious Epoch." Van Vechten's *The Tatooed Countess* and Wylie's *Jennifer Lorn* both owe much to Cabell's sophisticated irony. Cabell is pictured here at center holding court on Halloween, 1923, at the West Chester, Pennsylvania, country club. He and others were there visiting Joseph Hergesheimer (third from left). Seated to Hergesheimer's right (second from left) is Priscilla Cabell. Elinor Wylie is on Cabell's left. Van Vechten, behind the woman in the large white hat, appears to be dressed as a sailor. H. L. Mencken, hair parted, in bow tie, is toward the back right. Blanche and Alfred Knopf, publishers, are on the front to the far right. Inasmuch as Phoebe Gilkyson, an aspiring writer who would publish in the *Reviewer*, was also of West Chester and sent this photograph to Cabell, she may be the animated talker to his right.

98          3201 MONUMENT AVENUE

For the first twelve years of their marriage, James and Priscilla Cabell lived in Dumbarton Grange, the large frame house just north of Richmond that her first husband had built on the Dumbarton railway stop. In 1925, with her children grown, they moved to 3201 Monument Avenue in Richmond. The house, despite its appearance of size, was considerably smaller, built on a triangular strip, all facade with no rear yard. "And at 3201 Monument Avenue she allotted to me yet another library upstairs wherein to write books," wrote Cabell. It was another triple-windowed room, on the left above. The parlor, also on the left, later became a bedroom because of Priscilla Cabell's arthritis, and here Cabell died on May 5, 1958.

99       THE AUTHOR OF THE BIOGRAPHY

This photograph of Cabell was used by Frank C. Pape for an etching copyrighted 1930, the year the Storisende Edition of the Works of James Branch Cabell completed its appearance. Cabell was then fifty-one. This photograph may have been made somewhat earlier or the art of the retoucher may have evened his hairline, a symbolic gesture in accord with certain retouchings Cabell had made in the "completed" Biography.

CABELL AS HOST

Burton Rascoe, Ellen Glasgow, Cabell, Priscilla Cabell, and Eliott Springs pictured in the dining room of 3201 Monument. This room on the west later became the living room when the latter, to the east, was made into a downstairs bedroom owing to Priscilla Cabell's arthritis. A small reception room opposite the front door became the new dining room; in it Cabell installed the white marble mantel from his grandmother's house at 101 East Franklin. This mantel is now the focal point of the Cabell Room in the James Branch Cabell Library. Cabell was sensitive to the symbols of "old family" gentility, as his pygmalion transformation of Rebecca P. Shepherd to Priscilla Bradley Cabell attests.

MARGARET FREEMAN, LATER THE SECOND WIFE OF CABELL

Margaret Freeman, drawn here in the early 1920s, was one of the four editors of the *Reviewer*, credited with stimulating the renaissance in southern letters. In *As I Remember It*, Cabell tells us he first glimpsed her in 1918 when she was twenty-four and that later as guest editor of the *Reviewer* he "did not argue with Margaret Freeman, who waited with her chin raised defiantly." He urged Hunter Stagg, another editor, to propose to Margaret, but Hunter was turned down. Margaret made a career for herself in New York as an interior decorator. Some thirty years later, the widowed Cabell himself proposed and was accepted, after Margaret Freeman consulted with Hunter Stagg.

When Priscilla Cabell developed nearly crippling rheumatism in 1936, the Cabells gave up their annual summer sojourns to Mountain Lake as their cottage there stood on a steep hill. They elected to spend their summers near Ophelia, Virginia, "in low-lying Northumberland County," and bought a building site at the mouth of the Potomac looking northward into Chesapeake Bay. Priscilla Cabell dispensed with an architect's services. "She accomplished this task through the forthright process of telling the local carpenters exactly what she did want and just exactly where she wanted it put," Cabell wrote in *As I Remember It.* "She improvised and she perfected any number of architectural betterments while the building was in progress. But among her very first requirements, as I recall matters, was a glass-enclosed small porch-room, so that in the summer time Mr. Cabell would have somewhere to write his books. . . . And always after that we spent each summer at Poynton Lodge, quietly and with contentment, among a loyal assemblage of her children and of her grand-children." Margaret, Cabell's second wife, continued the leisurely rituals here, large meals, gardening, shopping for fresh fish and produce, entertaining relatives and friends.

103       CABELL AND MARGARET FREEMAN, ON THEIR WEDDING DAY

Margaret Freeman was fifty-six, Cabell seventy-one when they married June 19, 1950. Priscilla Cabell had died the year before, and Cabell was concerned for Ballard's welfare as well as his own domestic comforts. Ballard, then nearly thirty-five, suggested that his father marry the "vibracious" Margaret Freeman who did "not ever put up with any foolishness from anybody." Margaret debated the choice between her declining career in New York as a decorator and that of homemaker for a man she had known in her youth but had never dreamed of marrying. Margaret consulted Hunter Stagg; Cabell consulted Marjorie Rawlings, his neighbor in Florida. Ballard was her fate. She continued the routines congenial to Cabell: summers at Poynton Lodge in Ophelia, winters in Saint Augustine, spring and fall in Richmond. She nursed Cabell in his final illness in 1958 and made a home for Ballard until his death in 1980. *Courtesy of the Richmond* Times Dispatch

104         THE PORCH OF 3201 MONUMENT AVENUE

In pre-air-conditioned Richmond, porch-sitting was respectable, and as 3201 had no rear garden in an older tradition, its front porch served as a pleasant sitting area to observe a minuscule garden of camellias on the east (through the lattice arch). Summers were spent by Cabell and his family for some fifteen years at Mountain Lake, Virginia, and then at Poynton Lodge for the remainder of his life. In 1935, owing to Cabell's annual bouts with pneumonia, they began to spend their winters in Saint Augustine, Florida. Accordingly, 3201 Monument Avenue became primarily a spring and fall residence, congenial seasons in Richmond.

105        BALLARD CABELL

        Cabell wrote of his son: "Ballard had developed into that which the advertisements of 'special schools' call tactfully 'the exceptional child.' His body had grown quite normally, I mean, although it remained dwarfish; but his mind must stay forever—so said the omniscient grave doctors—the mind of a child. Yet I found as the years passed that his mind was astute and nimble and remarkably well balanced throughout its entire extent. The trouble was, so nearly as anybody could phrase this matter, that a part of his mind was missing. Of mathematics, here to cite his main lack, Ballard had not ever any notion." But Ballard's excellent memory for faces, his courtesy, his pleasure in meeting people won for him many friends. Margaret Cabell interested him in painting in gouache, an opaque watercolor technique, and his work was accorded critical recognition in a number of art shows. He is pictured here in his fifties; he died in 1980 in his sixty-fifth year.

106       <small>CABELL IN HIS SEVENTIES</small>

Cabell is here pictured in his small writing room just off his library on the second floor of 3201 Monument. He continued writing up until his final illness. His last book, *As I Remember It*, was published in 1955, three years before his death. His library is now housed in the Cabell Room of the James Branch Cabell Library of the Virginia Commonwealth University, while many of his papers are at the University of Virginia. He was first buried in the cemetery of Emmanuel Episcopal Church at Brook Hill, Virginia, next to Priscilla, his wife of thirty-six years, but Margaret Cabell, his wife of eight years, then elected to move both to Hollywood Cemetery in Richmond, leaving a space between for Ballard and reserving a space for herself next to Cabell.

107      THE CABELL ROOM

Margaret Cabell stands in the room she designed to house Cabell's
personal library in the James Branch Cabell Library of the Virginia Commonwealth
University. She took as her model the Victorian style of the house Cabell was born in,
101 East Franklin (see the photograph on page 83), and the marble mantel shown
here is one from that house. On the right stands a mahogany bookcase which Cabell
bought with the first money he earned from the sale of his early stories. In this case he
kept the leather-bound copies of the first editions of his works. Over the bookcase
hangs a portrait of Ballard Cabell. On the opposite wall (unseen) hangs a portrait of
Cabell painted after his death from a photograph; Margaret wanted him to appear as
the man she was married to. His earlier portraits were given to other institutions. Margaret Cabell likewise designed Cabell's tomb in Richmond's Hollywood Cemetery, a
Renaissance-style sarcophagus sculpted in Italy.

# JAMES BRANCH CABELL
## *The Life of His Design*

### W. L. Godshalk

When I was invited to speak at the James Branch Cabell Centennial Celebration, I was asked—almost immediately—for the title of my talk. The phrase "the life of his design" popped into my head, and I determined to use it. Only several months later did I recognize the significance of my apparently inadvertent choice. "The life of his design" is derived, of course, from Shakespeare's *Troilus and Cressida*. In a scene central to that play, the Trojans debate the essential pros and cons of keeping Helen from the Greeks. The Helen we see and hear in that play is hardly Cabell's unattainable queen, and Shakespeare's Hector—the Trojan policy leader—points out the irrefutable reasons why this minx should be returned and the war ended. Then, curiously, as he concludes his carefully reasoned speech, he abruptly changes his mind, deciding that Helen must be kept at all cost—"For," he says, "'tis a cause that hath no mean dependance / Upon our joint and several dignities" (II. ii. 192–93).[1] His conclusion is shockingly at variance with his former argument, but none of his auditors onstage seems to notice or care. Young Troilus is especially heartened by Hector's final commitment to keeping Helen and shouts: "Why, there you touch'd the life of our design!" (line 194). In his youthful enthusiasm, Troilus is driven by thoughts of "glory" and "fame." It is doubtful if he in any way understands or even glimpses the ironies of Hector's speech, but, of course, we do. When Troilus speaks of the life of their design, he refers specifically to Hector's specious conclusion and

---

1. G. Blakemore Evans (ed.), *The Riverside Shakespeare* (Boston: Houghton Mifflin, 1974), is the text used.

its emphasis on "dignity," that is, worldly appearance, the Trojan public image. Though Troilus may accept the conclusion at face value, we—who stand apart from the action—see that the life of the play's design is a tension between the reality of lust and war, and the assertion of dignity. The myth of the Trojan War that Shakespeare could count on his audience to know is superimposed on a sordid struggle between cuckolds and lechers. For us, the life of Shakespeare's play is epitomized in Hector's speech; the play is based on the deeply felt and unresolved tension implicit in this double vision of the world.

But what does this have to do with Cabell? I believe that those familiar with Cabell's fiction will acknowledge that it is based subtly or blatantly on the same unresolved tension. However, when the title of this essay popped into my head, I had no idea what it had to do with Cabell's work, and I had no idea what the actual topic of my talk would be. It became rapidly apparent, nevertheless, that I wished to focus my attention on *Figures of Earth*, Cabell's novel that concentrates on bringing designs to life and the many ironies involved in that process. But what has *Figures of Earth* to do with Shakespeare's *Troilus and Cressida*? Although I do not believe that Cabell was thinking of Shakespeare's play when he wrote the novel, there are interesting links between the two works and I believe that they are profoundly similar at the deepest level where the design of each comes to life. I shall return briefly to this idea later, but now I wish to concentrate on some aspects of *Figures of Earth*.[2]

The work is divided into five parts, each dedicated to a different literary figure, and each prefaced with a quotation from Cabell's fictitious source. In the foreword addressed to Sinclair Lewis, Cabell calls this source *Les Gestes de Manuel*, but the quotations are all in English—obviously from a Renaissance translation. The preliminary indications suggest that we are reading a romance; and this is the primary level of the narrative. The first part of the romance, dedicated to Wilson Follett, is called "The Book of Credit." It deals with Manuel's youth. When we meet him, he is a young swineherd staring into the pool of Haranton, daydreaming. "His gravest care in life" appears to be a "figure which [he] had made out of marsh clay from the pool of Haranton" (p. 3). At this point, he meets Miramon Lluagor, the maker of dreams, and receives instruction for his first quest, along with the magic sword Flamberge, which, according to legend, makes

2. James Branch Cabell, *Figures of Earth: A Comedy of Appearances* (New York: Robert M. McBride, 1921), second printing, is the text used in this essay. I select this text as being closest to Cabell's (corrected) original purpose.

its bearer invulnerable. Manuel is to rescue the Count of Arnaye's lovely daughter who is being held captive, Miramon says, by a magician at the top of Mount Vraidex. With Flamberge strapped to his side, Manuel begins his ascent, and meets Niafer, who is also climbing the mountain. At each dreadful encounter, Manuel reaches for magic Flamberge, but Niafer forestalls him by deceiving each of the four monsters. The mountain is successfully climbed through Niafer's deceptions and with no heroic act performed by Manuel. At the top, Manuel unexpectedly finds Miramon Lluagor, the magician who set him the quest and gave him the sword—in order to have himself conquered. Farcically, Miramon is married to the Count of Arnaye's lovely daughter and wishes her to be rescued so that he may live and practice the art of dream-making in peace. Manuel is given the choice, here, between Gisèle, the count's talkative and domineering daughter, and Niafer, Gisèle's simple waiting woman. Apparently infatuated by Niafer's tricking of the monsters, he chooses her. What he does not know is that Niafer's tricks came from the same source as Flamberge—Miramon himself. Unfortunately, as the happy couple descend Vraidex to be married, they meet Grandfather Death, and Manuel allows Niafer to die in his stead; the implication is that he actually murders her. At the same time, Manuel learns the secret of worldly success from Horvendile, and the rest of Part 1 shows Manuel using a goose feather to bring wisdom to King Helmas, holiness to King Ferdinand, and the unattainable princess, in this case, Alianora, to himself. It is after his meeting with King Ferdinand and being made Count of Poictesme (if he can only get it away from the incumbent ruler) that Manuel assumes his lifelong motto: "*Mundus vult decipi.*" "The world desires to be deceived." In each court he visits, Manuel continues his work as sculptor, making, in each case, a figure that mixes the features of his host or lover with his own.

Dedicated to Louis Untermeyer, Part 2 of the romance is called "The Book of Spending." Having attained the unattainable princess, Manuel implicitly rejects her for his interest in sculpture, and she explicitly rejects him to become Queen of England. Manuel now desires to bring his figures of earth to life, and he learns that the easiest way to do that is through the good graces of Queen Freydis, the Queen of Audela, the land beyond the fire. After deceiving her into becoming his mate and into animating Sesphra—the figure that mixes Alianora and himself—the pair live happily for a brief while in Morven—a land of enchantment.

"The Book of Cast Accounts"—dedicated to H. L. Mencken—is the central part of the romance, in which Manuel rejects Freydis. Leaving her suddenly one evening, Manuel travels northward to Dun Vlechlan, "where the leaves [are] aglow with the funereal flames of autumn" (p. 166). Here he serves the disembodied head of Misery for one month—thirty days that become for him thirty years. At the end of his servitude, Manuel asks Misery to bring Niafer back from the dead—which he duly accomplishes. This part culminates with Manuel and Niafer meeting Alianora, Freydis, and their entourages. Alianora is traveling to England to become queen; Freydis is going to take possession of the Red Isles. The confrontation is replete with subdued antagonism.

Dedicated to the English novelist, Hugh Walpole, Part 4 is "The Book of Surcharge." This part begins with Manuel's failure to conquer Poictesme by military force and ends with Miramon Lluagor's conquest of Poictesme for Manuel by means of ten mythic figures. Between these two events, Manuel makes friends with the Philistines, arranges with the stork to have babies delivered in a method prescribed by the prudish Philistines, dwells briefly with Freydis where Niafer has their first child (delivered by the stork, of course), and has a strangely homosexual affair with his animated creation (Sesphra) who is now married to Freydis. As this part comes to an end, Manuel rejects Freydis completely, and Miramon transforms him into a Christ figure—though the redemption of Poictesme is hardly Christian in nature.

The fifth and final part, dedicated to Joseph Hergesheimer, is "The Book of Settlement." Now Manuel prospers, reaching the height of his worldly power and wealth. He travels to England, fathers a male child upon Alianora, and never sees her again. He then spends his time in the Room of Ageus, until one day he realizes that the third window in that room does not open out onto reality, but onto the realm of Queen Suskind—apparently the same girl who had loved him in his youth. Finally, because of Suskind's hold on his child Melicent, Manuel murders Suskind, and in the last chapter confronts, once more, Grandfather Death. This time Manuel is given a choice between going himself or sending Melicent; he elects to die himself. Passing through Lethe, Manuel returns, strangely, to the beginning of his eventful history. Once again, he is a young man at the pool of Haranton, and Miramon Lluagor, the brother of Death, is preparing to send him on his initial quest.

I realize that this attempt at giving a bird's-eye view of the total structure of the romance leaves much unsaid and that a synopsis at its best is never completely rewarding. Indeed, I confess that I have, in the foregoing paragraphs, been a paraphrastic heretic. For one thing, my paraphrase does nothing to capture the haunting figure of Suskind who lurks at the edges of the action from the very first chapter onward. But, with this rather large disclaimer, I do think that this outline allows us to see a few essential aspects of Cabell's design.

One of the recurrent ideas of the novel—an idea that is part of much of Cabell's fiction—is that for each attainment a price must be paid. Life is a series of trade-offs; if you take that, you lose this. The idea is simple, easy to state, and profound in its effects on life; it is a basic principle in Cabellian economics. As Horvendile tells Manuel, "It is always possible, at a paid price, to obtain whatever one desires. . . . But I must tell you the price also, and it is that with the achieving of each desire you will perceive its worth" (pp. 48–49). The implication is that the object is not worth the achieving.

In *Figures of Earth*, Cabell puts this cost analysis into the very structure of the fiction. In this connection, it is well to remember that *manuel* in common law means, in part, "a thing whereof present profit may be made." In Part 1, Manuel is willing to trade Gisèle and to pay Niafer for his own life. It is at this point in the narrative that Horvendile explains the principle of cost to Manuel, and, in a sense, we can then see that Manuel has given Niafer for Alianora—paid his beloved serving girl for the unattainable princess. In the second part, Manuel pays the price for this attainment by realizing its worth. "Yes," Manuel says, "you and I are second-rate persons, Alianora, and we have found each other out. It is a pity. But we will always keep our secret from the rest of the world, and our secret will always be a bond between us" (p. 111). Of course, Alianora must be given up to attain Freydis, while, in Part 3, Freydis must be paid and Misery served to regain Niafer. Misery here explains the terms of repayment: "When you have this Naifer," Misery tells Manuel, "I shall return to you in the appearance of a light formless cloud, and I shall rise about you, not suddenly but a little by a little. So shall you see through me the woman for love of whom your living was once made high-hearted and fearless . . . and you will ask forlornly, 'Was it for this?'" (p. 187). Nevertheless, as Alianora is attained in Part 1, Freydis in Part 2, Niafer is the prize of Part 3. In the next part, the thing to be purchased is Poictesme, and the price to be paid is more complex: Manuel must ally himself with the Philistines, reject Freydis utterly, and become one of the Redeemers, no longer quite human. "Thus," Cabell observes, "did Dom Manuel enter into the imprisonment of his own castle and into the bonds of high estate, from which he might not easily get free" (p. 286).

In the final part of the romance, the object of purchase and the price to be paid are more difficult to state, more ambiguous. The problem centers upon the third window in the Room of Ageus. We know that *Ageus* is an anagram for *usage*, and so the Room of Ageus apparently implies conventions both social and personal. To dwell in the Room of Ageus is to live conventionally, according to one's habits and the general status quo. In order for Manuel to do this, Alianora must be rejected—and she is. That price is, to all appearances, easily paid. But a problem remains: there is another vista in this Room of Usage, a vista into the misty world of Suskind. *Suskind*, we know, is an anagram for *Unkiss'd*. And when one enters the Kingdom of Suskind, one leaves behind a locket of one's hair as the price of entrance. That Manuel is forced to leave a locket as paid tribute to Suskind does not seem to trouble him, but he is extremely troubled when his daughter Melicent pays a locket of her hair. Apparently Melicent's initiation into Suskind's kingdom is part of the price Manuel himself must pay in order to enjoy that kingdom's mystic pleasures. But, Manuel tells Suskind, "You . . . have demanded the one price I may not pay" (p. 336). Melicent, Manuel hopes, will remain as untroubled by thoughts of Suskind as is her mother Niafer. To ensure this, Suskind is murdered and the third window is mortared up. The Kingdom of Suskind is a symbol of the unattainable desires that man always has—even Manuel. And when these desires are finally destroyed—when Suskind is murdered—Manuel is ready for Grandfather Death. Manuel appears to believe that death is his final payment, that he will now obtain peace.

The five parts of *Figures of Earth* fit together as a complex series of purchases, of debts and prices to be paid. The financial subtitles point in this direction, and what we watch in the five books is the increasingly high price of earthly success; we see the cost of selling out as well as its inevitability. Again I would like to enter a caveat and emphasize that I have recorded only a few of Manuel's major financial transactions. The other characters are also involved in their own financial speculations and purchases, for Manuel is not alone in conducting his personal life in terms of economy.

In tracing Manuel's financial record, Cabell recurrently uses, in talking of Manuel, the language of bondage. From the beginning of his story, Manuel is bound. In the first pages, we learn that he feels constrained by a geas put upon him by his mother. He tells Miramon: "My mother, sir, was always very anxious for me to make a figure in the world, and when she lay a-dying I promised her that I would do so, and then she put a geas upon me to do it. . . . It is what you might call a bond or an obligation, sir, only it is of the particularly strong and unreasonable and secret sort which the Firbolg use." But in accordance with his own desires, Manuel interprets his mother *literally*: in order to "make a figure in the world" he has become a sculptor. Miramon is more than dubious. "Are you certain," he asks, "it was this kind of figure she meant?" silently deliberating the question "if any human being could be as simple as Manuel appeared" (p. 5). Of course, Manuel is not at all simple; he has *simply* interpreted his mother's geas to suit his own desires. His elaborate pun on "figures" is as intentional as Cabell's. Saying good-bye to his pigs, Manuel tells them, "I shall travel everywhither, and into the last limits of earth, so that I may see the ends of this world and may judge them while my life endures" (p. 9). Manuel makes this statement of his desire again and again, with variations, throughout most of the romance. But, the point to be made and emphasized is that here the bond is interpreted to fit the man.

As the story progresses, the bondage becomes a far different sort, and Manuel is caught ultimately in his role as Redeemer of Poictesme; he assumes a preestablished role; he is no longer unique, merely one of a series of mythic heroes. Manuel himself recognizes this bondage. "Certainly I think there is no escape for me upon this side of the window of Ageus," he admits. "A bond was put upon me to make a figure in this world, and I discharged that obligation. Then came another and yet another obligation to be discharged. And now has come upon me a geas which is not to be lifted either by toils or by miracles. It is the geas which is laid on every person, and the life of every man is as my life, with no moment free from some bond or another" (p. 327). It is Manuel's tragedy that he comprehends the extent of his confinement. But he also sees its necessity. "There is no help for it, and no escape," he says, "and our old appearances must be preserved . . . in order that we may all stay sane" (p. 337). We are trapped by life.

Only Grandfather Death can offer him liberty from Usage, and yet even as Death prepares to give him freedom and welcomes him to talk freely, Manuel refuses: "Even at the last there is the bond of silence," he says, "I shall never of my own free will expose the naked soul of Manuel to anybody" (p. 343). In one sense, anyway, Manuel's bondage is self-imposed, the price he has had to pay for what he has made of himself and what he is—a figure of earth. In the end, he is not a man who interprets the bond to meet his desires, but a man who increasingly accepts and is bound by the desires of others.

Manuel's silence is puzzling. Even at the last, there is the bond of silence. Cabell himself points to this aspect in his prefatory letter to Sinclair Lewis. Contrasting Jurgen and Manuel, Cabell initially suggests that "Dom Manuel is the Achilles of Poictesme, as Jurgen is its Ulysses." "Yet," he goes on, "minute consideration discovers, I think . . . a more profound, if subtler, difference, in the handling of the protagonist: with Jurgen all of the physical and mental man is rendered as a matter of course; whereas in dealing with Manuel there is, always, I believe, a certain perceptible and strange, if not inexplicable, aloofness. . . . never anywhere have I detected any firm assertion as to Manuel's thoughts and emotions, nor any peep into the workings of this hero's mind" (p. xv). Cabell concludes that this is, in fact, the way we must deal with all our fellow creatures, "whether they wear or lack the gaudy name of heroism" (p. xvi). Obviously, Manuel is silent because it suits Cabell's purpose.

Cabell never explicitly tells us that purpose, but Manuel's silence is surely connected with the subtitle of the novel: "A Comedy of Appearances." Since we are never allowed to glimpse Manuel's thoughts or feelings, we must judge him by appearances, and part of the experience of reading *Figures of Earth* is our attempt to judge the real and the illusory, to discriminate between them. But Cabell's use of appearance is not that simple. Manuel's motto—"*Mundus vult decipi*"—expresses Manuel's belief, a belief founded on the facts of the world as he finds it, that humans desire to be deceived. Deception gives us holiness, wisdom, and love; deception is the very basis of human transactions. The romance itself is merely appearance, and Cabell has Horvendile—his surrogate—say, "All the living in this world," that is, the world of the romance, "appears to me to be only a notion of mine" (p. 46). The fictional reality is exploded. And all things, Cabell hints, both inside and outside the story, are appearance; nothing is surely real. The superiority of the reader is destroyed, much as is the smugness of the audience at the end of Genet's *The Balcony*.

Cabell gears Manuel's silence to his education in appearances. When Manuel's sister tells him piously, "The coat does not make the man," Manuel replies, "It is your belief in any such saying that has made a miller's wife of you, and will keep you a miller's wife until the end of time" (p. 53). And so Manuel begins his second quest dressed appropriately in Sunday black. After his multiple deceptions with a goose feather, Manuel meets the Zhar-Ptitza—the Fire-Bird—whose cry is: "Fine feathers make fine birds." Manuel seems driven to point out to the bird that this is not the true proverb, and "such perversions . . . they tell me, are a mark of would-be cleverness." Of course, the reader knows that Manuel has already learned the lesson of sartorial appearance, but the Zhar-Ptitza does not, and the bird responds: "So it may seem to you now, my lad, but time is a very transforming fairy. Therefore do you wait until you are older . . . and then you will know better than to doubt my cry or," the bird concludes archly, "to repeat it" (pp. 102–103). And, of course, this is the very touchstone to Manuel's character. He becomes the public man, a gray eminence, a public voice mouthing meaningless platitudes. He becomes a husk of his former self, and at the end we intuit that Manuel's silence now results from his inner emptiness. He has lived superficially so long that there is nothing else left. When Grandfather Death arrives, Manuel insists on his prerogatives: "In Poictesme the Count of Poictesme goes first in any company. It may seem to you an affair of no importance," Manuel tells Death, "but nowadays I concede the strength as well as the foolishness of my accustomed habits, and all my life long I have gone first" (p. 351). However we may interpret the accuracy of Manuel's final assertion, it is a nice touch, and it captures him perfectly. Even in the face of Death, appearances must be kept; they have become habitual. His recognition that these habits are foolish again indicates that he is not unaware of what has happened to him.

Manuel's silence, then, is tragic. He is not imperceptive; he is not uncreative; he does not lack emotions. But to achieve public success, he has allowed appearances to replace genuineness in his character; he has taken deception for his reality.

But there is another reason for Manuel's silence, and this reason has to do with the genre in which Cabell is, at least in part, working. Beneath the trappings of romance, *Figures of Earth* is an allegory. As Cabell himself insists, comparison of *Jurgen* with *Figures of Earth* is inevitable. *Jurgen*, I would like to argue, is not allegorical, although it may approach allegory in its use of symbolism. For example, the women whom Jurgen meets are symbolic of certain ways of life or human values. But his relationship to these symbolic women does not become allegorical because their actions—what the women say and do—do not *necessarily* indicate an *internal* change in Jurgen himself. The characters in *Jurgen* are related to the protagonist's various searches for meaning in the universe, but they do not mirror what is happening in Jurgen's psyche. In *Figures of Earth*, the characters do indicate what is happening in Manuel's psyche, and I believe the romance is capable of—in fact, can only be completely understood by—a sustained allegorical reading. I am not going to attempt a thorough allegorical reading here, but I do wish to show that the allegory is a substitute for Manuel's verbal revelations.

Since words are a facade for Manuel, not a way of getting at truth, it is highly appropriate that allegory is used to reveal what is happening to him. As we remember from our reading of Spenser, the allegorical protagonist does not express his emotions; they are expressed for him by the situation he is in and the characters he meets. When the Red Cross Knight enters the forest of Error, for example, he does not *say* that he is confused by a multiplicity of religious doctrines. His actions and the monster he fights with *symbolize* that confusion. A great deal—I am not prepared to say "all"—of *Figures of Earth* works precisely in this way. Of course, my adverb *precisely* is not quite accurate since allegory is not generally susceptible to precise interpretation as we know from the many conflicting readings of *The Faerie Queene*. Nevertheless, I would like to attempt a brief reading of Cabell's allegory while recognizing the necessary limitations of such an attempt.

At the beginning of the romance, Manuel is the artist-dreamer staring into the pool of Haranton and making his figures of earth, his artistic creations, from the fantasies engendered by the pool. It is a pool of common human experience that Manuel has yet to understand completely. He is approached by the master of dreams who tells him that one of his dreams can be made real: he can have the unattainable woman. Given an apparently magic weapon, Flamberge, he is told that he must climb Mount Vraidex, the mount of "ten truths." I take it that Manuel's conquest of Vraidex symbolizes his understanding that truth is not simple; there are many truths, and Manuel moves beyond naïve dualism into the world of multiplicity. Also, his climbing of Vraidex indicates the loss—by conquest—of his early dreams. If Manuel is the dreamer, Niafer is the embodiment of active common sense. During the climb, he learns that common sense is of more value than magic swords. For the artist-dreamer this is a valuable lesson.

At the top of Vraidex, Manuel must chose between Gisèle and Niafer—between the unattainable woman and the servant girl. Forced to give up his early dreams, he understands that by taking Niafer he is giving up "everything my elders have taught me to prize"—wealth, social status, broad lands, a lovely wife. His rejection of Gisèle is his last gesture of youthful romanticism as well as a rejection of his dreams. He accepts common sense.

The ensuing confrontation with Grandfather Death is Manuel's first realization that death is inevitable—even for him. Having conquered and left the world of youthful dreams, he must face the fact of personal extinction. In his fear, he sacrifices the person he loves most—Niafer, who dies for him. Her sacrifice symbolizes the death of initial, youthful purity as well as the rejection of conventional common sense. Manuel understands that common sense cannot save him, finally, from death. He is now instructed by Horvendile in the ways of success and (because of the in-evitability of death) learns that worldly success is worthless. Manuel runs scared.

Attempting to forget the loss of Niafer, he returns briefly to the pool of Haranton, rapes Alianora, and, after her flight, begins a second quest for the unattainable woman. The allegorical significance of Alianora is not immediately discernible, though we may believe, to begin with, that she is the embodiment of romantic love. In his quest for her, Manuel happens upon King Helmas, to whom he inadvertently gives the gift of worldly wisdom. During his sojourn with Helmas, Manuel learns the ways of wisdom, but at this juncture he has no desire, or perhaps need, to use them. His encounter with King Ferdinand gives him experience with what the world considers holiness, and he comes to understand that holiness of this kind is also not now what he needs. Finally, he attains the ironically unattainable Alianora, who, we finally recognize, is not the symbol of love, but of political power; or perhaps we may better see her as political power disguised as romantic love. In raping her, Manuel is forcing his way into politics. Manuel's liaison with Alianora is short-lived, but during his stay in the court of her father, he makes an image combining her features with his—a figure known as Sesphra, *i.e.*, "phrases." Manuel learns that the art of politics is an art of language, of making memorable patriotic phrases. At this point, Manuel and Alianora part company, apparently because Manuel is a second-rate politician and politics, he feels, is a second-rate activity. In this section, young Manuel experiments with wisdom, holiness, and political power as focuses for his life. He is disillusioned, but at no time does he utterly reject any of these possibilities. He will return to them in due course.

Manuel now desires to animate his figures of earth, and his new quest is for Queen Freydis, another unattainable woman, the Queen of Audela, *i.e.*, "over there." Wisdom, embodied in Helmas, tells him how to win her; the dictionary is the book of magic that must be used. Freydis is, of course, artistic inspiration; she is, if you will, the muse. Manuel's deception of her is the internal process of artistic creation, and her animation of Sesphra indicates that Manuel has become the talented verbal artist who is able to create lifelike characters. Manuel, however, does not like image makers (artists), satirizes them, and rejects Freydis—at least for the time.

Manuel's next quest is for the return of Niafer, for which he must serve the personification of Misery for a month of years, sacrificing his youth for her return. As I read it, Manuel's visit with Misery is not separable from his quests for political power and artistic distinction. Misery has become a part of his life, and it is not so much that he seeks Misery as that he wishes to be rid of it. He believes that a return to Niafer—improperly remembered, of course—will be a return to youthful happiness. For Manuel, she still symbolizes commonsense living, conventionality, a stable home, and babies. The misery of life brings back Niafer, or, we may say, the death of youth causes the rebirth of common sense.

At this point, Poictesme enters the allegorical picture. Given to him earlier by the holy Ferdinand—if only he can get it away from the Northmen who live there—Poictesme is the embodiment of materialism, and to attain his material desires, Manuel must court holiness, learn political rhetoric, and change his life to conform to conventional morality. Finally, to attain Poictesme he must espouse the religion of the Redeemer and become one with Christ. In passing, Queen Freydis and Sesphra along with their perverse and subversive natures must be rejected completely. The artistic temperament cannot exist in Poictesme. It is the home of conventional common sense.

In the final part of the allegory, Manuel has achieved the height of his material success; he has a last, brief flirtation with political ambition; and then he retires to the Room of Ageus—to Usage, to his ingrained habits. The Kingdom of Suskind is the symbol of his remaining unattainable desires, and, when he destroys Suskind, he in effect kills himself. His "soul" or what's left of it is gone.

What we have, then, in the narrative of Manuel's life is actually his inner story—the progress of his soul in its quests and in its defeats. An Everyman, Manuel is the artist *manqué*, the creative talent that sacrifices everything for material success only to realize its worthlessness.

I discern an interesting conflict in the novel between the manner and the matter. In general, the allegorical mode presupposes meaning and worth. Spenser will again give us a norm. Book II of *The Faerie Queene*, for example, is based on the supposition that temperance is a meaningful virtue that can give structure to life. This supposition, in turn, is based on the hypothesis that we live in an ordered and meaningful universe with ultimate justification. The educated reader, I submit, comes to an allegory with these expectations. Quite the reverse is true in *Figures of Earth*. Cabell supposes a meaningless universe, and his allegory (in itself meaningful) depicts the meaninglessness of human life. What we are presented with is almost a contradiction in terms: an ironic, satiric allegory.

In this context, two aspects of Cabell's allegory seem to me most significant: it is both fragmentary and circular. First let me explain what I mean by fragmentary. I am not using it pejoratively to indicate that Cabell lacks command of his medium. What I mean is that Cabell is the master of the discrete incident. He does not fragment reality as an author such as Thomas Pynchon does, but he refuses to interpret life as an organic whole, as a meaningful plot. In Cabell's vision, life is merely a succession of ironic incidents, and this vision affects the way the narrative is presented. Let us take as an example the end of Chapter 6 and the beginning of Chapter 7. In Chapter 6, Manuel talks with his sister Math after having raped Alianora at the pool of Haranton. He tells Math that he will no longer herd swine; he will follow his own thinking and his own desire. "Thereafter," Cabell writes, "Manuel kissed Math, and . . . set forth for the far land of Provence" (p. 54). We expect that the next chapter will logically follow from this sentence. It does not. Instead, Cabell violently shifts the perspective, and Chapter 7 begins from the viewpoint of King Helmas. "So did it come about," writes Cabell, "that as King Helmas rode a-hunting in Nevet under the Hunter's Moon he came upon a gigantic and florid young fellow, who was very decently clad in black" (p. 55). The focus of the narrative has changed, and the chapter might with ease be detached from the novel and read as a short story. This disjunctive experience is a constant in reading *Figures of Earth*. Many techniques contribute to the feeling: the surprising encounter (*e.g.*, Manuel and Niafer coming face to face unexpectedly with Freydis and Alianora), the rapid shift (*e.g.*, Manuel's first defeat in Poictesme), the mysterious entrance (*e.g.*, Hinzelmann), the inexplicable occurrence (*e.g.*, the apparent death of the knight in vermilion armor). Recurrently, the reader is challenged, thrown off balance, puzzled, forced to search for a meaning. In sum, the reader is stopped, for the allegorical nature of the narrative insists that he make sense of what's going on while the narrative incidents often militate against any such procedure.

Why does Cabell do this? I think the answer is that he wishes to destroy our feeling of narrative continuity. If life is not a meaningful whole, then the narrative should remind us of that fact. It should be puzzling and disjunctive, not clear and unified. I realize, of course, that this kind of explanation indulges in what has been called the "imitative fallacy." That is, if the artist wishes to express boredom, he writes a boring passage to bore his readers. Cabell, however, does not bore us, and the antagonism set up between the allegory of a man's life—with its roots in medieval and Renaissance art—and the disjunctive narrative is one of the basic ways, I believe, that Cabell gives life to his design.

But the narrative is also circular. As Grandfather Death leads Manuel through the river Lethe, Manuel asks what his destiny will be. "It is that of all living creatures, Count Manuel," replies Death. "If you have been yourself you cannot reasonably be punished, but if you have been somebody else you will find that this is not permitted" (p. 353). Manuel finds the statement incomprehensible, and so, I think, does the reader—at least initially. Part of the problem is the ambiguity of "this." Ultimately, I take "this" to mean "being somebody else." It is not permitted in this world to be another person, and that means, I believe, to live according to the ideals of others, exactly what Manuel has come to do. Manuel's punishment is to be returned to the beginning of his story, to be forced to try again. He is caught on the wheel of Karma, and, of course, all we can expect is that he will continue to fail. He is consigned to meaningless, repetitive failure.

Part of this repetitive quality is also carried by the mythology of the romance. A reading of the Cranwell and Cover *Notes* reveals that Cabell is using figures drawn from various mythological systems from Russian to Aztec.[3] As Redeemer of Poictesme, Manuel becomes the eleventh of the mythological redeemers that Cabell (or Miramon) assembles to conquer Poictesme. The point is that Manuel is not at all unique; he is merely one of a repetitious and mainly forgotten series.

But, as Grandfather Death points out, Manuel's destiny is the destiny of all living creatures. In a very tragic way, the defeat of Manuel is our defeat, for Manuel is Everyman, and we participate in his meaningless life. The only glimmer of hope is that even in defeat Manuel can assert—without much authority, it's true—his own worth. Grandfather Death skeptically asks, "What does it matter now?" (p. 347).

Now this essay, too, must come full circle. It should be clear by now, I think, how *Figures of Earth* resembles Shakespeare's *Troilus and Cressida*. Both are cynical works that rely on the tension between the real and the mythic for their vitality. The Trojan War and the redemption of Poictesme are glorious myths of golden times. Against these myths, Shakespeare and Cabell set an inglorious and rather sordid reality. The life of their designs relies on the disjunction we all feel between our desires and our actual accomplishments, between our beliefs and our deeds. Both works embody and gain life from this tragic duality.

3. John Philips Cranwell and James P. Cover, *Notes on "Figures of Earth"* (New York: Robert M. McBride, 1929).

# ENCHANTMENT AND DELUSION
## *Fantasy in the Biography of Manuel*

## Mark Allen

Even though James Branch Cabell's entire Biography of Manuel assumes the life and lineage of Dom Manuel, ruler and redeemer of Poictesme, only some of the individual stories use the history and mythology that Manuel and Poictesme provide. The works that do can be categorized as mythological tales, distinct from the historical and contemporary tales of the Biography, and from the nonnarrative, literary discussions that we get in the likes of *Beyond Life*. These works, too, are Cabell's contributions to fantasy literature, different from the rest of the Biography in certain formal respects, but more important, unusual in the imaginative license they allow. Among these works we find, as the tumblebugs would have it, Cabell's most scandalous: *Jurgen* and *The High Place*. We also find perhaps his most whimsical: *The Silver Stallion*. Certainly, we find here some of his most poignant in *Music from Behind the Moon* and *The Way of Ecben*. These works, along with *Figures of Earth, The Cream of the Jest*, and *Something About Eve*, pose for us a rich and sometimes startling array of nymphomaniacal witches and goddesses, an imaginary geography that is all but unique in fiction, and a series of narrative surprises that teach us to be on our toes while delighting our socks off. Indeed, the range of fantastic devices that Cabell uses can sometimes be suspected of sheer virtuosity, and if taken in doses too large, his fantasies can cloy just a bit, but he continually stands up to rereadings—a result, no doubt, of his linguistic and imaginative richness.[1]

1. For all of Cabell's fantasies, I have used the Storisende Edition (18 vols., New York: Robert M. McBride, 1927–30). All quotations are from this edition.

It is tempting to re-pose a comparison that has been posed before: between Cabell and his British contemporary, Lord Dunsany. Their similarity is a function of their common fantastic richness, for each regales in a particular type of imagination. Cabell is certainly more the ironist than Dunsany—using and debunking familiar or just less than familiar myths— while Dunsany is more the romantic—fabricating his own mythology of Pegāna. But behind this, there is a similarity that runs deep: both of them are capable of the grand rhythms of mythological prose. Dunsany's mythic names, for example, are richly evocative though purely imaginative, and his rhythms and syntax are downright biblical: "Before there stood gods upon Olympus, or ever Allah was Allah, had wrought and rested Māna-Yood-Sushāī."[2] If not always familiar, Cabell's names usually reward the efforts of research if we know where to look in Greek, Norse, Indian, and Russian mythology. A particularly interesting sample is his selection of the name *Horvendile* for his recurring figure of the poet and lover—a variation on the pre-Aesirian, Norse god Orvandel, and an analogue to Tolkien's Eärendil.[3]

But more important, Cabell's prose style—like Dunsany's and Tolkien's—reaches grand heights when necessary, even though he contrasts his "high" prose with matter-of-fact dialogue and sometimes brutally mundane characters. This point is an important one, since style is too often neglected in discussions of fantasy and too little noticed when Cabell is discussed in this respect. Ursula Le Guin has made the valuable observation that style is more important to fantasy than to other types of literature "because in fantasy there is nothing but the writer's vision of the world."[4] When Madoc, for example, pursues the "skirling" music of Ettarre, we have only Cabell's language to evoke in us a sense of what it is like "behind the moon." And what is remarkable is Cabell's ability to achieve this sense without relying wholly on descriptive detail. For unlike many less adept writers of fantasy—and very much like the adepts—Cabell portrays his otherworlds through an accumulated atmospheric sense as well as a visual one. His worlds, in many ways, are created not by *what* he says about them, but *how* he says it. Without descending to facile archaizing—without committing the sin of the "She-To-Whom Trap" that

2. Lord Dunsany, *The Gods of Pegāna* (Boston: John W. Luce, n.d.), 1.

3. Lin Carter, "Horvendile—A Link Between Cabell and Tolkien," *Kalki*, III (1969), 85–87.

4. Ursula Le Guin, *From Elfland to Poughkeepsie* (Portland, Ore.: Pendragon, 1975), 28. This essay has been reprinted in Le Guin's collected essays, Susan Wood (ed.), *The Language of the Night: Essays on Fantasy and Science Fiction* (New York: Putnam, 1979).

Le Guin defines—Cabell achieves a fine and subtle "distancing from the ordinary."

He avoids the false subjunctive mood and a forced archaic vocabulary; instead, he relies on rhythms and cadences that are uncommon without becoming febrile. His diction is generally simple and concrete, although he seems to delight in the single, unusual word that requires particular attention to its appropriateness. His prose is laced with rhetorical figures, but unless underscored for ironic effect, they rarely loom larger than the information they carry. This is the stuff of effective fantasy style, uncommon without being distorted: "It was a strange and troubling music she made there in the twilight, and after that slender mistlike woman had ended her music-making, and had vanished as a white wave falters and is gone, then Madoc could not recall the theme or even one cadence of her music-making, nor could he put the skirling of it out of his mind. Moreover, there was upon him a loneliness and a hungering for what he could not name" (IV, 253). We find here the choice simile of a wave and that wonderfully evocative word *skirling*, but the accumulative rhythm of the first sentence and the contrasting, falling rhythm of the second are what produce in us a feel for Madoc's yearning. For even if we do not know what *skirling* means, we know that it is music that haunts, that hangs on to the back of the mind without quite being heard. And if we do know that *skirling* means the sound of a bagpipe, the context somehow removes the instrument to a faraway hill where the harshness of the sound is softened and made alluring.

In a strange way, this paradox of alluring harshness epitomizes Cabell's style; it epitomizes the clash between romance and realism which carries his irony as well as his imaginative richness. I referred earlier to a similar, although broader paradox that typifies Cabell's fantasies: that clash which echoes between his unearthly settings and his pedestrian characters—best seen in the contrast between setting and dialogue. In *Figures of Earth*, chronologically the beginning of the Biography, Manuel ascends to the top of Vraidex, the mountain of the sorcerer, Miramon Lluagor. Later, he conjures up Queen Freydis of Audela and withstands the horrors of her shape-shifting. Later still, he passes through the Window of Ageus to the graylands beyond. Indeed, most of Manuel's exploits find him confronting characters, places, and situations that are the material of otherworldly fantasy. These actions come forth alive from Cabell's pen, creating a truly fantastic arena for Manuel and his fellow characters.

But when Manuel talks, we wonder if he is not missing something of the splendor that surrounds him. He speaks with such simplicity that we cannot be sure whether he is shrewd or blind, valiant or merely stupid. His repeated assertion that he must "make a figure in the world" is at once a recurring pun and strikingly at odds with the tasks he attempts in order to fulfill his goal. For when Manuel's mother told him to "make a figure in the world," she no doubt meant something quite different from either fashioning mud-figures in a swine wallow or magically enlivening statuettes. And even though Manuel pursues his tasks with heroic fortitude, Cabell's irony is apparent.

It is not only Manuel's misunderstanding, though, that produces the irony; it is also Cabell's deft touch with understatement and mundanity in dialogue. When Manuel is told of the great Miramon Lluagor, "lord of the nine kinds of sleep and prince of the seven madnesses," he recalls what he has heard of the sorcerer: "Yes, in the kitchen of Arnaye, also, such was the report concerning this Miramon: and not a person in the kitchen denied that this Miramon is an ugly customer" (II, 6–7). Or during Manuel's service to Béda, the head of Misery, our hero asserts that he has an immortal spirit. Béda pursues the issue, asking where the spirit resides. Manuel can only reply: "It is inside me somewhere, sir. . . . Well, I have always heard so, sir" (II, 145). In Manuel's diction and lack of conviction we have a challenge to the necessary awe and wonder of fantasy that comes close to satirizing the form itself. The danger is that the otherworldly atmosphere of the tale might dissipate before irony, social comment, and literary self-consciousness—as sometimes it does.

The work *Taboo* is a case in point. I have not included *Taboo* among Cabell's fantasies simply because it fails to maintain an atmospheric distance from irony and social comment. Indeed, unless we know that Horvendile here is a mouthpiece for Cabell's comments on literary censorship, the story makes little sense at all. This is not to say, necessarily, that *Taboo* is a poor tale, simply that it is not a fantasy. It is clever and rather engaging as a result, but it is not fantastic. What distinguishes *Figures of Earth* and its kin is the consistent backdrop of evocative language, even in the face of irony and near allegory. The language creates a sense of an otherworld and stands up to the irony in the works, allowing us to see where Cabell directs our attention, but rarely forcing us out of Poictesme back to actuality.

After all, it is Cabell's imaginary geography and cast of characters that are a great part of his power. Without Audela, Antan, Acaire, and hell, there would be no fantasy in the Biography. Without Ettarre, Freydis, Yaotl, and Horvendile, Cabell's more realistic characters would not be lead to otherworlds. If fantasy requires a language all its own, it is built in realms of its own making. And Cabell builds such a variety of imaginative sets for his characters that a list of them would be formidable. In *The Silver Stallion* alone we find not only Poictesme, hidden somewhere in central medieval Europe, but Miramon's magic mountain, The Place of the Dead where Coth pursues Manuel, the realm of the gods where Donander plays the game of creation, and more. The work represents well Cabell's imaginative range since it is a collection of interlocking tales that allow for broad variety.

The action opens at the castle, Storisende, of the now dead Manuel, located near the center of Poictesme. The medieval setting is familiar enough in fantasy, valuable for its distancing from the ordinary and for its flavor of high romance. The setting, too, carries with it an implicit sense of adventure that is manifested when seven of Manuel's nine lords attempt the quests laid upon them by Horvendile. Gonfal, Miramon, Coth, and Guivric pursue the four points of the compass, Kerin descends, Donander ascends, and Ninzian remains to wrestle with saints and spirits.

If Coth's experiences are the most varied, Guivric's are in a way the most fantastic. For even though Donander becomes a god and Miramon shakes the universe, Guivric travels east only to find himself where he began. His tale is fantastic not only in setting and character, but formally as well. Guivric pursues Glaum the Sylan only to find that Glaum is pursuing him. While seeking to free himself from Glaum's enchantment, Guivric finds that he has only to submit to achieve a sort of victory. This circular pattern is a surprisingly effective device that capitalizes upon Guivric's venture into a magical realm: the narrative "trick" of the tale depends upon the magic of Glaum "beyond the wall of the Sassanid." Through his magic, Glaum takes over Guivric's body and offers his, condemning the hero to wraithdom or freeing him from the shackles of humanity—we are not sure which. Guivric leaves his study only to reenter through, apparently, Glaum's doorway and confront the image of himself. We find a wry sort of *doppelgänger* that is possible only in an otherworld.

Eric Rabkin, in his *The Fantastic in Literature*, poses a somewhat labored term, *anti-expected*, for the unfamiliar occurrences that we encounter in fantastic realms.[5] Labored though it is, the term is curiously applicable to the narrative surprises that we find in Cabell's fantasies. The magic of Glaum's shape-change is, I suppose, anti-expected, but in a way it is only

5. Eric Rabkin, *The Fantastic in Literature* (Princeton, N.J.: Princeton University Press, 1976), 10.

a means of posing the narrative trick that countermands our expectations of a quest. Here is clear anti-expectation: we set out on a quest to a realm of mystery and high magic, and we find ourselves entering the study we left some pages earlier. The essence of a quest is the testing of the questor and the accomplishment of the task, and Guivric not only gets nowhere, he literally loses himself without ever having moved. The device, of course, depends upon magic—a new set of phenomenological laws—and as such it is the stuff of fantasy. Indeed, it may be the final trick that an author of fantasy can use on his audience.

But if it is the final trick of the fantasy author, Cabell does not know when to quit. *Music from Behind the Moon, Jurgen, Figures of Earth, The High Place*, and other tales from *The Silver Stallion* all use similar narrative ploys, each one dependent upon the power of some character, some talisman, or the magic that seems to be Poictesme's fate. Madoc rescues Ettarre by altering the book of the Norns—of past fate. Jurgen asks Koshchei the Deathless to return him to the wife he is simultaneously running from and rescuing. Manuel discovers that the coming of Grandfather Death replaces him on the treadmill that has been his life—the final scene of the work duplicating the initial one. The third wish of Miramon in *The Silver Stallion* counteracts the effects of his having won three wishes in the first place. And Florian of *The High Place* dreams an entire life, only to awaken again as a drowsy ten-year-old.

This latter case is of particular interest to the fantasist because it accomplishes the difficult task of maintaining fantasy in a dream-frame, a peculiar form of counteracting expectation. Like Lewis Carroll's adventures of Alice, *The High Place* casts its fantastic setting as the figment of a child's imagination, and like Carroll's work too, *The High Place* succeeds where similar attempts fail. The difficulty lies in posing the dream so that the sense of the otherworld does not dissolve before the rationalizing effect of the dream itself; fantasy requires credibility for the marvelous, not explanation, and if the action of the story is the record of a child's dream—and only this—the story destroys its own marvelous equipment. In *The High Place*, however, Florian's dream is much more than a child's imagination at work. Since Florian awakens with full recollection of his dream, and since his dream includes a range of experience unknown to any ten-year-old—especially aesthetic and sexual experiences—we understand that Florian has lived on some other plane in the dream, however unexplained. The dream is simply one way of passing from the familiar to the fantastic and back again. Like Jurgen's ride on the back of the centaur or the Sylan's magic in *Something About Eve*, Florian's dream is a form of portal between two realms of differing phenomenological laws—a portal between magic and mundanity that transports the characters while playing loose with our expectations. We have a dream that is more than a dream and a magical realm that is, for Florian, somehow more than real. The reader can maintain belief in Florian's dreamworld because the world is internally consistent and sufficiently detailed. When we find that the tale is a dream, our belief is modified but not destroyed.

Cabell uses a somewhat different technique in *The Cream of the Jest*, and yet we have a similar sense of a narrative trick. Perhaps his most fascinating talisman of power—the sigil of Scoteia—here functions as the portal. When Kennaston toys with the sigil and is transported haphazardly through time and space, we cannot help but wonder whether he is enchanted or insane. He becomes Horvendile through the power of the sigil, pursuing Ettarre and visiting out-of-the-way corners of history. When we discover that the sigil is only half of a broken cover to a jar of cold cream, the jest seems complete. But this is only the cream; the jest is Cabell's own when the talisman is decoded. All men, we find, pursue Ettarre in their own ways, and all men, too, share in Kennaston's enchanted insanity—or insane enchantment. The levels of irony and narrative play echo throughout the work, all of them dependent upon the fantastic talisman. If the other portals in Cabell's works are more familiar in fantasy, few of them support as much ironic weight or such broad interplay of narrative levels.

I have hurried through a representative description of Cabell's otherworlds and the narrative devices they pose to find myself discussing his portals. The accident is appropriate. Even better than his various imaginative worlds, Cabell's portals demonstrate his range as a fantasy writer. Whereas the sigil of Scoteia and Florian's dream are two of Cabell's more elaborate portals, others are not far from hand. Earlier, I mentioned Jurgen's ride on the centaur: the journey takes the level-headed pawnbroker on a race with the sun, ending in the fabulous garden between the dawn and sunrise. Guivric's exchange with Glaum anticipates Gerald Musgrave's encounter with Guivric/Glaum that transports him to lands of enchantment in *Something About Eve*. Donander's death in *The Silver Stallion* is his portal to otherworlds, as Kerin's fall down the Well of Ogde is his.

Indeed, nearly all imaginable types of portals are found in the Biography. We have simple journeys across boundaries, magical ventures through windows and doorways, sudden transformations of dream and vision, death and rebirth. We find conjuring spells like Manuel's invocation of Freydis, objects of power like Miramon's Bees of Toupan, sending spells by which Dolores projects Jurgen into hell. In each case, the device offers us a means to glimpse new sets of laws with the characters, unfamiliar geographies, and purely imaginative experiences. Through Cabell's portals the reader of the Biography can walk, dream, or wish himself from one realm to another, participating in the release from the familiar that makes fantasy refreshing. Even when we begin in magical Poictesme, we travel to other realms that function differently, and the very process of magical movement provides us with the simple gratification of travel, while giving a chance to do what we cannot do in automobiles, jets, or even rockets—we break the rules and find new rules, impossible rules of magic and fantasy.

These rules and the portals that discover them are of course Cabell's. As such we expect the irony that they carry. His realms are frequently those we might not want to visit—hell, for one—and his laws are not always appealing. The rules of religion and morality, in particular, lack something of the idealism that is expected in fantasy, but Cabell's rules are as fully developed as their complements in other works of fantasy. Where a work like George MacDonald's *Phantastes* poses chastity as an ideal, Jurgen's adventures pose a different morality to say the least. Where Tolkien or Dunsany assumes a spiritual hierarchy, Cabell's gods are distinctly relative. What is important though is the consistency between law and action in a work of fantasy. Even if it be the consistency of chaos, the work must pose its own rules and play by them. As the battlefield victory of *The Lord of the Rings* parallels its moral hierarchy, so Jurgen's ironic profligacy is paralleled by his final return to his shrewish wife. In a similar way, Manuel's wry stupidity anticipates all the various perspectives on romanticism and realism that the later characters embody. The portals in the Biography are consistent with Cabell's pervasive theme that things are not always as they appear to be—in Poictesme any more so than twentieth-century Virginia.

Cabell's fantasies reflect one more of the elements essential to fantasy: a love of language. As discussed earlier, he writes with the easy precision of a word-shaper, fully capable of creating an atmosphere that is rich, alluring, and tangible. As well, his works are thematically concerned with language and its power. Spells, quotations, and promises all play important parts in Cabell's tales and they rarely are fallow when employed. Jurgen receives a cantrap (cantrip) from the Master Philologist early on in his exploits and tries frequently to use the spell. Only when he seeks to move from heaven to hell does he discover the wry power of the words: he capitalizes on the apparent accident of history that so long left heaven without a Pope John XX. Jurgen claims the spot and is justly (?) rewarded. *Something About Eve* follows Musgrave's pursuit of the same Master Philologist. Madoc writes with a feather from the Father of All Lies. Indeed, the entire mythology of Manuel relies upon the *word* of the young Jurgen who said he saw the Redeemer last.

As is apparent, language can delude as well as enchant in Cabell's worlds and for his readers. Manuel spends much of his life seeking to "make a figure in the world," but he does not understand the meaning of his mother's geas. He strives valiantly to rescue Niafer from death because she so cleverly talked their way to the top of Vraidex, yet he does not see that all Niafer's cleverness is a ruse. And we are never quite sure how much else is a ruse. Cabell uses language as a double-edged tool and sometimes we get cut. Where Tolkien fashions his own Elven language, Cabell falsely documents his poems and tales. Where Le Guin's Earthsea trilogy relies heavily on the mythic power of names, Cabell shields irony in puns and anagrams. Where the riddles in Patricia McKillip's Riddle-master trilogy are the sources of power for the characters, Cabell's riddles pose dilemmas for his readers. In each case, language is magic, and magic, language. But with Cabell, language is also a game to play with his audience; we see the power of language in its extraordinary uses, and we find it challenging.

There is irony here as well as elsewhere in Cabell's fantastic imagination. It permeates his style, his themes, and all the devices of fantasy that he employs. But his irony rarely displaces the temporary belief we have when reading his fantasies. In conversation, yes, we discuss his sly puns and absurd characters, but when we read, we live for a time in Poictesme, the land where anything can happen and usually does. Like Cabell's own characters, we learn that delusion is a way of the world—a way of the world that can well lead to otherworlds, enchanted ones.

# THE RETURN OF JAMES BRANCH CABELL; OR, THE CREAM OF THE CREAM OF THE JEST

## Leslie A. Fiedler

I first read James Branch Cabell's *Jurgen* in 1932 or 1933 as a gesture of contempt (I was then fifteen or sixteen years old) to the world of my elders: a way of asserting my independence of the taboos imposed on me in particular—and more generally on all writers and readers of the time—by what I had already learned from H. L. Mencken to call the "booboisie," and what Cabell himself taught me, long before I discovered Matthew Arnold, to refer to as "Philistia." *Jurgen*, I knew before I picked it up, had been not so many years earlier a banned or almost-banned book. And I thought of it, therefore, in the context of other once-forbidden novels like Dreiser's *Sister Carrie*, Lawrence's *Lady Chatterly's Lover*, and James Joyce's *Ulysses*; so that flaunting it in the face of parents and teachers seemed to me quite as revolutionary an act as publicly reading Marx's *Das Kapital* or joining the Young Communist League—which I also did at the same moment, with a similar sense of daring, and none at all of the contradictions involved.

That Cabell despised Joyce and Lawrence, the whole adventure of modernism with which I had misguidedly identified him, I was as bliss-fully unaware as I was that, quite unlike those avowed enemies of convention and organized religion, he dutifully attended church, appeared in formal dress at cotillions, and refrained from typing on Sundays lest he offend his stuffier neighbors. Nor did I suspect that his politics were as far to the right as mine then were to the left, though it was already on record that he wished Hindenburg had triumphed in World War I and Stonewall Jackson had carried the day in the Civil War. In any case, I still believed that the main point was to *épater la bourgeoisie* from either flank; and that a chief weapon in that fundamental conflict between an enlightened Us and a benighted Them was the production of what They considered pornography. I was dimly conscious, though it scarcely seemed to matter, that what Cabell wrote was a special *kind* of pornography—soft, genteel, perhaps a little pretentious; which is to say, pornography euphemized and camouflaged with recondite literary allusions, learned mythological references, and quotations from acknowledged "great books," preferably in Greek and Latin, or at the very least, French.

I would, moreover, have denied vehemently that the pleasure I found in reading *Jurgen* (culture-climbing adolescent that I was, for all my radical jargon) had anything in common with the titillation derived from the same book by those "chorus girls" who Heywood Broun had reported thumbed through its pages, ignoring everything but certain "phallic" passages of which they had heard on the subcultural grapevine. And certainly I, a boy from the streets of Newark, New Jersey, felt nothing in common with those other young ladies in suburban or semirural finishing schools whose continued sniggering interest in his book prompted fan letters which enraged Cabell. Nor did my appreciation of his erotic masterpiece, I assured myself, resemble even the somewhat more sophisticated response of Zelda Fitzgerald, who, pleading that she could not find a copy in her local bookstore, wrote to ask Cabell to send her one; backing up her plea (she knew a nympholept when she encountered one) with a particularly fetching photograph of her very young and quite beautiful self.

Yet, I now realize, whatever my aesthetic or political rationalizations, I must have turned with relief (and the kind of thrill appropriate to my age) from the dutiful perusal of grim texts like Friedrich Engles' *Anti-Dühring* or Lenin's *What is to be Done?* not just to *Jurgen*, but to such other purportedly antibourgeois soft porn as James Huneker's *Painted Veils*, Anatole France's *Penguin Island*, and Pierre Louys' *Aphrodite*. Such books were available in those days in garishly illustrated cheap reprints, along with erotic "classics" like Flaubert's *Salammbô* and Boccaccio's *Decameron*, as well as more blatant examples of up-to-date mytho-pornography like Viereck and Eldridge's *My First Two Thousand Years*. And they were typically stacked up on bargain tables in chain drugstores and cut-rate *schlock* emporia, which peddled them side by side with exploding cigars and cutesy genre pictures of sleeping nude boys whose peckers were being nibbled at by geese.

I first read *Jurgen*, that is to say, in the context of a kind of exploitative popular culture against which I thought I had been immunized by long exposure to "high art," particularly in its avant-garde manifestations. Was I not, at the very moment, for instance, following breathlessly in succeeding issues of *transition* sections from the book which eventually became *Finnegans Wake*, but was then known by the few who were aware of it at all as *Work in Progress*? And had I not long since graduated from taking seriously the kind of *fin de siècle* pop novel which Cabell had begun by imitating, Anthony Hope's *Prisoner of Zenda*, for example, and Henry Harland's *The Cardinal's Snuffbox*? Even the romances of Booth Tarkington, about which Cabell remained ambivalent to the end of his career, the unspeakable *Seventeen* and the insufferable *Monsieur Beaucaire*, I had left behind with junior high school. Nor had I ever really developed a taste for the kind of middle American, middle-class, pseudorealistic best sellers by Harold Bell Wright and Gene Stratton Porter, which Cabell felt obliged to vilify long after they had lost their mass audience. It was as if he never outgrew the need to prove (to himself, to certain forgotten newspaper reviewers, like Burton Rascoe, to readers like me) that he was something altogether different: neglected, perhaps, by most Americans, but for his virtues rather than his faults.

What was Cabell to do, however, when he became—thanks not only to professional enemies of Philistia like me, plus finishing-school students and chorus girls, who were at least young, but to the very middle-aged Philistines who read Wright and Porter—a best seller? This was, indeed, the cream of the jest (but on *whom?*): a jest belatedly compounded by the fact that even now, if any of his books is remembered at all, it is likely to be that anomalous marketplace success, *Jurgen*. Long before his death in 1958, Cabell had recorded, not once but many times, his dismay over the fact that that single book overshadowed all the rest—most movingly perhaps in a much rewritten novel, entitled appropriately enough, *The Cream of the Jest.*

In it, an author called Felix Kennaston (one of Cabell's many thinly disguised fictional surrogates) is described as having produced after some distinguished failures a best seller, *Men Who Loved Alison*—"one of those many books which have profited very dubiously indeed, by having obtained, in one way or another, the repute of being indecent." Such books, which Cabell-Kennaston tells us include "the sloppy and soporific catalogues of Rabelais . . . and the unendurably dull botcheries of Boccaccio," are read, he goes on to explain, by an audience consisting of "immature persons who are content to put up with the diction and stylistic devices for the sake of the atoning talk of unnatural amours, which, however sparsely . . . adorns and opens the pornoscopic reader's laborious way."[1] Despite the multiple ironies, Cabell's point is clear. There are two types of best sellers: those read by a mass audience responding to the trash they really are; and those (usually erotic or suspected of being erotic) responded to for what they are *not* by the kind of reader who finds their essential best a distraction and a bore. But it is to the latter category that Cabell, despite everything, believed *Jurgen* to belong.

To have confessed otherwise, even to himself, would have undercut not only his aesthetic faith in himself as essentially different from the darlings of the literary marketplace but also his political belief that the majority of Americans (perhaps the majority of mankind) is always wrong in its choices in the bookstore as well as the polling place. Had he not declared as early as 1919 in *Jurgen* itself that "The religion of Hell is patriotism, and the government is an enlightened democracy"?[2] And was he still not insisting, looking at the best-seller lists of 1945 and finding them as disheartening as those of his youth, that "a nation which upon three separate occasions hand running re-elected Franklin Roosevelt has abandoned all claims to intelligence?"[3] Like most Americans by the end of World War II, I found such unreconstructed anti–New Dealism absurd, and the antidemocratic bias it betrayed reprehensible; yet even at that point I was no more able than Cabell to grant that in the literary arena as well as the political, popular judgment might sometimes be superior to that of a self-appointed aristocracy of taste.

But in the case of Cabell's *Jurgen* at least, time has proved the mass audience right. *Jurgen* (contrary to what Cabell himself thought) *is* the best of his novels—not despite its pornographic passages and because of its "fine writing," but despite that "fine writing" and because of its appeal to prurience. Had Cabell or any of the critics who first touted him understood so much, they would have been able to surmise what they did not in fact foresee: that his work was ironically destined to survive not as "high literature," belles lettres, "serious art"—but as a kind of "pop" appealing primarily to adolescents of all ages. Indeed, in this sense, his fate resembles that of Edgar Allan Poe, another native of Richmond, Virginia, and the only nineteenth-century American author he could bring himself

---

1. James Branch Cabell, *The Cream of the Jest: A Comedy of Evasion* (New York: Ballantine Books, 1971), 8–9.

2. James Branch Cabell, *Jurgen: A Comedy of Justice* (New York: Grosset and Dunlap, 1919), 277.

3. Edward Wagenknecht (ed.), *The Letters of James Branch Cabell*, (Norman: University of Oklahoma Press, 1975), 222.

to praise without qualification; though Poe, who like Cabell considered himself a "dandy" in the realm of art, has ended as the favorite reading matter of high school students and the source of plots for the kind of Class B movies they prefer.

Certainly, I myself did not realize this essential truth about Cabell even after my first enthusiasm for him wore out. At that point I not merely stopped reading him, I stopped thinking about him at all. If I recalled occasionally my former affection for *Jurgen*, it was as a juvenile lapse of taste, indulged in shamefully after I was old enough to know better: a yielding not only to what Cabell would have called my "pornoscopic" impulses, but also to a taste for overwriting and ingroup allusiveness—obvious appeals to reigning fashion and the snobbism of the culturally insecure, to which I had believed myself immune. Even my change of heart, however, turned out to be in tune with the changing times; for as the depression grew deeper, it no longer seemed possible to praise his effete efforts as H. L. Mencken and Burton Rascoe, for instance, once had. Besides, I asked myself, who the hell were *they* anyhow, those newspaper hacks without real standards or any deep theoretical understanding of what literature was? Almost imperceptibly, I and my contemporaries had begun to think of our times not as a postwar but as a prewar era; which is to say, memories of Wilson's ill-fated War to End All War, which so obsessed Cabell, faded and intimations of FDR's war-to-come began to haunt our troubled sleep.

It was "realism," in any case, which carried the day in the thirties, whose preferred novelists were Dos Passos and Farrell and Steinbeck: that very "realism" against which Cabell had vainly protested all his life long; though he had exempted from his censure such twenties forerunners of that movement as Sinclair Lewis and Theodore Dreiser—largely because they were his friends and had publicly touted his work. Other twenties writers whom he admired and praised, however, like Joseph Hergesheimer, came to be considered in the gray days of the depression too effete, elegant, involuted, affected, and "decadent" to be endured. Nor were their reputations redeemed in the post–World War II reaction against the ideological excesses of the thirties. Though by the time the fifties arrived, critical consensus had begun to turn against not just Farrell and Dos Passos and Steinbeck but Lewis and Dreiser as well, this did not mean the rediscovery of Hergesheimer and Cabell. Rather like their realist contemporaries and successors, such dandies of the twenties were measured by post–World War II critics against two somewhat younger contemporaries, Faulkner and Hemingway, who came—however slowly and with whatever ups and downs—to represent the major achievement in fiction of the post–World War I sensibility.

But Cabell refused, with what seems at this remove a touchingly transparent defensiveness, to measure himself against them. Urged by literary correspondents to read them and register an opinion, he responded, "I cannot protest that Hemingway is quite my favorite author," and "as goes Faulkner, I have to date [he is writing in 1953] read none of his books, I confess blushingly. They did not attract me somehow and besides that I felt duty bound to dispose of *Gone with the Wind* [first]." The last sentence is intended, of course, as the ultimate put-down, since he had already declared of Margaret Mitchell's super–best seller in 1936, "I did not find *Gone with the Wind* to be even readable, far less a masterpiece."[4]

The conjunction of the two authors and their simultaneous dismissal though natural enough, inevitable, perhaps, is also symptomatic and revealing. After all, Faulkner is far and away the chief contender for the title of greatest southern novelist of the twentieth century, to which Cabell had clearly aspired; and Margaret Mitchell (also a Southerner, committed to imprinting on the popular imagination that region's myth of the Civil War and Reconstruction) had written the most successful best seller of the century, as Cabell seemed for a little while to fear (but, one cannot help suspecting, also to hope) he might have done. Such a rejection of the two chief fictional spokesmen for the American South seems consistent, at first glance, with his interior expatriation: his attempt to write from his retreat in Richmond if not quite as if from outside the South, at least from outside the South as a part of America—from outside of America.

He sets the action of his most characteristic books in an imaginary kingdom whose boundaries may be vague, but whose climate is Mediterranean, and whose language is French, or rather, I suppose, Provençal; and he attaches himself to a literary tradition rooted in late medieval France and Restoration England. No wonder then that he was contemptuous of what he called the "spiritual descendants of Walt Whitman," especially Waldo Frank, whom he parodically portrays as calling out, "Come, let's be sturdy and fearless pioneers, and grow real hair on our chests, and develop our splendid innate qualities without truckling to tradition and effete foreigners."[5] The moment at which Cabell was travestying the cultural rediscovery of America was, however, precisely the moment at which

---

4. *Ibid.*, 198, 108, 103.
5. *Ibid.*, 94.

not just for younger native writers but for the whole world, the literature produced in the United States in the middle of the nineteenth century was becoming an inspiration and model. "Classic American Literature," D. H. Lawrence called that flowering of prose and verse which for him climaxed in *Leaves of Grass*; and the American critic F. O. Matthiessen labeled it even more honorifically "The American Renaissance." But Cabell is apparently as immune to the appeal of the fiction of that period as he is to its poetry. Of the author of *Moby Dick*, for instance, he remarks coolly that "When it comes to Melville, I feel I lack appreciation." And this is comprehensible enough after all; since as Cabell himself never managed to say, but must somehow have intuited, the erotic myths of chivalry and gallantry, domnei and the service of women which inform his fiction have little in common with the peculiarly American myth of interethnic male-bonding which moved novelists otherwise as different from each other as Cooper, Melville, Mark Twain, and Faulkner.

There is oddly enough one American book which appeared at that magical point in the mid-nineteenth century about which Cabell has a good word to say; though it is one ignored by both Lawrence and Matthiessen, and distrusted by almost all elitist critics—precisely because, perhaps, it has been a favorite of the popular audience everywhere in the world except the American South. I am referring, of course, to Harriet Beecher Stowe's *Uncle Tom's Cabin*, of which Cabell was driven to write, despite his abhorrence for Mrs. Stowe's abolitionism, her shameless sentimentality, and her unflattering portrayal of the region he loved, "It is badly written, and has nothing to do with any South which ever existed, but its power is undeniable." What moved him to such a declaration was not simple perversity, as I was at first tempted to believe, but that deep yearning for the "romantic" rather than the "realistic" which joined him to the most frivolous readers of best sellers and separated him from the "serious" critics of his time. "I grieve to report," he said by way of explanation, "that as a romance the book is excellent."[6]

His instinctive and unquenchable love for the romance, moreover, not only separated Cabell from the neo-Whitmanians, populists, nativists, and realists, who flourished largely in the Northeast of the United States, and whose politics were more often than not left of center. It drove a wedge also between him and that rival school, the self-styled New Poets and New Critics, many of whom (from John Crowe Ransom to Allen Tate) were not merely Southerners like him, but shared both his rightist politics and

6. *Ibid.*, 224, 207.

his distrust of the author of *Leaves of Grass*. Though like Cabell, they, too, turned to Europe as a source of inspiration, their models were the *symbolistes*, the founding fathers of modernism, which Cabell despised. Not only did he eschew *vers libre* in favor of conventional stanzaic form, refusing either to "break the iamb" or abandon the clichés of traditional poetic diction; he disavowed as well their favorite European novelist, James Joyce. T. S. Eliot, on whose taste the southern Agrarians based their own, had given *Ulysses* his blessing; but Cabell contemptuously associated its prose style with the empty rhetoric of American politics. Looking back on certain popular books he had loved in his earliest youth, for instance, he observes that he now finds them "to be as sad twaddle as a Congressional Record or the effusions of the late Gertrude Stein and James Joyce."[7]

Once more, his judgment is consistent with his practice, since the definition of the modern novel, the art novel, implicit in *Ulysses* challenges the basic assumptions about the nature of prose fiction which underlie the mannered prose, the whimsical structure, the romantic tone of the legend of Manuel and his descendants. Indeed, so long as the critical establishment continues to share Joyce's assumptions rather than his, Cabell stands little chance of being considered ever again (the words are V. L. Parrington's and were written at the peak of his fame) "the supreme comic spirit thus far granted us."[8] Despite the heroic efforts of Edmund Wilson to refurbish his fading reputation in the years immediately before his death and the continuing adulation of a shrinking circle of parochial admirers, Cabell has in fact disappeared almost completely from the consciousness of practicing writers and literary pundits. Not only has it become impossible to think of him any longer as a "great writer," but even as a minor one of real interest; so that Frederick Hoffman in a comprehensive book on the literature of the 1920s published in 1955 did not even list him in an extensive bibliography, much less discuss any of his novels at length.

Yet in 1980, at least seven of his books, all from the Poictesme cycle, were once more in print as paperbacks, and were displayed side by side with current best sellers in the bookstalls of airports and supermarkets. But this time around they are presented as under the aegis of "fantasy and science fiction," in a series which also includes reprints of L. Frank Baum's Oz books and is clearly aimed at the audience which has turned

7. James Branch Cabell, *Quiet, Please* (Gainesville: University of Florida Press, 1952), 27.
8. Vernon L. Parrington, *Main Currents in American Thought* (3 vols.; New York: Harcourt, Brace & World, 1958), III, 345.

the *Rings* trilogy of J. R. R. Tolkien, Frank Herbert's *Dune*, and Robert Heinlein's *A Stranger in a Strange Land* into pop classics. Cabell, that is to say, at the very moment of his exclusion (permanent and irreversible, I fear) from the ranks of "high literature" threatens to return as a "youth best seller," sharing the fate of certain of his nineteenth-century predecessors like Bram Stoker and H. Rider Haggard, who were remanded to the outer darkness by the critical establishment, but—in part for that very reason—prized by a student underground. And this seems scarcely surprising in the light of the facts of which I have been reminding you, particularly the early popularity of *Jurgen*.

This time, however, Cabell appeals to a new generation of what he considered the mindless young (the grandchildren of his original audience) not as a pornographer or an old-fashioned spinner of romantic yarns, but as a writer of up-to-date fantasy. Cabell is "probably the only American fantasy writer of genius," Lin Carter writes of him, apparently forgetting that other Richmond author, Edgar Allan Poe. But we are dealing with "hype" rather than criticism: an introduction to a series of Cabell reprints which Ballantine Books obviously hoped would reach in the late seventies the ready-made audience for what Edmund Wilson was already describing in 1956 as "juvenile trash," meaning specifically *The Lord of the Rings*. At that point, Wilson still thought it possible to distinguish between the fairy tales of Tolkien, which he was proud to despise, and the fantasy of Cabell, which he was not ashamed to admire. The former, he believed, demanded of adult readers, eager to share the enthusiasms of the young, the abrogation of all "standards," ethical as well as aesthetic, normally associated with maturity and sophistication.[9]

It seems to me, however, that though there is a real difference between the two, it is one of degree rather than kind, Cabell substituting for the naïveté of extended childhood the callowness of prolonged adolescence. The pleasure, therefore, which despite myself I continue to find in his fiction, seems to me an understandable but rather ignoble response to what are essentially the wet dreams of an eternal fraternity boy, wish-fulfillment fantasies set in a realm between dawn and sunrise, in which time is unreal and crime without consequence. In this crepuscular Neverland, all males are incredibly urbane and phallic, all women fair and delightfully stupid up to the point of marriage. After that dread event,

9. Lin Carter, "About *The High Place* and James Branch Cabell," in James Branch Cabell, *The High Place* (New York: Ballantine Books, 1970), xi; Edmund Wilson, *The Bit Between My Teeth: A Literary Chronicle of* 1950–1965 (New York: Farrar, Straus and Giroux, 1965), 326–32.

the former become genitally inadequate, and the latter shrewish and nagging, though dedicated, for reasons never made quite clear, to nurturing and protecting their doddering mates so that they can produce romances celebrating not those wives, of course, but certain phantom girls whom they have not married and who consequently remain forever desirable and eighteen.

How is it possible today to respond without guilt to Cabell's travesties of male/female relations, when women everywhere around us are protesting such stereotypes of them and us? Indeed, they had already begun to do so at the moment Cabell was publishing his first books; nor was he unaware either of that protest or of the leveling politics which underlay it; the inevitable extension, it seemed to him, of egalitarianism from class to gender. Nonetheless, though he observed in 1935—with typical snide irony—that "the lady is climbing down to full equality with the butler and the congressman," he refused to give ground; declaring that as a "Romanticist" and a member of what he liked to call "the gentry," he could never agree to "regard women as human beings." Yet guilty or not, we who do regard our sisters as human, read him still in large part, I suspect, not in spite of his "sexism" but because of it; since in the unreconstructed dark underside of our minds the notion of the eternally unattainable lady which we do not dare to confess in full daylight continues to lead a crepuscular life.

Indeed, it would seem as if popular "fantasy" exists precisely in order to indulge "immortal longings" in us which our conscious pities and allegiances have taught us to continue. Cabell, to be sure, had completely different notions about the function of nonmimetic art. To him the enemy was "realism," which he identified not just with the bourgeois world of compromise and accommodation, but with the best sellers that celebrated its values. His elite "romances" he thought of as subverting and transcending that world in the imagination, thus preparing a chosen few for achieving in fact an evolutionary leap to a new level of humanity. But the survival of his books as merely another kind of best seller (preferred above all others at the moment by the youth audience) suggests that their function may all along have been "regressive" rather than "progressive," though therapeutically so—encouraging, as the psychiatrists would put it, "regression in service of the ego."

They afford us, that is to say, ways of expressing, harmlessly, symbolically, certain juvenile wishes and primordial fears that we have learned to be ashamed of but from which we can never quite deliver ourselves: ways— to use a metaphor which might well have appealed to Cabell, but somehow did not—of "giving the Devil his due." Though a working title of the novel eventually called *Jurgen* was "Go to the Devil," and Cabell actually described in it a Black Ritual invented by that infamous Satanist and sexologist, Aleister Crowley, he was deeply embarrassed when a grateful Crowley hailed him as "a world genius of commanding stature."[10] He refused in fact ever to answer his insistent letters, dismissing him as one of the nameless "hordes of idiots and prurient fools . . . of dabblers in black magic" from whom in genteel dismay he sought to dissociate himself.[11] Yet it is surely dishonorable motives rather like Crowley's which have made it possible for me to return to Cabell; ten of whose novels I read with unseemly relish before I could manage to stop, preferring this time around *The High Place*, a work really wicked, rather than, like *Jurgen*, merely naughty. And surely I could not have done so, if I had not realized that I was dealing not with "high art" but with "juvenile trash," which like all trash—indeed, like all books which "please many and please long"— was of the Devil's party without knowing it.

10. Aleister Crowley, *The Confessions of Aleister Crowley* (New York: Hill and Wang, 1969), 739.

11. James Branch Cabell, *As I Remember It* (New York: Robert M. McBride, 1955), 238.

# JAMES BRANCH CABELL
*A Bibliographical Essay*

## Ritchie D. Watson, Jr.

### BIBLIOGRAPHY

There have been a number of Cabell bibliographies published, including several which appeared during and shortly after the height of the author's popular and critical acceptance in the 1920s and early 1930s. Merle Johnson's *A Bibliographic Check List of the Works of James Branch Cabell* (New York: F. Shay, 1921), with an epistolary preface by Cabell himself, listed his books chronologically through 1921. Johnson's bibliography was quickly superseded in 1924 by Guy Holt's *A Bibliography of the Writings of James Branch Cabell* and in 1932 by a bibliography by I. R. Brussel with an identical title. Both of these works were published in Philadelphia by the Centaur Book Shop. Both Holt and Brussel provided collations and descriptions of first editions of Cabell's works as well as listings of his contributions to books and periodicals and selected secondary criticism. However, Brussel's work was naturally more inclusive and contained, as well, descriptions of subsequent editions of Cabell's individual works.

A twenty-five-year bibliographical hiatus ended with the publication of Frances Joan Brewer's *James Branch Cabell: A Bibliography of His Writings, Biography and Criticism* (Charlottesville, Va.: University Press of Virginia, 1957). In many respects Brewer's work remains the definitive bibliography of Cabell's published writings. Drawing on earlier bibliographies, Brewer presents her material in three parts. Part I lists Cabell's fifty-two books according to the series which he had created to divide his work, beginning with *Beyond Life* (New York: Robert M. McBride, 1919), designated as the first volume of the Biography of the Life of Manuel, and ending with *Of Ellen Glasgow* (New York: Maverick Press, 1938), the eleventh volume of the series entitled X Y & Z. Cabell's active participation in the preparation of this bibliography may well explain Brewer's decision to list the books in this order.[1] But one regrets the absence of a critical preface that would explain the rationale behind such an organization, since one might more logically assume the volume would be arranged alphabetically or chronologically.

Aside from this rather confusing arrangement, there are few criticisms that can be made of the contents of Part I. In addition to standard bibliographical information, Brewer's work provides a precise physical description of the first edition of each work, as well as the characteristics which distinguish subsequent impressions of that edition; and it lists later editions, with descriptions of those editions that contain significant revisions. The contents of each work are listed, as well as those portions of the book which were published originally in other books, in magazines, or in journals. Since Cabell customarily reused his material by incorporating shorter pieces into his books, this information is especially helpful. Bibliographical descriptions conclude with selected reviews of the work as well as other pertinent information. For example, Brewer provides a partial listing of books, pamphlets, and magazine articles dealing with *Jurgen's* suppression, and she informs us that the novel inspired a Deems Taylor musical composition performed by the New York Symphony in 1925.

Part II of Brewer's bibliography is an alphabetical listing of Cabell's 223 contributions to books and magazines. Omitting reprints from any of the author's books, the list includes essays, short stories, poems, reviews, and introductions to books. Cabell observed in his foreword to this bibliography that Brewer had included "everything I have managed to get published," and there is no reason to doubt the veracity of his remark. Brewer gives the magazine or journal in which the work was published and indicates its subsequent incorporation into Cabell's books.

The third part of the Brewer bibliography lists 257 secondary sources covering the years 1903 through 1956. These biographical and critical writings, arranged alphabetically by author, include book-length studies, commentaries in books, and magazine, journal, and newspaper articles. Part III is followed by a chronological listing of Cabell's books and of his contributions to books and magazines through 1955, with cross-references

---

1. See George E. F. Brewer, "Frances Joan Brewer's Bibliography: Its Genesis," *Cabellian*, II (Autumn, 1969), 28–29.

to the fuller listings of Parts I and II; by a chronological listing of critical writings, with cross-references to the alphabetical listings of Part III; and by a list of prior Cabell bibliographies. Complementing all this information is a thorough and useful index.

Frances Brewer's bibliography represents the first of a two-volume set, the second volume being Matthew J. Bruccoli's *Notes on the Cabell Collection at the University of Virginia* (Charlottesville, Va.: University Press of Virginia, 1957). As Bruccoli explains in his brief but clear and informative introduction, his work is "basically a listing of all the impressions of all the editions of James Branch Cabell's works now in the Alderman Library of the University of Virginia." Using fifty pages as a reliable sampling, Cabell's books (with the exception of the fully collated *Jurgen*) have been collated with the aid of the Hinman collating machine for textual variants in different impressions of an edition. In addition to such collations, other techniques have been employed, such as the measuring of gutters at the centers of page gatherings and the noting of type damage.

Bruccoli's work also contains notes on special Cabell material at the Alderman Library, including a descriptive calendar of 414 of Cabell's letters, spanning the period from 1915 to 1949. The list includes abstracts of each letter, with emphasis on the details of Cabell's literary career. Except for the Guy Holt letters, all correspondence to Cabell is omitted. Though one might have wished otherwise, Bruccoli decided to expurgate details of Cabell's private life from the abstracts. As with the Brewer bibliography, Bruccoli's volume contains a thorough and complete index.

In 1968 Maurice Duke added to standard bibliographical information about Cabell with a doctoral dissertation entitled "James Branch Cabell's Library: A Catalogue" (University of Iowa). This dissertation provides an alphabetical catalogue of 3,363 volumes in Cabell's personal library, including 767 autographed and inscribed books and 577 letters found within the books. The great majority of these books and letters have subsequently been presented by the author's widow, Margaret Cabell, to the James Branch Cabell Library of Virginia Commonwealth University. As Duke explains in his "James Branch Cabell's Personal Library: A Summary" (*Cabellian*, I [Fall, 1968]), the library is a tangible record of what Cabell read during his lifetime and is an important source of letters, autographed first editions, and other memorabilia.[2]

One of the most concise of Cabell bibliographies, by Dorothy B. Schle-

---

2. For a more complete description of Cabell's collection see Maurice Duke, "James Branch Cabell's Personal Library," *Studies in Bibliography*, XXIII (1970), 207–16.

gel, appeared in Louis D. Rubin's *Bibliographical Guide to the Study of Southern Literature* (Baton Rouge: Louisiana State University Press, 1969). Prefaced with a brief but informative description of the vicissitudes of Cabell's critical reputation from the 1920s to the 1960s, the list of thirty-two secondary sources is highly selective; nevertheless, Schlegel's bibliography, pointing to the best known and most significant critical writings, provides a useful starting point for the uninitiated student.

In 1974 the Revisionist Press of New York issued the cheaply printed but highly priced *James Branch Cabell: A Complete Bibliography*, by James N. Hall. Unfortunately this bibliography is not at all complete. However, its first section, which lists Cabell's works according to series, does include considerably more impressions of a given edition than Brewer and lists some editions which are absent from Brewer's work. The listings for *Jurgen* provide a good illustration of the nature of this additional material. Frances Brewer describes the first, second, third, and eighth impressions of the first edition. Hall's bibliography lists twenty impressions, though the thirteenth and fourteenth are listed as not having been seen and though the other printings are described as being identical texts of either the third, eighth, or eighteenth impressions. Hall does list one significant impression of *Jurgen* not included by Brewer, the eighteenth, which he describes as containing a number of minor revisions "intended to tie in *Jurgen* more closely with the Biography of Manuel." In addition, he lists paperback editions of the novel published since 1957 and seven foreign language editions. Based on this additional bibliographical information, the Cabell scholar would do well to consult Hall's first section as a supplement to the first part of Brewer's bibliography.

The second part of Hall's bibliography, entitled "Cabelliana," lists sixty-three shorter works, including material by Cabell appearing for the first time "in a form other than a magazine or newspaper," material originally published in a magazine or newspaper making its first appearance in a book not written or edited by Cabell, and periodical contributions not reprinted in any of Cabell's books. The mystery of this section is that Hall would include it at all, since all the items he lists can be found in Brewer's work, which Hall describes as definitive. Unlike Brewer, Hall does include twenty works or excerpts reprinted in anthologies. But even this list is not completely inclusive, omitting, for example, the Cabell selection which appears in the text edited by Richard Beale Davis, C. Hugh Holman, and Louis D. Rubin, Jr., *Southern Writing: 1585–1920* (New York: Odyssey Press, 1970).

The portion of the Hall bibliography devoted to secondary criticism is divided into five sections. Section 1 contains books about Cabell, listed in chronological order with no annotations. Section 2 lists prior bibliographies. Section 3 is entitled "Cabellian Art" and includes books "which are primarily in the artistic fields," with an alphabetical listing of Cabell's illustrators. Section 4 contains an index of all the issues of the *Cabellian* and of the contents of *Kalki* through Volume 6, Number 1. It is the fifth section, entitled "Miscellaneous," which illustrates most glaringly the deficiencies of this portion of Hall's work. The twenty-four items are obviously uninclusive and seem to reflect the mere whims of the bibliographer. Ellen Glasgow's *They Stooped to Folly* is included, apparently because it contains a dedication to Cabell, and Thomas Wolfe's *You Can't Go Home Again* seems to have been cited for a single reference to the "land of Cocaigne." None of the important essays which revived interest in Cabell, such as those by Edmund Wilson and Louis D. Rubin, Jr., are included.

In summary, James N. Hall's bibliography is in many respects seriously inadequate. Its listing of Cabell's books should be used as a supplement to Brewer's more detailed collations, and its appendix, by Nelson Bond, giving the values of Cabell's books current in 1974, may be of interest to the collector of Cabelliana. But its listing of Cabell's shorter works adds nothing to the Brewer bibliography, and its survey of Cabell criticism is completely unsatisfactory.

The need for a Cabell bibliography which provides a more complete compilation of scholarship, especially of scholarship which has appeared since the Brewer bibliography in 1957, has recently been addressed with the appearance of Maurice Duke's *James Branch Cabell: A Reference Guide* (Boston: G. K. Hall, 1979). The format of Duke's guide is chronological, beginning with 1904 and ending with 1975. Each year is divided into two sections; Section A lists books and Section B includes shorter writings on Cabell.

Culling Cabell's personal scrapbooks in the Alderman and James Branch Cabell libraries—scrapbooks which contain thousands of clippings—Duke has selected hundreds of newspaper and magazine reviews for inclusion in his work. His bibliography contains a large number of entries not listed by Brewer, many of them anonymous, and it will be especially helpful for those interested in the critical response to Cabell's writing during his early career. For example, Brewer lists five entries for 1919, while Duke lists thirty-six. However, two of Brewer's five entries, including an article in the Chicago *Tribune* by Burton Rascoe, are not included in Duke's guide. Thus, the fastidious researcher will want to check Duke's listings against Brewer's.

Helpful though Duke's reference guide may be, it is not without its flaws. Its index includes "only significant entries," but Duke does not describe his criteria for compiling the partial index. He indexes, for example, Edgar E. MacDonald's 1970 article, "Cabell's Richmond Trial," which appeared in the *Southern Literary Journal,* but not MacDonald's "The Influence of Provençal Poetry on James Branch Cabell," which was published in the same year in the *Cabellian*.[3] Neither from the titles nor from the brief annotations which follow is it clear why one article would have been considered more significant than the other.

One may also raise objections concerning the accuracy of some of the guide's annotations and the helpfulness of others. Duke describes Edd Winfield Parks's 1953 essay, "James Branch Cabell," as one that "views Cabell in light of twentieth century literature in the South." In fact this essay focuses on what Parks terms Cabell's romantic brand of humanism and makes no direct reference to his southern milieu. Describing Fred C. Hobson's *Serpent in Eden: H. L. Mencken and the South,* Duke informs us that "the author makes references to Cabell throughout this book." However, the annotation fails to note that an entire chapter of Hobson's book, Chapter 6, is devoted to the Mencken-Cabell friendship.

Finally, Duke's reference guide omits a few articles which ought to have been included in any reasonably complete survey of Cabell scholarship. Richard Warner's 1975 article, "The Illusion of Diabolism in the Cabellian Hero," is not listed. Neither is Edgar MacDonald's "Glasgow, Cabell, and Richmond," an omission all the more strange because the article was included in a special issue of the *Mississippi Quarterly* in 1974 to which Duke himself contributed. The researcher would be well advised to supplement Duke's reference guide with Jerry T. Williams' *Southern Literature 1968–1975: A Checklist of Scholarship* (Boston: G. K. Hall, 1978), with the annual supplements which have appeared in the *Mississippi Quarterly* since 1975, and with the annual *MLA International Bibliography.*

### EDITIONS

First and later editions of Cabell's works are described in Frances Brewer's *James Branch Cabell: A Bibliography of His Writings, Biography and Criticism* and in James N. Hall's *James Branch Cabell: A Complete Bibliography.* Both of these books are assessed in the first part of this essay.

---

3. The works by MacDonald, Parks, Hobson, and Warner discussed in the last three paragraphs of this section are described more fully in Section V of this essay.

Beginning with the third printing of *Jurgen* in December, 1919, Cabell's works, which were being published by R. M. McBride and Company, began appearing in brown cloth with a gilt kalki device in the lower right-hand corner. This kalki binding was given to later printings of *The Rivet in Grandfather's Neck* (1915), *The Certain Hour* (1916), *From the Hidden Way* (1916), and *The Cream of the Jest* (1917), as well as to the first edition of the works which followed *Jurgen*, beginning with *Figures of Earth* (1921). In 1920 Cabell began revising and republishing his early fiction, incorporating these revised works into the Kalki Edition. *The Eagle's Shadow* (1904), *The Line of Love* (1905), *Gallantry* (1907), *Chivalry* (1909), and *The Cords of Vanity* (1909) were reissued between 1920 and 1923. *The Soul of Melicent* (1913) was published in 1920 in the Kalki Edition as *Domnei*.

The Kalki Edition is important because it is obviously a precursor to the better-known Storisende Edition of *The Works of James Branch Cabell*, published by McBride from 1927 through 1930 in eighteen volumes. The development of the Kalki Edition described in the previous paragraph lends support to Edgar E. MacDonald's hypothesis, presented in "The Storisende Edition: Some Liabilities" (*Cabellian*, I [Spring, 1969]), that the Biography of the Life of Manuel was not conceived as early as 1901, as Cabell asserted at a number of points in his writing, but that the concept began to form in 1917 with *The Cream of the Jest* and was confirmed in 1919 by *Jurgen* and *Beyond Life*. The revision of Cabell's earlier works for the Kalki Edition strongly suggests that the decision to include them in the Biography was made sometime between 1917 and 1920.[4]

*The Works of James Branch Cabell* thus represents the revised and final form of the Biography of the Life of Manuel, which was initially developed in the Kalki Edition. Excluding three of Cabell's early genealogical studies, the Storisende Edition includes all of his works published through 1930. In addition, Volume XVIII, *Townsend of Lichfield*, contains material never before published. The prefaces to each volume were reprinted in *Preface to the Past* (New York: Robert M. McBride, 1936).

At the present time hardbound editions of eleven of Cabell's works are available. With the exceptions of the University Presses of Florida's *Quiet Please* and Peter Smith's *Jurgen*, these facsimile and reprint editions are expensive, ranging in price from $10.50 to $40.00. The Limited Editions Club published in 1976 a deluxe edition of *Jurgen* selling on the rare book

---

4. For an assessment of the Biography that advances an interpretation of composition considerably closer to that of Cabell's see John Macy, "Introduction," *Between Dawn and Sunrise* (New York: Robert M. McBride, 1930).

market in 1980 for $50.00. This edition was illustrated by Virgil Burnett and includes a brief introduction by Edward Wagenknecht.

Seven of Cabell's novels now appear in paperback. Most of these have been made available through Ballantine Books' Del Rey Fantasy Classic Series. Thanks to Ballantine Books and Dover Press, several of Cabell's strongest and most important novels not available hardbound—*Figures of Earth, The High Place, The Silver Stallion*—have been made accessible to readers. Cabell enthusiasts might well hope that in the future more of his novels will become available in less expensive hardbound editions. Even more welcome would be new editions of Cabell's charming and perceptive essay collections, such as *Let Me Lie*.

### MANUSCRIPTS AND LETTERS

The largest collection of manuscripts and letters is in the James Branch Cabell Archive at the Alderman Library of the University of Virginia. This collection covers the years 1896–1958 and is especially rich in materials from the period between 1920 and 1940. At the Alderman are reposited manuscript copies of many of Cabell's books, including *Figures of Earth, The Silver Stallion, The High Place, The Cream of the Jest,* and the first, second, and final drafts of *Jurgen*. There are also manuscripts of a large number of articles and stories as well as thirteen scrapbooks, which contain clippings—many dealing with the attempted suppression of *Jurgen*—and correspondence to Cabell. The archive includes approximately two thousand original letters and eight hundred microfilm or xerox copies, many of them from correspondents such as H. L. Mencken, Burton Rascoe, Sinclair Lewis, Joseph Hergesheimer, Hugh Walpole, Ellen Glasgow, Carl Van Doren, Carl Van Vechten, and Guy Holt.[5] A descriptive calendar of Cabell letters in the archive as of 1957 is included in Matthew Bruccoli's *Notes on the Cabell Collection at the University of Virginia*, described in the first part of this essay. There are over sixty letters from Cabell in the Ellen Glasgow Collection and additional Cabell material in the Fishburne, Mary Johnston, and Florence Stearns papers.

The Cabell Collection of Virginia Commonwealth University's James

5. A description of the archive is given in "The James Branch Cabell Collection in the University of Virginia Library," compiled by Mary Faith Pusey and Donna L. Purvis (July, 1971). Copies are available in the Barrett Collection at the University of Virginia, Charlottesville, and in the Cabell Collection at Virginia Commonwealth University, Richmond.

Branch Cabell Library contains nearly six hundred letters to Cabell and approximately fifty letters from Cabell. The majority of these letters were inserted in the books of Cabell's personal library, which were given by his widow to Virginia Commonwealth University, and are indexed in Maurice Duke's dissertation, "James Branch Cabell's Library," described in the first part of this essay. Cabell material at Virginia Commonwealth also includes three scrapbooks containing both clippings and letters; two notebooks containing genealogical material; one book of edition notes; and two miscellaneous notebooks containing, among other items, holograph copies of Cabell's verse.

Manuscript holdings in other libraries are listed in *American Literary Manuscripts* (Austin: University of Texas Press, 1960), in Albert Robbins' *American Literary Manuscripts: A Checklist of Holdings* (Athens, Ga.: University of Georgia Press, 1977), and in the annual volumes of *The National Union Catalogue of Manuscript Collections*. Significant Cabell holdings are in the Burton Rascoe and Horace Liveright papers at the University of Pennsylvania, the George Jean Nathan Papers at Cornell, the Carl Van Doren and F. Scott Fitzgerald papers at Princeton, and the Cabell Collection at the University of Texas. The New York Public Library, the Houghton Library of Harvard, the Beinecke and Sterling Memorial libraries at Yale contain substantial material distributed through a number of collections. Betty Adler's *Man of Letters: A Census of the Correspondence of H. L. Mencken* (Baltimore: Enoch Pratt Free Library, 1969) locates 404 of the letters Cabell and Mencken exchanged and also includes the correspondence of other writers associated with Cabell, including Emily Clark, Joseph Hergesheimer, and Sinclair Lewis.

Two major collections of Cabell's correspondence have been published. In 1962 Margaret Freeman Cabell and Padraic Colum brought out *Between Friends: Letters of of James Branch Cabell and Others* (New York: Harcourt, Brace & World, 1962).[6] Graced with a solid introduction by Carl Van Vechten which admirably describes the milieu for the letters, the book provides a generous sampling of correspondence from 1915 to 1922, a period during which Cabell was moving from relative obscurity to fame and notoriety. There are substantial numbers of letters between Cabell and Guy Holt, Sinclair Lewis, Burton Rascoe, Joseph Hergesheimer, and H. L. Mencken. Other correspondents include F. Scott Fitzgerald, Theodore Dreiser, Louis Untermeyer, Robert McBride, and Carl Van Vechten.

6. Padraic Colum was coeditor of this volume in name only. For an account of the compiling of these letters see Edgar E. MacDonald's review of *The Letters of James Branch Cabell* in *Southern Literary Journal*, IX (Fall 1976), 104–105.

The emphasis of this selection is on *Jurgen* and on the unsuccessful attempt to suppress its publication.

Edward Wagenknecht's *The Letters of James Branch Cabell* (Norman, Okla.: University of Oklahoma Press, 1975) was evidently an attempt to provide Cabell enthusiasts with a more inclusive sampling of his correspondence. Unfortunately the book cannot be judged a definitive collection. Essentially Wagenknecht's volume includes portions of a selected number of Cabell's letters. Few letters are presented whole, some fragments consist only of a few lines, and no letters to Cabell are included. There are letters to nineteen correspondents, including Guy Holt, Joseph Hergesheimer, Burton Rascoe, and Ellen Glasgow, with each correspondent given a separate chapter. The editor provides the briefest of introductions and very few explanatory notes. The lack of notes is a more marked deficiency because one is reading only one half of an epistolary exchange.

In addition to these book-length selections there are several articles devoted to portions of Cabell's correspondence. Frank Durham, in "Love as a Literary Exercise" (*Mississippi Quarterly*, XVIII [Winter, 1964–65]), quotes from the surviving letters of a "playfully amorous and playfully literary" correspondence Cabell carried on with Miss Norvell Harrison, a cousin who lived in Brooklyn, during his "three year exile" in New York City from 1898 to 1901. Durham believes that the letters reveal a youthful writer using the exchange as "an ideal laboratory in which to experiment with several literary styles as he sought the right one for himself." Maurice Duke's "Letters of George Sterling to James Branch Cabell" (*American Literature*, XLIV [March, 1972]) presents eight edited letters from the San Francisco poet to Cabell between 1920 and 1924. Louis Cheslock's "*The Jewel Merchants*, an Opera: A Case History" (*Cabellian*, IV [Spring, 1972]) includes the text of forty letters written from 1929 to 1940 between Cheslock, Cabell, and H. L. Mencken regarding the creation and performance of Cheslock's opera, based on the Cabell play.

The published letters of three prominent American literary figures will be of interest to Cabell scholars. *The Letters of H. L. Mencken*, edited by Guy Forgue (New York: Alfred A. Knopf, 1961), contains letters to correspondents such as Burton Rascoe, Guy Holt, and Theodore Dreiser which include interesting observations about Cabell. There are over 150 references to Cabell in the index of *Ingenue Among the Lions: The Letters of Emily Clark to Joseph Hergesheimer* (Austin: University of Texas Press, 1965), edited by Gerald Langford.[7] Edmund Wilson's *Letters on Literature and*

---

7. Edgar E. MacDonald, "Another Opinion of *Ingenue Among the Lions*," *Cabellian*, II

*Politics: 1912–1972* (New York: Farrar, Straus and Giroux, 1977) includes eight letters to Cabell or to others concerning Wilson's reawakened interest in Cabell's writing and his seminal essay which appeared in the *New Yorker* of April 21, 1956.

### BIOGRAPHY

In 1932 Carl Van Doren observed: "The legend which [has] grown up about Mr. Cabell no doubt owes its exuberance to the scarcity of the facts upon which it has been fed." Indeed, an aura of mystery, secrecy, and innuendo surrounded Cabell for much of his life, and it is therefore extremely unfortunate that to this date no definitive biography has appeared to provide a fully developed portrait of the writer. Joe Lee Davis includes a convenient nineteen-page biographical summary in his *James Branch Cabell* (New York: Twayne, 1962), but there are no book-length biographies.

Several of Cabell's essay collections are sources of biographical information, although it must always be kept in mind that these autobiographical statements are written by a master of irony and obfuscation who cultivated his privacy and who was probably not entirely displeased by his reputation as a faintly satanic and mysterious gentleman from Richmond-in-Virginia. *These Restless Heads* (1932), *Special Delivery* (1933), *Let Me Lie* (1947), *Quiet Please* (1952), and *As I Remember It* (1955) all provide glimpses into Cabell's private life, but the latter two books are especially interesting. *Quiet Please* contains descriptions of Cabell's amorous adventures as a young bachelor as well as an account of his life in Saint Augustine, which he frequented for his health after 1935. *As I Remember It* includes sketches of Cabell's first and second wives and assessments of many writers and editors he met during his long writing career. It is also interesting for the light it sheds on his relationship with Ellen Glasgow and on his collaboration in the revising of the final drafts of her books *In This Our Life* and *A Certain Measure*.

Maurice Duke's *James Branch Cabell: A Reference Guide* (see the first part of this essay) lists a number of newspaper and magazine interviews which Cabell gave during his life. One of the best and most extensive of the early essay-interviews is David Karsner's "Censored into Fame" (New York *Herald Tribune*, July 24, 1927). Julian R. Meade's *I Live in Virginia* (New

---

(Autumn, 1969), 30–31, warns us against accepting the letters as an accurate assessment of Cabell or of his family.

York: Longmans, Green, 1935) contains a brief but nicely written account of a meeting with Cabell which leads to the conclusion that he is "scholarly, impersonal, solitary" and that he belongs in his library "with his own amusements." Two later newspaper interviews are also notable. Guy Friddel's feature story in the Richmond *News Leader* (October 31, 1955) quotes Cabell liberally and includes his defense of his treatment of Ellen Glasgow in *As I Remember It*. Louis D. Rubin, Jr., conducted one of the last interviews with Cabell for the Baltimore *Evening Sun* (July 6, 1956). A recent feature story in the *News Leader* by George Edmonson (October 10, 1979) contains Emmet Peter's assessment of the story that Cabell spent two years working in the coalfields of West Virginia.

The most significant event in Cabell's career—an event which thrust him into national prominence—was the attempt by the New York Society for the Suppression of Vice to block the sale of *Jurgen*. Scholars interested in the *Jurgen* controversy should consult *Jurgen and the Censor* (New York: E. H. Bierstadt, 1920) and *Jurgen and the Law* (New York: Robert M. McBride, 1923), edited by Guy Holt. The first book includes a preface by Cabell; the report of the emergency committee formed to defend the novel, recounting the history of the action taken to suppress the novel and the formation of the committee; a list of signers who protested the suppression; twenty-nine letters of support from prominent writers and cultural figures; and extracts of press accounts of the controversy.[8] Holt's book begins with an introductory essay surveying the action which preceded the trial and includes the "Brief for the Defendants" submitted by the attorneys for Robert McBride and the decision of Judge Charles C. Nott, which directed the jury to bring a verdict of acquittal. It also prints the text of the Walter Kingsley letter which appeared in the New York *Tribune* and which prompted John Sumner to indict the publishers.

There are a number of brief reminiscences of Cabell written by people who were personally and professionally linked to him. In 1925 Hunter Stagg wrote a short sketch in the March/April issue of *Brentano's Book Chat* entitled "The Absence of Mr. Cabell" in which he sought to counter the myths surrounding the much-talked-about writer, including notions that he had been "born in a colonial mansion overlooking the River James" and that he knew more about "what went on at the witches' Sabbath than

---

8. Critics interested in the genesis of *Jurgen* will want to consult a letter Cabell wrote to Burton Rascoe describing how the book came to be written. The text of this letter was included in Rascoe's essay on Cabell in *Prometheans, Ancient and Modern* (New York: G. P. Putnam's Sons, 1933), described in Section V of this essay, and was also included in Colum and Cabell (eds.), *Between Friends*, 127.

a Virginia gentleman had any business knowing." Emily Clark's *Innocence Abroad* (New York: Alfred A. Knopf, 1931), an account of the founding and publication of the *Reviewer*, devotes its second chapter to Cabell's association with the little magazine. Clark describes Cabell's rather aloof and enigmatic personality, but also emphasizes his kindness to her, quoting from some of the letters she received from him.[9] Burton Rascoe's *Before I Forget* (New York: Doubleday, Doran, 1937) includes a description of Cabell's early career and of Rascoe's discovery of him, material which had originally appeared in the April, 1936, issue of *Esquire*. It also presents three of the four letters exchanged between Rupert Hughes and Cabell concerning Hughes's objection to the serialization of *Beyond Life* in the Chicago *Tribune*. In "Happy Birthday, Dear Mr. Cabell," an article which appeared in the April, 1951, issue of *Town and Country*, Joseph Hergesheimer recounts his first meeting with Cabell on a visit to Richmond in 1921 with H. L. Mencken.

Ellen Glasgow devotes a brief chapter of her autobiography, *The Woman Within* (New York: Harcourt, Brace, 1954), to her friendship with Cabell, which began with her visit to Williamsburg when Cabell was a senior and the object of homosexual innuendos. She also focuses on the 1901 Richmond murder mystery in which Cabell was rumored to have killed John W. Scott because of his involvement with Cabell's mother. Though Glasgow sees Cabell as the innocent victim of the "mob spirit," critics have rightly questioned her motive in choosing to focus only on the two most painful episodes of Cabell's life. In *Fragments from an Unwritten Autobiography* (New Haven, Conn.: Yale University Press, 1955) Carl Van Vechten recalls his introduction to Cabell through Joseph Hergesheimer and paints a portrait of a reserved, correct, and proper Virginia gentleman, devoted to his native state and city in spite of their indifference to him.[10]

There have been two more recent reminiscences of some biographical importance. Warren A. McNeill's "James Branch Cabell 'In Time's Hourglass'" (*Cabellian*, III [Spring, 1971]) provides an account of McNeill's meetings with Cabell. Desmond Tarrant's "On Visiting the Master" (*Kalki*, VI, no. 3 [1974]) is a brief description of a visit paid to Cabell on Thanksgiving Day, 1957, a few months before the author's death, in which Cabell

9. The account in *Innocence Abroad* originally appeared as "The Case of Mr. Cabell vs. the Author of the Biography," *Virginia Quarterly Review*, V (July, 1929), 336–45.

10. The material in *Fragments from an Unwritten Autobiography* appeared originally in "Mr. Cabell of Lichfield and Poictesme" in *Yale University Library Gazette* (July 23, 1948), 1–7.

comments on Hemingway, Faulkner, Mencken, and southern race relations.

In addition to personal remembrances, a number of scholarly articles have contributed significantly to Cabell biography. Emmet Peter's "Cabell: The Making of a Rebel" (*Carolina Quarterly*, XIV [Spring, 1962]) recounts Cabell's academic career at William and Mary College and gives details of the Williamsburg scandal, of Cabell's failure to be named editor of the student magazine, and of the John W. Scott murder in Richmond in 1901. Peter believes that these events were important keys to Cabell's "moral rebellion" and that they served "to sharpen [his] perception" and to enrich his artistry. In "James Branch Cabell at William and Mary: The Education of a Novelist" (*William and Mary Review*, V [Spring, 1967]), William Godshalk provides a more detailed account of Cabell's college years, including information about specific classes he took and descriptions of his contributions to the college monthly. Godshalk's analysis of the homosexual incident concludes that Cabell and all the others rumored to have been involved were fully absolved by the college faculty. In a rather diffusely structured essay entitled "Mencken and Cabell" (*Cabellian*, I [Fall, 1968]), Richard Ruland discusses Mencken's defense of *Jurgen* and the role Ruland believes Mencken played in the creation of the novel. He concludes that Mencken's sometimes ambivalent but generally positive judgment of Cabell's writing is related to the fact that he "always judged books as substantive statements in the cultural battles of his day."

Edgar E. MacDonald has contributed two informative biographical articles. "The Glasgow-Cabell Entente" (*American Literature*, XLI [March, 1969]) details the aid Cabell gave Glasgow in the writing of *In This Our Life* and *A Certain Measure*, argues convincingly that Glasgow's concept of her novels as a unified social history of Virginia originated with Cabell, and describes the estrangement that resulted from Cabell's burlesque review of *A Certain Measure*. Although theirs was a "careful" friendship nurtured by mutually flattering reviews, MacDonald believes their literary alliance was not "accompanied by the close personal relationship that many people suppose." In "Cabell's Richmond Trial" (*Southern Literary Journal*, III [Fall, 1970]), MacDonald concentrates on the John Scott murder, detailing the family ties which linked Cabell's mother to Scott, the rumors which associated them romantically, the divorce Mrs. Cabell won from her husband in 1907, the suppression of the identity of the murderer by the Scott family, and the bitter allusions to this personal disaster Cabell made in *The Cords of Vanity* and *The Rivet in Grandfather's Neck*. His thesis is that Cabell's "Olympian pose of remoteness and imperturbability" was a mask carefully constructed in response to the Williamsburg and Richmond scandals.

Critical biographies of Sinclair Lewis and Elinor Wylie contain brief glimpses of Cabell. Mark Schorer's *Sinclair Lewis: An American Life* (New York: McGraw-Hill, 1961) includes an account of Lewis' visit to Cabell at Rockbridge Alum Springs,[11] briefly discusses Lewis' defense of *Jurgen*, and mentions a later visit Lewis paid to Cabell in Saint Augustine. *Elinor Wylie: A Biography* (New York: Dial Press, 1979), by Stanley Olson, describes Wylie's visit to Richmond and Cabell's early admiration for her, which changed to disappointment with the publication of *The Orphan Angel*. A number of references are made to the Cabell-Glasgow relationship in E. Stanly Godbold's biography, *Ellen Glasgow and the Woman Within* (Baton Rouge: Louisiana State University Press, 1972), though most of the information is a reworking of material originally presented in Edgar MacDonald's "The Glasgow-Cabell Entente."

### CRITICISM

#### *1918–1929: "He Has Drunken of the Holy Bottle"*

Certainly the most extraordinary aspect of the history of Cabell criticism is the precipitous plunge his reputation sustained between the middle twenties, when he was the darling of the American intelligentsia, and the late forties and early fifties, when he was almost uniformly dismissed and forgotten by critics. The irony of this critical peripeteia is made complete when one realizes that the sudden flowering of Cabell's renown had been preceded by years of relative obscurity. Although Cabell had published his first book in 1904, it was not until 1918 that he began attracting a significant number of critical admirers.

Chief among these early champions were Burton Rascoe, writing in the Chicago *Tribune*, and H. L. Mencken, writing in the Baltimore *Sun*. On July 3, 1918, Mencken wrote an article for the New York *Evening Mail*, published later in that year by Robert M. McBride as a leaflet, in which he described Cabell as "the only first-rate literary craftsman that the whole

---

11. Schorer's description of this visit is supplemented by a brief but interesting account written by Grace Hegger Lewis in *With Love from Gracie* (New York: Harcourt, Brace, 1955).

South can show."[12] By 1918 Mencken and Rascoe had been joined by other critics. Writing in the *Dial* (April 25, 1918) Wilson Follett asserted that the starting point for a proper appreciation of Cabell was "his inestimable gift of hocus-pocus." However, Follett believed that Cabell's capacity for jesting was inextricably linked to a serious philosophical viewpoint. As he expressed it: "His little world in which the artist is a jester at the expense of the gullible is only one convolution of the greater cosmos in which life is an inscrutable jester at the expense of us all."

Cabell's critical following was substantially enhanced by the publication of *Jurgen* in 1919 and by the controversy which subsequently surrounded it. Hugh Walpole, in a pamphlet entitled *The Art of James Branch Cabell* (New York: Robert M. McBride, 1920), decried the anonymity in which the writer had languished until *Jurgen* and concluded that though his fiction would "always be a sign for hostilities," he was the most arresting literary personality on either side of the Atlantic.[13] Writing in the *New Republic*, XXVI (April 13, 1921), Robert Morss Lovett was somewhat less positive. Lovett felt that Cabell's satire was neither so trenchant nor so original as that of Anatole France, the writer with whom he had been frequently compared. Yet he believed that in repudiating the "herd instinct" in American letters Cabell had contributed to national literature a variety and individuality it badly needed.

By the early twenties Cabell had gained many of his most powerful and eloquent admirers. Carl Van Doren, in an essay on Cabell published in the *Nation*, CXII (June 29, 1921), and reprinted in a slightly revised form in his *Contemporary American Novelists, 1900–1920* (New York: Macmillan, 1922), described the concept of the dynamic illusion presented in *Beyond Life*. Although he wished that Cabell had trained his sights more on contemporary Virginia, he believed that his subject was far superior to those of other popular romancers. They were "unconscious dupes of the demiurge whereas he, aware of its ways and its devices," employed this romantic force "almost as if it were some hippogriff bridled by him in Elysian pastures." In *The Beginnings of Critical Realism in America* (New York: Harcourt, Brace, 1921; reprinted in *Main Currents of American Thought* [New

12. For a detailed treatment of Mencken's early advocacy of Cabell see pages 121–25 of Fred Hobson's *Serpent in Eden*, reviewed later in this section. Burton Rascoe's account of his discovery of Cabell is given in *Before I Forget*, described in Section IV of this essay. Those interested in Rascoe's support of Cabell should also consult Donald M. Hensley's *Burton Rascoe* (New York: Twayne, 1970).

13. Walpole's pamphlet was republished in revised form in 1925 and republished again by the Kennikat Press in 1967.

York: Harcourt, Brace, 1930]), Vernon Parrington observed that Cabell's comedy, based as it was on the sense of man's limitations, was pessimistic, but not cheap or shallow or escapist. In Cabell's world, romantic idealism confronted pessimism; out of this conflict came a profound cosmic irony. Parrington concluded that Cabell stood apart from lesser American writers "as Mark Twain stood apart, individual and incomparable." Writing in the *Double Dealer*, IV (July, 1922), Louis Untermeyer maintained that the underlying idea of all of Cabell's work was the romantic and poetic concept that the dream and the quest to attain the dream were "more real than reality." In *Heavens* (New York: Harcourt, Brace, 1922) Untermeyer illustrated his concept in a pastiche of the Poictesme novels in which Ortnitz, the questor, rejects the calls of realism, shallow romanticism, decadence, and lyric poetry. He seeks instead a heaven that he is bound to attain, even though he discovers it to be an empty place.

A number of other critics in the early twenties reserved a chapter for the discussion of Cabell's work in their book-length treatments of contemporary literature. Vincent Starrett, in his *Buried Caesars* (Chicago: Covici-McGee, 1923), asserted that *Jurgen* was the summit of Cabell's fictional achievement, followed closely by *Beyond Life*, *The Cream of the Jest*, and *Figures of Earth*. Starrett was convinced that Cabell was "dead" because, in his opinion, the great works had been completed and would not be matched again. Paul Jordan-Smith's *On Strange Altars* (New York: Albert and Charles Boni, 1924) agreed with Burton Rascoe that Cabell was the Anatole France of America and asserted further that his works constituted "the best writing that has come from this continent since Hawthorne."

Cabell's fame also spread to England and France. Carl Bechhofer observed in his *The Literary Renaissance in America* (London: William Heinemann, 1923) that Cabell had entered the lists in delightful and valiant combat against Puritanism. From Paris, Regis Michaud included an analysis of Cabell in *Le Roman Americain d'Aujourd'hui* (Paris: Boivin, 1926), an assessment that was substantially repeated in his *American Novel Today* (Boston: Little, Brown, 1928) and in *Les Romanciers Americains* (Paris: Boivin, 1931). Michaud believed that Cabell's artistic philosophy had been strongly influenced by Walter Pater and Anatole France.[14]

14. Two other French language articles of interest to Cabell scholars are described in some detail in Edgar E. MacDonald's "Cabell Criticism: Past, Present, and Future," *Cabellian*, I (Fall, 1968), 21–25, described later in this section. MacDonald discusses Joseph Mainsard's "L'Evasion de James Branch Cabell" (*Les Cahiers du Sud*, November, 1929) and Maurice Le Breton's "James Branch Cabell Romancier" (*Revue Anglo-Americaine*, December, 1933; February, 1934).

Although most treatments of Cabell during this period were general descriptions, there were a few articles which focused on more specific areas or characteristics of his writing. Carl Van Doren's "Irony in Velvet: The Short Stories of James Branch Cabell" (*Century Magazine*, CVIII [August, 1924]) examined the revisions in the early short stories Cabell made for the Kalki Edition, revisions which "cut away an earlier softness" and sentimentality. Van Doren compared the stories to the "smaller chapels braced against the central structure" of the "towered cathedral" of the later novels, with an irony of vision that linked them to the later work. Joseph Warren Beach, in "The Holy Bottle" (*Virginia Quarterly Review*, II [April, 1926]), recounted how he was won over to Cabell by the insights of *Beyond Life* and by a style that had "precision as well as flavor" and was perfectly suited in its archaic quality to the writer's thinking and purpose.[15] In the ironic humor and the mingled pity and scorn of Cabell's prose Beach heard echoes of Lamb, Carlyle, and Swift. He had, the critic concluded, "drunken of the Holy Bottle."

In 1924 a small book of essays on Cabell entitled *A Round Table in Poictesme: A Symposium* (Cleveland: Colophon Club, 1924) was published. Cabell contributed an introductory essay which described an imaginary conversation with himself as a young man about to launch into the writing of *The Eagle's Shadow*. Other essays, some as short as a page, were written by Ernest Boyd, Don Bregenzer, Samuel Loveman, Ben Ray Redman, Frank L. Minarik, M. P. Mooney, Christopher Morley, Edwin Meade Robinson, Howard Wolf, and H. L. Mencken. Among the more significant essays were those by Boyd, which treated Cabell's early novels; by Bregenzer, which emphasized the blindness of critics to his early work; and by Minarik, which detected a resemblance between Cabellian and Aristophanean comedy.

From 1927 to 1929 four short book-length studies of Cabell's fiction appeared. H. L. Mencken's *James Branch Cabell* (New York: Robert M. McBride, 1927) was a highly provocative analysis, written in Mencken's inimitable style, that revealed as much about the author as his subject. Mencken asserted that "what [ailed]" American literature was "a delusion of moral duty." Cabell, he believed, stood "outside the praying band." Mencken saw Cabell's later work, and especially *Jurgen*, as part of the 1920s attack on Babbittry and viewed his subject as "the most acidulous

15. Similar versions of this article appeared in "Pedantic Study of Two Critics," *American Speech*, I, (March 1926), 289–306, and in *The Outlook for American Prose* (Chicago: University of Chicago Press, 1926; reprinted 1968).

of all the anti-romantics." *Cabellian Harmonics* (New York: Random House, 1928), by Warren A. McNeil, sought to explain the "harmonic plan" on which the complete Biography of Manuel had been constructed. McNeil saw the whole as symphonic and implicitly embraced the notion that Cabell's work was from the beginning unified in concept. He interpreted each book as a single movement of a prose symphony in which one of the three recurring themes of the Biography was developed. In addition, each book contained certain passages written in what McNeil—borrowing Cabell's phrase—called "contrapuntal prose," prose which summed the plan of the entire Biography.[16] Although the book's supporting analysis was dry and pedestrian, it constituted the first detailed book-length critical analysis of Cabell's fictional method.

James P. Cover's *Notes on "Jurgen"* (New York: Robert M. McBride, 1928) was a glossary of those sources and allusions in *Jurgen* which the author had been able to trace. The notes identified characters, referring the reader to other novels in which they had appeared, and detailed the mythical and historical origins of many of Cabell's fictional creations. Cover collaborated in 1929 with John Phillips Cranwell in the writing of *Notes on "Figures of Earth"* (New York: Robert M. McBride, 1929). This book had an organization identical to the 1928 title, but it also contained concluding appendices in which the authors identified W. R. S. Ralston's *Russian Folk Tales* and Sabine Baring-Gould's *Curious Myths of the Middle Ages* and *Legends of the Patriarchs and Prophets* as major sources for the folklore of *Figures of Earth*.

In 1928 Joseph Hergesheimer wrote an essay on Cabell in the January issue of the *American Mercury* in which he elegantly expressed "without apology" his admiration and devotion to the man and his work. In spite of its eloquence, Hergesheimer's article betrayed a defensive tone which suggested that by the late twenties critical currents were beginning to turn against Cabell. Indeed, significant critical disclaimers had been written as early as 1923. Percy Boynton, in "Mr. Cabell Expounds Himself" (*English Journal*, XII [April, 1923]; reprinted in *Some Contemporary Americans* [Chicago: University of Chicago Press, 1924]), had taken exception to the writer's pedantry and to his painstakingly fabricated style and had concluded airily that he saw no need to consider the writer "either arch-fiend or demi-god." In *Men Who Make Our Novels* (New York: Dodd, Mead, 1924), C. C. Baldwin faulted Cabell for often being "a bore, repetitious

---

16. Edd Winfield Parks discusses McNeil's thesis in some detail in "James Branch Cabell," *Hopkins Review*, V (Summer, 1953), 37–47, reviewed later in this section.

and affected." Even more serious was Baldwin's charge that Cabell had plagiarized directly from John Millington Synge. "His matter," he contended, "was lifted bodily from the Irish, his rhythms from Yeats and Synge, his wit from Wilde and Swift and Moore."

Negative voices were heard with greater frequency toward the end of the decade. Upton Sinclair indicted *Jurgen* in *Money Writes* (New York: Albert and Charles Boni, 1927) as "one of the most depraved and depraving books ever published in America." In *The Demon of the Absolute: New Shelburne Essays* (Princeton, N.J.: Princeton University Press, 1928), Paul Elmer More brought the tenets of the New Humanism to bear upon Cabell's writing, finding it lacking in ethical content. If art dealt with life as it "ought to be," as Cabell insisted, then what, asked More, ought life to be? He concluded that for Cabell it meant following "the petty vagaries of vice without any of the ugly consequences that overtake the sinner in the actual flesh." Henry Seidel Canby, assessing Cabell in his *American Estimates* (New York: Harcourt, Brace, 1929), reached the somewhat similar conclusion that Cabell had "wasted on ingenious obscenity energies which might have gone into invention and the pruning of a luxuriant style."

One of the more interesting of these later critical assessments was Edward Niles Hooker's "Something About Cabell" (*Sewanee Review*, XXXVII [April, 1929]). Hooker contended that Cabell was a writer worthy of serious consideration, and he praised his style and the irony of fate which underlay and gave thematic unity to his work. Yet he believed that Cabell had yet to write his best work and that the recently published *Something About Eve* indicated a potentially disastrous movement in the direction of inferior fiction. The doubts raised by Hooker, Canby, and More would be heard more loudly, more insistently, and with more negative vehemence as the Wall Street panic of 1929 ushered in the depression decade of the 1930s, with its emphasis on literary realism and socially relevant fiction.

*1930–1955: "A Grossly Overestimated Third-rate*
*Anatole France"*

Only eight years separated Joseph Hergesheimer's adulatory assessment of Cabell and Arthur Hobson Quinn's *American Fiction* (New York: D. Appleton-Century, 1936; reprinted 1964); but as early as 1936 Quinn was describing Cabell's rapid rise and equally sudden fall in critical esteem as "a phenomenon of American letters." Indeed, after 1929 Cabell's reputation was assailed from all directions. Fred Lewis Pattee questioned, in *The New American Literature* (New York: Century, 1930; reprinted 1968), whether Cabell's work could seriously be considered fiction. He went on to observe that the writer's message was "a philosophy of negation thrown into narrative form." From the South, Allen Tate contributed an evaluation entitled "Mr. Cabell's Farewell" (*New Republic*, LXI [January, 1930]) which, though it contained interesting insights, was largely negative in its conclusion. Tate saw the creation of Poictesme as a response to the destruction of the Old South. Behind the artistic impulse was "the blind impulse to vindicate the psychology of defeat." Cabell's big mistake, Tate believed, was his attempt "to escape from the Old South by making Poictesme a place of his own creation" and by thus making it "bloodless, mechanical, repeating itself in a vacuum."

In his *Expression in America* (New York: Harper, 1932) Ludwig Lewishon labeled Cabell an escapist, a derogatory epithet commonly applied to him in the 1930s. "The fields of earth are on fire," he complained, "and Cabell offers us the daydreams of a romantic adolescent." Newton Arvin, reviewing *These Restless Heads* in the *New Republic*, LXX (March, 1932), called Cabell "a grossly overestimated third-rate Anatole France, whose creative equipment rests largely on the foundations of a stale Confederate culture [and] whose romanticism has the emptiness of adolescence without its spontaneity." Granville Hicks, not surprisingly, excluded Cabell from his "great tradition" of proletarian American fiction (*The Great Tradition* [New York: Macmillan, 1933]). He declared Cabell a double fraud. He was a "sleek, smug egoist" whose desire for a bygone aristocracy made him dissatisfied with the present; yet he had "not enough imaginative vigor to create a robust world in which deeds of chivalry and gallantry" might be performed.

As the depression intensified, so did critical assaults against Cabell. Clifton Fadiman, writing in the *Nation*, CXXXVI (April 12, 1933), theorized that Cabell's brand of escapism appealed to two groups of readers— the American gentlemen who found his romantic irony soothing because they could find no support in American pragmatism for their position of privilege, and the literary young men and women who found "industrial civilization very unpleasant to confront." In "The James Branch Cabell Period" (*New Republic*, LXXXIX [January 13, 1937]; reprinted in *After the Genteel Tradition* [Carbondale, Ill.: Southern Illinois University Press, 1964]), Peter Munro Jack saw the Cabell vogue of the 1920s as a product of "the surprising impact of estheticism on post-war American literature," an estheticism whose flame had already died in England and France. Jack threw Cabell in with other writers of the period whom he considered second-rate—Elinor Wylie, Joseph Hergesheimer, Ben Hecht, and Scott Fitzgerald. The philosophy of this pretentious escapist, he concluded, had been expressed by other writers, but none had "reiterated it so monstrously and monotonously."

There were thus many strong critical denunciations of Cabell in the thirties, but it would be an oversimplification to assert that Cabell had lost all of his admirers. Indeed, he continued to receive a number of critical accolades during this decade. Perhaps the most substantial voice was that of Carl Van Doren, whose small book, *James Branch Cabell* (New York: Literary Guild, 1932), was an expanded version of an analysis which appeared under the same title in 1925. Van Doren's essay was divided into three parts. In "Cabell Minor" the critic reviewed the early work, which he judged too slight and too far removed from Cabell's most important subject matter. "Cabell Major" focused on what Van Doren considered Cabell's greatest work, the Poictesme novels—especially *Figures of Earth*, *Jurgen*, *The Silver Stallion*, and *The High Place*. In "Scholia" Van Doren traced the development of the Biography of Manuel with reference to *The Lineage of Lichfield, Beyond Life*, and *Straws and Prayerbooks*. Van Doren believed that the object of his study was one of America's great romantic writers, equal to Hawthorne and Melville in "wit and loveliness." This was a judgment slightly tempered in his subsequent study of American fiction, *The American Novel, 1789–1939* (New York: Macmillan, 1940).

Other voices were also raised in support of Cabell through the 1930s. Ellen Glasgow, in an essay entitled "The Biography of Manuel" (*Saturday Review*, VI [June 7, 1930]), regretted that her fellow Richmonder's writing contained so little of the "passion of love." Yet she predicted that his writing would last because it embodied the detachment and irony common to all "courageous thinkers who refuse to flatter and dare examine our destiny." Pelham Edgar's *The Art of the Novel* (New York: Macmillan, 1932; reprinted 1965) contained a brief survey of Cabell's work and maintained that the importance of his unique contribution to American literature was "unquestioned." Burton Rascoe defended Cabell as he had done in earlier years on the Chicago *Tribune* in his *Prometheans* (New York: G. P. Putnam's Sons, 1933). Rascoe marveled at the cohesiveness of the Biography of Manuel and called Cabell, not a novelist, but "a historian of the human soul." Harlan Hatcher's *Creating the Modern American Novel* (New York: Farrar and Rinehart, 1935) diagnosed Cabell's 1920s popularity as the product of the appeal of a type of "up-to-date romance" that was also "brittle with urbanity and aloofness." But this urbanity, Hatcher asserted, was matched with a satirical sense rare in American letters. Benjamin DeCasseres, in *The Elect and the Damned* (New York: B. DeCasseres at the Blackstone Publishers, 1936), endorsed Cabell with the same enthusiasm that had characterized his analysis in *Forty Immortals* (New York: J. Lawren, 1926). DeCasseres placed Cabell with Cervantes, Jules de Gaultier, and other "renegades from reality" and judged him the most remarkable American writer since his fellow Virginian Poe. From London, C. John McCole contributed an analysis of Cabell in *Lucifer at Large* (London: Longmans, Green, 1937) which—though it quarreled with him for making "a cabala of the commonplace" and for burying "his head in disillusion"—concluded that his style, intelligence, wit, and irony marked him "one of the most brilliant of present-day writers."

A number of articles dealing sympathetically with Cabell's fiction appeared in scholarly journals. In "Mr. Cabell's Cosmos" (*Sewanee Review*, XXXVIII [July–September, 1930]), Clara McIntyre emphasized characteristics of his fiction which she believed reflected the preoccupations of the modern age—the desire for escape to keep the horrors of life at bay, the emphasis on the joy of being young, the frankness in dealing with sex, and especially the desire to believe in our own importance in the face of the knowledge of our insignificance in the universe. She found Cabell's central theme, the persistence of the dream in the human heart, to be thoroughly modern in temper. Gay Wilson Allen's "Jurgen and Faust" (*Sewanee Review*, XXXIX [October–December, 1931]) analyzed the similarities and differences between these two characters. Allen observed that both *Faust* and *Jurgen* were epic spiritual odysseys and that both protagonists displayed "divine dissatisfaction" with life. But Goethe's drama was inherently optimistic and Christian, while Cabell's novel was cynical, satirical, and "non-Christian"—its hero a master of compromise. William R. Parker, in "A Key to Cabell" (*English Journal*, XXI [June, 1932]), contended that Cabell had advanced no further than a form of skepticism in his fictional quest for meaning. Parker summarized what he believed was Cabell's prevailing attitude toward life: "Make the best of life as it is, not only understanding its inadequacies, but also giving occasional exercise to your highest human faculties by imagining things *as they ought to be*. It is a kind of pragmatic idealism."

Leon Howard, in an article entitled "Figures of Allegory: A Study of James Branch Cabell" (*Sewanee Review*, XLII [January–March, 1934]), used three novels to illustrate his thesis that Cabell employed allegory to advance three primary themes. According to Howard, *Figures of Earth* presented allegorically the theme that "all is vanity." *Jurgen* conveyed the idea that man can find "a certain degree of salvation in the power of romance or poetic illusion." And *Something About Eve* revealed that the revolt against reality involves great difficulty and sacrifice and is often unsuccessful. In "*Jurgen* and *Figures of Earth* and the Russian Skazki" (*American Literature*, XIII [January, 1942]), Paul Brewster detailed the strong influence of the Russian fairy tale, or *skazki*, on Cabell's language, his motifs and episodes, and his use of proper nouns.

In 1937 Walter Klinefelter published *Books About Poictesme: An Essay in Imaginative Bibliography* (Chicago: Black Cat Press, 1937), an elaborate fictional bibliography much in the spirit of Cabellian ruse. Klinefelter identified the main sources of Cabell's Poictesme as *Les Gestes de Manuel* and *La Haute Histoire de Jurgen*, imaginary medieval epic cycles. The fanciful bibliography came complete with listings of subsequent editions of the cycles and descriptions of the surviving manuscripts of Nicholas de Caen, a fictional source Cabell himself had invented years before.

There was, therefore, a substantial chorus of critical approval for Cabell during the 1930s, but a review of some of the names of the critics who blasted Cabell—Tate, Arvin, Hicks, Fadiman—indicates that the weight of a newly emerging critical generation was being applied largely to depress his reputation. In the long run the combined attacks of Marxist criticism, the New Humanism, and the New Criticism prevailed. Percy Boynton, who had been mildly disapproving of Cabell's work in the 1920s, was even more condescending in his *America in Contemporary Fiction* (Chicago: University of Chicago Press, 1940). Expanding his analysis to include comments on the later novels, Boynton concluded that Cabell was still the same writer, "picturesquely diverting" though "a little tiresome." A more devastating verdict was delivered by Oscar Cargill on the eve of World War II in his *Intellectual America* (New York: Macmillan, 1941). In this book Cargill labeled Cabell "beyond all shadow of doubt, the most tedious person who has achieved high repute as a *literatus* in America." Beside the Biography of Manuel, he observed, "the Congressional Record is sprightly entertainment and the *Novum Organum* a bacchanalian revelry." A year later Cargill's judgment was seconded by Alfred Kazin in his *On Native Grounds* (New York: Reynal and Hitchcock, 1942). Kazin believed the collapse of Cabell's reputation was caused by something in his fiction "so stringy in its poverty, so opposed to all that is high, noble, and intense in art, that nothing could long conceal it."

Proof that the anti-Cabell critics had won the field can be easily found by glancing at Maurice Duke's bibliography of secondary criticism. From the years immediately preceding World War II through the early fifties, Cabell criticism, which had approached figuratively the volume of a torrent in the 1920s, receded to a mere trickle. When Cabell was mentioned at all by newly emerging critics, such as Frederick J. Hoffman in *The Modern Novel in America* (Chicago: Henry Regnery, 1951), it was with total disdain. A handful of critics, however, continued to admire him. Edward Wagenknecht, in his *Cavalcade of the American Novel* (New York: Holt, 1952), presented a survey of Cabell's entire canon and a useful interpretive outline of the Biography of Manuel.[17] Wagenknecht rejected the assertion that the writer was an escapist. Though he allowed for flaws in his writing, he believed that ultimately Cabell's fiction spoke for nothing "smaller or more limited than the human spirit itself." In *The Confident Years* (New York: E. P. Dutton, 1952), Van Wyck Brooks called Cabell a "writer of integrity" who had "developed an aesthetic philosophy that was quite his own," though ultimately, comparing him to the great romantics, he found him rather "pale and thin." Western naturalist Vardis Fisher's *God or Caesar?* (Caldwell, Idaho: Caxton Printers, 1953) continued an advocacy of Cabell which had begun in the 1930s.[18] Fisher contended that Cabell wrote in the service of artistic principle, or God, as opposed to money and fame, and he believed that he was a great realist because he dealt "with the profound truths of myths which underlie the surface of life."

In addition to treatments of Cabell in books, there were also two scholarly articles of note during this period. Raymond Himelick's "Cabell, Shelley and the 'Incorrigible Flesh'" (*South Atlantic Quarterly*, XLVII [January, 1948]) noted that in both Shelley and Cabell there was an "intense preoccupation with man's hopeful and determined quest for beauty and harmony of existence that is somehow epitomized by the woman dream." But though the idealistic Shelley refused to believe the dream was unattainable, the cynical and realistic Cabell understood "that to have perfection in one's grasp is to find it flecked and marred." Edd Winfield Parks's "James Branch Cabell" (*Hopkins Review*, XV [Summer, 1952]) presented the thesis that Cabell was in part a humanist.[19] Though he doubted the existence of God, he had "an abiding faith in man's spirit." His faith was ultimately placed, not in the priest, but in the artist—who could help direct man on his quest, his "improbable journey toward perfection, toward self-

17. The assessment in *Cavalcade of the American Novel* is a revision of Wagenknecht's "Cabell: A Reconsideration," *College English*, IX (February, 1948), 238–46.

18. For a more complete analysis of Vardis Fisher's championing of Cabell, see Joseph M. Flora, "Vardis Fisher and James Branch Cabell," *Cabellian*, II (Autumn, 1969), 12–16.

19. This article was republished with minor modifications in Louis D. Rubin, Jr., and Robert D. Jacobs (eds.), *Southern Renascence* (Baltimore: Johns Hopkins University Press, 1953).

realization." Among Cabell's works Parks believed that *Figures of Earth* and *Jurgen* best embodied his perversely humanistic philosophy.

### *1956–1980: "The James Branch Cabell Case Reopened"*

The inception of the recent period of Cabell scholarship is conveniently and felicitously marked by Edmund Wilson's seminal essay, "The James Branch Cabell Case Reopened," which appeared in the April 21, 1956, issue of the *New Yorker*. Scholarly interest in Cabell, as we have seen in the previous section, had sporadically manifested itself in the late forties and early fifties; but there can be no doubt that Wilson's article was a significant factor in the modest resurgence in Cabell's reputation that has taken place in the last twenty-five years. Wilson saw Cabell as the product of a vanquished region fundamentally at odds with the rest of the nation in its view of history. Caught between his lack of belief in the old legends and his disdain for the New South, Cabell had plunged into Poictesme—a dreamworld made of "quicksilver," confronting the reader with "continual metamorphoses" which led ultimately to a deep understanding of life's radical uncertainty. Wilson's penetrating analysis of Cabell's work was followed by an obituary tribute in the *Nation* (CLXXXVI [June 7, 1958]) in which he detected what he believed was the "misanthropic sadism" and the "blackness of imagination" of the *Nightmare* trilogy—works which he had not read for his first article. He continued to define the source of the writer's bitterness in regional terms, seeing it as being related to "the bitterness of the South at having had [its] dream proved a fiction, and then somehow having had still to live on it."

Wilson's reawakened interest in Cabell was quickly seized upon by others. In an editorial in the Richmond *News Leader* (June 5, 1956) Louis D. Rubin, Jr., speculated that "The Prospects of a Cabell Revival" were distinctly favorable. Raymond Himelick observed in "Cabell and the Modern Temper" (*South Atlantic Quarterly*, LVIII [Spring, 1959]; reprinted in his *James Branch Cabell and the Modern Temper* [New York: Revisionist Press, 1974]) that if our nation were able to reacquire a respect for the writer's Voltaire-like irony, and if the age were ever again to understand "that negation need not always wear a hair shirt, then the case of Cabell [might] not be entirely closed."

Rubin and Himelick were partly accurate in their speculation that a Cabell revival might be in the offing. The sixties and seventies have witnessed an increase in Cabell scholarship, with several new books and two journals devoted to the analysis of his writing. The following summary of recent scholarship follows a more traditional bibliographical paradigm, dividing the criticism into assessments of books, of chapters and commentaries in books, and of articles.

BOOKS  Joe Lee Davis' Twayne volume, *James Branch Cabell* (New York: Twayne, 1962), is rather overambitious in its claims for its subject. But it is also a very useful work, with extensive and helpful interpretations of Cabell's mythology. A brief biographical sketch is followed by an analysis of the Biography of Manuel, which is viewed in terms of the Cabellian attitudes of chivalry, gallantry, and poetry. A chapter on the later writings follows, and the study concludes with a final assessment. Davis categorizes Cabell as an allegorical realist who utilizes Old World subject matter and sources to explain and give form to current Virginia traditions and attitudes. Cabell's understanding of life, Davis believes, is a realistic one; at the same time his form violates the rules of realism.

*Jesting Moses: A Study in Cabellian Comedy* (Gainesville, Fla.: University of Florida Press, 1962), by Arvin Wells, is probably the most interesting book on Cabell that has yet appeared. Wells's thesis is that Cabell is essentially a comic poet, in the tradition of Rabelais, who evolves in his major novels a new kind of comedy, one which balances between tragedy and comedy "without being tragi-comedy." Focusing almost entirely on the novels in the Biography of Manuel, Wells sees *The Cream of the Jest* as a transitional work in which Cabell's complex comic pattern first fully emerges. That pattern is based on the contrast between man's dreams and illusions and the imperfections of his real world, and it involves his rebellion against these finite imperfections and his eventual acceptance of the human condition. In the major novels—which Wells identifies as *Jurgen*, *Figures of Earth*, and *Something About Eve*—the Faustian quest for the unattainable is balanced by the Odyssean pattern of reconciliation to home, wife, and security. Yet the Faustian quest gives meaning to and enriches the questor's life.

Desmond Tarrant, in *James Branch Cabell: The Dream and the Reality* (Norman, Okla.: University of Oklahoma Press, 1967), sees his subject as a great mythmaker. In an exegesis that shows the influence of Jungian theory, Tarrant depicts Cabell as a romancer who probes into the unconscious world and brings away the universal elements of the human saga, which are dramatized in the life of Manuel and of his descendants. Both the early and later novels are treated, with high praise accorded *Hamlet Had an Uncle*. The analysis is marred by errors of fact, some of which Cabell noted in a letter to Tarrant included in the book, and by a critique which too often strays from its thesis into plot summary and description of details of composition. Even more than Davis' work, Tarrant's analysis is weakened by an excessively eulogistic approach to Cabell.

In 1974 and 1975 the Revisionist Press published four short books of essays by Cabell scholars: Raymond Himelick's *James Branch Cabell and the Modern Temper* (New York, 1974), William Leigh Godshalk's *In Quest of Cabell* (New York, 1975), Geoffrey Morley-Mower's *Cabell Under Fire* (New York, 1975), and Dorothy B. Schlegel's *James Branch Cabell: The Richmond Iconoclast* (New York, 1975). Virtually all of the essays in these works appeared in journals prior to their inclusion in a book, and thus they will be described separately in the section of this essay that deals with recent articles.

CHAPTERS AND COMMENTARIES IN BOOKS  Wayne Booth's brilliant study of point of view, *The Rhetoric of Fiction* (Chicago: University of Chicago Press, 1961), uses *The Cream of the Jest* as a key example in a chapter entitled "The Uses of Authorial Silence." Here Booth discusses the advantages of not providing a clear central narrator and of producing deliberate confusion in the reader through an observer who is himself confused. The three narrators of Cabell's novel—Felix Kennaston, Horvendile, and Richard Fentnor Harrowby—"break down the reader's conventional notions of what is real" by undermining "the reader's normal trust in what the narrator says." *Minor American Authors*, edited by Charles A. Hoyt (Carbondale, Ill.: University of Southern Illinois Press, 1970), contains an essay on Cabell by Fred B. Millet that briefly surveys the *Jurgen* censorship controversy and moves on to a general discussion of the *Biography of Manuel* and an account of Cabell's critical rise and fall. Millet concludes that Cabell's experimentation in style and form and his antirealism and exotic myths make it "distinctly possible that [he] is more relevant to the current literary atmosphere than he has been to any period since the twenties." Allen Churchill, in his *The Literary Decade* (New York: Prentice Hall, 1971), considers Cabell a footnote in our cultural history; yet he points out that to Mencken, Sinclar Lewis, and Malcolm Cowley, Cabell and Joseph Hergesheimer were perceived as writers who had liberated American fiction "from the Genteel Tradition and the Hoosier School."

Chapter 6 of Fred C. Hobson's *Serpent in Eden: H. L. Mencken and the South* (Chapel Hill: University of North Carolina Press, 1974) contains an extended discussion of the Mencken-Cabell friendship. Addressing the question of why these two opposite types were in such sympathy, Hobson maintains that Mencken was attracted to Cabell because he believed Cabell represented the finest aspects of southern aristocracy, because he viewed Cabell as an isolated, outcast artist who had chosen to satirize his native region, and because he applauded Cabell's rejection of the moralism inherent in the New Humanism. Hobson parts company with Richard Ruland, who believes the Cabell-Mencken alliance was one of time and circumstance.[20] Mencken, Hobson contends, had a perceptive understanding of Cabell's work as literature, a perception that derived from a spiritual affinity between the two.

RECENT ARTICLES    One of the most important general analyses of Cabell's fiction is Louis D. Rubin, Jr.'s "Two in Richmond: Ellen Glasgow and James Branch Cabell," in his and Robert D. Jacobs' *South: Modern Literature in Its Cultural Setting* (Garden City, N.Y.: Doubleday, 1961). This long essay is a slightly revised version of the second part of Rubin's short book, *No Place on Earth: Ellen Glasgow, James Branch Cabell, and Richmond-in-Virginia* (Austin: University of Texas Press, 1959). In the section of his essay dealing with Cabell, Rubin argues that Mencken was right when he termed Cabell "the most acidulous of all the anti-romantics." There is, he believes, something of Ellen Glasgow's social history in his novels. Cabell's understanding of man's paradoxical need for the illusion of myth is conditioned by his understanding of his region's embracing of its postbellum legends. Jurgen's meditations on the statue of Manuel, observes Rubin, "are no less serious because they were occasioned by events in legendary Poictesme, rather than by a contemplation of the statue of George Washington in Capitol Park in Richmond." Dorothy B. Schlegel, in "Cabell's Translation of Virginia" (*Cabellian*, II [Autumn, 1969]), is in broad agreement with Rubin that, in dealing with Poictesme, Cabell deals by indirection with Virginia. Through his medieval legends he is able to evaluate the myths of his fellow Virginians—their faith in God, their faith in the aristocratic code of honor, and their devotion to the idea of the southern lady.

In "James Branch Cabell and the Comedy of Skeptical Conservatism" (*Midcontinent American Studies Journal*, VI [Spring, 1965]) Robert H. Canary contends that Cabell's work is not escapist, but that it embodies a social philosophy that is skeptical and conservative, much like that of H. L.

20. Ruland's "Mencken and Cabell," is discussed in the biography section of this essay.

Mencken. Cabell's idea that one must accept one's society as it is, is made most explicit, according to Canary, in the *Heirs and Assigns* trilogy. Raymond Himelick, in "Figures of Cabell" (*Modern Fiction Studies*, II [Winter, 1956–57]), believes that Cabell's novels convey his understanding of life as a "grotesque comedy" in which "romantic passion succumbs to romantic appetite, and romantic appetite is annihilated by consummation." Himelick shares Rubin and Canary's conviction that Cabell is fundamentally antiromantic in spirit. Another article emphasizing the darker aspects of Cabell's fiction is Dorothy Schlegel's "Cabell's Comic Mask" (*Cabellian*, IV [Autumn, 1971]). For Schlegel Cabell's mask of comedy hides "the deep sense of tragedy which [lies] at the heart of most of his work." The darker side of Cabell's treatment of sexuality is the subject of Robert Canary's "Cabell's Dark Comedies" (*Mississippi Quarterly*, XXI [Spring, 1968]). Cabell's novels, Canary believes, are characterized by "a general distrust of the female principle in life and a particular rejection of active female sexuality." *Jurgen, Something About Eve,* and *The King Was in His Counting House* reveal a deep sexual ambivalence and reflect patterns of attitude associated with the Oedipus complex.

Edgar E. MacDonald, in "Cabell's Hero: Cosmic Rebel" (*Southern Literary Journal*, II [Fall, 1969]), discusses the recurring themes of aspiration and damnation that are associated with Cabell's protagonists. In creating his heroes, MacDonald maintains, the author draws on both the Don Juan and Faust legends, though as his fiction develops his characters become more and more "demonic and speculative in the Faust tradition." Cabell was, he concludes, drawn to create "hungering heroes" whose dissatisfaction with reality leads them toward the forbidden and unknown. In a more recent article, entitled "The Illusion of Diabolism in the Cabellian Hero" (*Novel*, VIII [Spring, 1975]), Richard Warner rejects this theory of Cabell's diabolic protagonists. Explicating three episodes from *Figures of Earth, The Cream of the Jest,* and *The High Place,* Warner argues that none of Cabell's characters are motivated in their traffic with evil by sheer perversity or "a manifest sympathy with evil for its own sake." He sees their romantic rebellion as redemptive, not damning.

Cabell's relationship to his critics has been the subject of a number of articles. Dorothy Schlegel's "Cabell and His Critics" (in Richard K. Meeker [ed.], *The Dilemma of the Southern Writer* [Farmville, Va.: Institute of Southern Culture Studies, 1961]; reprinted in the *Cabellian*, III [Spring, 1971]) examines Cabell's relationship with both his fellow Virginians and with critics outside the state. She believes that Cabell was inherently ambivalent in his attitude toward his public. He deeply needed adulation, yet he was often contemptuous of people who did not understand his work. Schlegel concludes that both Cabell and his critics "had good reasons for feeling hostile to each other." James Blish, in "To Rhadamanthus Snarling: Cabell Against His Critics" (*Kalki*, II, no. 3 [1968]), agrees with Schlegel that the writer was inordinately sensitive to criticism. "His vendetta against the critics, in consequence, loses considerable of its effect, by seeming as much the petulance of a spoiled child as the anger of a wronged man." M. Thomas Inge's "The Unheeding South: Donald Davidson on James Branch Cabell" (*Cabellian*, II [Autumn, 1969]) reprints Davidson's negative review of *Something About Eve* and finds it ironic that the Agrarians themselves eventually foundered on the same criticism that they used to attack Cabell—that they were men trying to escape into a romantic past. Geoffrey Morley-Mower's "Cabell Under Fire" (*Kalki*, VII, no. 1 [1975]) focuses on the hostile review given *Figures of Earth* by Maurice Hewlett and on Cabell's response.

Two articles have been concerned with general assessments of Cabell's critical fortunes. In "Recent Cabell Criticism" (*Cabellian*, I [Fall, 1968]) Joe Lee Davis presented an interesting survey, briefly but expertly outlining the rise and fall of his reputation and concentrating more fully on what he believed were the most significant recent studies. Davis discussed in some detail the Tarrant and Wells books as well as five unpublished Cabell dissertations. Edgar E. MacDonald's "Cabell Criticism: Past, Present, and Future" (*Cabellian*, I [Fall, 1968]) found it a good sign that *Jurgen* was no longer the exclusive focus of criticism and that critical analyses were no longer dominated by the literary clichés of the 1920s and 1930s. The essay is also interesting for its summary of two French-language articles not found in other bibliographical sources—Joseph Mainsard's "L'Evasion de James Branch Cabell" (*Les Cahiers du Sud*, November, 1929) and Maurice Le Breton's "James Branch Cabell Romancier" (*Revue Anglo-Américaine*, December, 1933; February, 1934).

Several analyses of Cabell take a biographical approach to understanding his work. Geoffrey Morley-Mower, in "Cabell's Black Imagination" (*Kalki*, VIII, no. 1 [1980]), contends that the increasingly bitter tone of his writing is related to "his ill-fortune in having an only son who could not carry on his name" and that the happiness reflected in his last two works derives from his late marriage to Margaret Freeman. In "The Re-Evolution of a Vestryman" (*Kalki*, II, no. 4 [1968]) James N. Hall traces evidences of Cabell's religious attitudes in his books—from the increasing cynicism of the early and middle periods, to the bitter agnosticism and occultism of the later period, to an abrupt shift back to conventional Episcopalianism in the last years. John Boardman's "The Two Cabells" (*Kalki*, III, no. 3 [1969]) hypothesizes that Horvendile, the maker or romancer, and Kennaston, the spectator and reporter who brings the news, both represent aspects of Cabell's character. "Cabell's Game of Hide and Seek" (*Cabellian*, IV [Autumn, 1971]), by Edgar E. MacDonald, stresses that Cabell was conditioned by the circumstances of his early years in Richmond and at William and Mary to turn "instinctively to the literary mask." With *The High Place*, however, the author removes his mask, attributing his book to no other author. "The game of hide and seek is over." Louis Untermeyer examines rather superficially Cabell's use of masks in a pamphlet entitled *James Branch Cabell: The Man and His Masks* (Richmond: Associates of the James Branch Cabell Library, 1970).

A number of critical articles have been directed toward the examination of influences on Cabell's aesthetic philosophy. In "James Branch Cabell and Southern Romanticism" (in Francis Butler Simkins (ed.), *The South in Perspective* [Farmville, Va.: Longwood College, 1959]; reprinted in R. C. Simonini (ed.), *Southern Writers: Appraisals in Our Time* [Charlottesville, Va.: University Press of Virginia, 1964]), Dorothy Schlegel investigates "the extent to which James Branch Cabell was both influenced and repelled by Southern Romanticism." She finds that young Cabell was strongly affected by the chivalric aspect of southern romanticism as well as by the ironic preference of the southern romantic for gallant eighteenth-century tastes and standards, combined with a poetic yearning for another age and reality, usually the medieval age. Schlegel contends that though the South furnished Cabell "with the initial dynamics governing his philosophy of life and of art," he eventually ventured in his writing far beyond the boundaries of his native region. In "James Branch Cabell: A Latter-Day Enlightener" (*College Language Association Journal*, XII [March, 1969]), Schlegel examines how the eighteenth-century French Enlighteners, especially Voltaire, shaped Cabell's use of irony, exaggeration, understatement, and the affected pose of innocence to attack intolerance—in this case the fundamentalism of the Bible Belt South. James Blish's "Cabell as Voluntarist" (*Kalki*, III, no. 4 [1969]) links his artistic principles to the late-nineteenth-century voluntarism of Schopenhauer and Nietzsche, which stresses the malleability of objective reality to the will and idea of the human mind.

Edgar E. MacDonald's "The Influence of Provençal Poetry on James Branch Cabell" (*Cabellian*, III [Autumn, 1970]) finds that the writer's three major philosophic and thematic attitudes have their origins in his discovery at William and Mary of Provençal poetry. This discovery resulted in the early verse, "springs which flow into the mighty current that becomes the Life of Manuel." MacDonald's "Glasgow, Cabell, and Richmond" (*Mississippi Quarterly*, XXVII [Fall, 1974]) and Maurice Duke's "Cabell's and Glasgow's Richmond: The Intellectual Background of the City" (*Mississippi Quarterly*, XXVII [Fall, 1974]) examine the relationship of these Richmond writers to their milieu. Duke demonstrates that cultural activity was rather vigorous in nineteenth-century Richmond and that it helped to form the "personal intellectual background" of both Glasgow and Cabell. MacDonald observes that though Glasgow could look on Richmond with a degree of detachment, Cabell "could not write of Richmond objectively until after his major work was accomplished."

A considerable number of critical articles have been concerned with tracing specific sources for Cabell's myths, characters, and symbols. Lin Carter's "Horvendile—A Link Between Cabell and Tolkien" (*Kalki*, III, no. 3 [1969]) reveals that his study of the Teutonic and Scandinavian sources of Tolkien's fiction, entitled *Tolkien: A Look Behind "The Lord of the Rings,"* led him to the discovery of the source for Cabell's Horvendile. In "Another Mirror for Pigeons" (*Kalki*, III, no. 3 [1969]), Emmet Peter offers an explanation of Cabell's symbolic pigeons and mirrors, using *The Arabian Nights* and Sir Richard Burton's translation of *The Book of the Thousand Nights and a Night*. Roger Staples, in "The Lance and the Veil" (*Kalki*, IV, no. 1 [1969]), examines Cabell's adaptation of Aleister Crowley's Gnostic Mass for the Lance Ceremony in *Jurgen*. In "Cabell and MacDonald" (*Kalki*, IV, no. 4 [1970]) James Allen asserts that Cabell's *The Cream of the Jest* and *Jurgen* were influenced by George MacDonald's *Phantastes* (1858). G. N. Gabbard examines the narrative sources of *The High Place* in "Fairy Tales in *The High Place*" (*Kalki*, IV, no. 4 [1970]). Two other articles by Gabbard present a rather strained argument for an Ibsen influence on Cabell: "*Jurgen* and *Peer Gynt*" (*Kalki*, V, no. 1 [1971]) and "Count Manuel and *Peer Gynt*" (*Kalki*, VI, no. 4 [1973]). Roger Bryant's "Manuel Magus" (*Kalki*, V, no. 1 [1971]) draws a connection between Count Manuel and the magus-hero of ancient legend. Illustrating the multiple symbolic meanings of Cabell's mirrors in "Cabell's Mirrors and (Incidentally) Pigeons" (*Kalki*, VI, no. 2 [1974]), William Godshalk suggests another source for the symbol—Edmund Spenser's *Faerie Queene*. Maggey Mateo's "Cabell and *The Mabinogion*" (*Kalki*, VII, no. 2 [1976]) contends that the Welsh legends collected in *The Mabinogion* are "an important source for names, places, and descriptions in Cabell's works."

There have also been a number of examinations of similarities between Cabell's fiction and the work of other modern writers. Nathan Halper argues, not very convincingly, in "Joyce/Cabell and Cabell/Joyce" (*Kalki*, IV, no. 1 [1969]) that there are striking resemblances between Cabell and Joyce. Joe Lee Davis explores the responses of Cabell and George Santayana to the New Humanist attack on American culture in Cabell's *Some of Us* and Santayana's *The Genteel Tradition at Bay* in "Cabell and Santayana in the Neo-Humanist Debate" (*Cabellian*, IV [Spring, 1972]). Davis concludes that their rejections of the conformity and of the rigidity which they perceived in the New Humanist attitude have complementary critical value. Nancy McCollum, in "Glasgow's and Cabell's Comedies of Virginia" (*Georgia Review*, XVIII [Summer, 1964]), contends that both Richmond writers deal ironically but delicately in their novels of the Old Dominion with the worship by their fellow Virginians of the chivalric tradition. In "The Ornate Wasteland of James Branch Cabell" (*Kalki*, VI, no. 3 [1974]; reprinted in Warren French (ed.), *The Twenties: Fiction, Poetry, Drama* [Deland, Fla.: Everett-Edwards, 1975]), Maurice Duke maintains that both Cabell and T. S. Eliot see the world from a similar point of view and that Eliot's wasteland is not far removed from Cabell's Poictesme, though Cabell seeks to conceal the cancer at the heart of contemporary culture while Eliot exposes it in his poetry.

William Godshalk detects a similarity between Cabell and more recent fiction in "Cabell and Barth: Our Comic Athletes" (in *The Comic Imagination in American Literature* [New Brunswick, N.J.: Rutgers University Press, 1973]). Godshalk believes that Cabell's "resolute frivolity" is similar in tone to Barth's "cheerful nihilism." Both writers are "comic athletes," players of literary games who call all into question, even man's most sacred myths. In "Cabell as Precursor: Reflections on Cabell and Vonnegut" (*Kalki*, VI, no. 4 [1975]), Joseph Flora argues, through an inspection of the fiction of both writers, that Cabell and Vonnegut are products of ages of cynical disillusionment who counsel acceptance of things as they are in their fiction through the use of romantic fantasy. The affinity between Cabell and Vonnegut is indirectly suggested in Conway Zirkle's "Circular Time Travel" (*Kalki*, IV, no. 3 [1970]). Zirkle believes that Cabell demonstrates time and again in his novels that he approves of circular time travel in which characters end where they began.

Robert H. Canary presents a stimulating analysis of Cabell's relation to modern literature in "The Contexts for Cabell" (*Kalki*, VII, no. 2 [1977]). Canary links the absence of Cabell from the English curriculum to "the failure of either period or region to provide an appropriate context" for considering his work. Drawing on Irving Babbitt's *Rousseau and Romanticism*, Canary would have us see Cabell in the context of modern romanticism, which includes many works labeled realistic and naturalistic. This contemporary brand of romanticism posits the artist who lives "at least partly in a world of his own creation" and who serves as "a paradigm of modern man."

In recent years, as Edgar MacDonald observed in his 1968 article on Cabell criticism, critics have abandoned their preoccupation with *Jurgen* and have expanded their consideration to include many of Cabell's individual works. Joseph Flora, in "From Virginia to Poictesme: The Early Novels of James Branch Cabell" (*Mississippi Quarterly*, XXXII [Spring, 1979]), believes that the four early Virginia novels should be examined "to see Cabell developing a style and a subject matter." Flora focuses on the characters of John Charteris, Felix Kennaston, and Richard Fentnor Harrowby to examine what he believes is a major theme of the Virginia novels: the "portrayal of the life of the mature artist, particularly as seen in relationship to his married life." In "Cabell's *Cream of the Jest*" (*Modern Fiction Studies*, II [May, 1956]) Edd Winfield Parks analyzes Cabell's frequently repeated phrase. Although Parks points out that there are several meanings, he believes the essential jest is that we are forced to support ourselves with truths that may well be fictions. Yet by confronting the world with faith, man can "set at bay the jest that he is merely a puppet." In "Cabell's *Cream of the Jest* and Recent American Fiction" (*Southern Literary Journal*, V [Spring, 1973]), William Godshalk points out that Felix Kennaston, in his desire to escape reality, stands in a line of schizophrenic, mentally abnormal modern protagonists that include Kurt Vonnegut's Billy Pilgrim and John Barth's Eben Cook.

There have been two interesting treatments of *Beyond Life*. In his "Introduction" to the Johnson Reprint Company's 1970 edition of *Beyond Life* (reprinted in *Kalki*, IV, no. 2 [1970]), William Godshalk details the sources for Cabell's critical ideas and traces the growth of this important essay collection. Evelyn Hinz and John Teunissen, in "Life Beyond Life: Cabell's Theory and Practice of Romance" (*Genre*, X [Fall, 1977]), assert that *Beyond Life* is Cabell's best expression of his artistic credo. They believe that Cabell identifies romance with a cosmic perspective which enables man to see beyond life, history, time, and place and which rejects with encompassing irony the nostalgic and primitive attitudes ordinarily associated with romanticism. In the face of evolutionary naturalism and Christian linear time Cabell the romancer seeks to restore man's "mythic heritage," which is reconstructed in his fiction through cyclically recurring archetypes.

Emmons Welch bases his interpretation of *Jurgen* on the principles set forth in *Beyond Life* in his article, "*Beyond Life* and *Jurgen*: The Demiurge" (*Cabellian*, II [Spring, 1970]). Welch argues that the central philosophical notion of the novel, the demiurge, makes *Jurgen* a comedy of justice. In *Jurgen* extramarital love represents man's impulse to escape reality. The novel's justice, Welch observes, is a paradox: man, like *Jurgen*, is "permitted his illusions and protected from the knowledge of his inadequacy of these illusions." Julius Rothman's "Jurgen, the Rabelaisian Babbitt" (*Cabellian*, I [Fall, 1968]) sees the protagonist as a sort of Babbitt, who would also be a poet. Rothman maintains that through Cabell's characterization of Jurgen, the vanity, greed, and pride of all men are satirized. In "'Some Ladies and Jurgen'" (*Kalki*, VII, no. 2 [1976]), Paul Spenser demonstrates the relation between Cabell's novels and the original magazine stories from which many of them are constructed by focusing on "the convoluted growth of *Jurgen*" from a short story entitled "Some Ladies and Jurgen." Spenser details how Jurgen's simple quest for women in the short story is transmuted into a more profound symbolic quest "for an answer to the riddle of life." In a similar approach, Spenser analyzes the transformation of Cabell's first published story, "An Amateur Ghost," into the Smoit episode of *Jurgen* in "Jurgen and the Ghost" (*Kalki*, VII, no. 4 [1978]). The thesis of Geoffrey Morley-Mower's "Cabell's Reputation and *Jurgen*" (*Kalki*, V, no. 1 [1971]) is that Cabell is neither atheist, blasphemer, nor pornographer and that *Jurgen* is a useful antidote to the diseases of youth—vague idealism and sensual escapism.

In 1970 and 1971 several articles devoted to an analysis of *The Silver Stallion* appeared in *Kalki*. Joseph Flora's "The Structure of *The Silver Stallion*" (*Kalki*, IV, no. 2 [1970]) observes that the ten books of this novel are ordered to provide great variety of action as they lead the reader to the inevitable conclusion that the dream is more significant than reality. In "Stallion and Legend" (*Kalki*, IV, no. 2 [1970]), Desmond Tarrant defines *The Silver Stallion* as a comedy of redemption which ultimately stands for the satisfaction of faith. Robert Canary's "Fables of Art in *The Silver Stallion*" (*Kalki*, IV, no. 2 [1970]) sees the legend of Manuel as "a fable of art, in praise of that romance which enables men to ward off the thought of the tempting grey nothingness." Joanne Yocum traces the acceptance or rejection of the legend of Manuel by the seven lords of the Fellowship of the Silver Stallion in "The Triumph of Romantic Realism" (*Kalki*, V, no. 3 [1971]). Romantic realism, she concludes, ultimately turns all these knights "into true children of the spirit of Manuel, though most of the lords perversely [resist] seeing themselves in that way."

A few articles have analyzed Cabell's later works. James Blish's "The

Long Night of a Virginia Author" (*Journal of Modern Literature*, II [September, 1972]) begins his study of *The Nightmare Has Triplets* by detailing the resemblances between *Smirt*, *Smith*, and *Smire* and James Joyce's *Finnegans Wake*. Though Blish acknowledges that neither writer influenced the other, he finds his comparison interesting because it shows two writers attempting to follow up in similar ways on major and successful work. Blish thinks that Cabell should have spent less time attacking critics in his trilogy, and he believes that too much of his nonfictional writing was injected into the narratives. Yet, he concludes, "the two-thirds of the *Nightmare* that are relevant are also brilliant, original, and very moving." In Desmond Tarrant's analysis of "Cabell's *Hamlet Had an Uncle* and Shakespeare's *Hamlet*" (*Cabellian*, III [Autumn, 1970]), he points out that Cabell uses the "ancient, historical, and legendary Hamlet as well as Shakespeare's" in creating his character. The death of Hamlet and the triumphant survival of his uncle signifies the triumph of objective reality and makes *Hamlet Had an Uncle* perhaps "the subtlest of Cabell's later works of art." In "James Branch Cabell's Flirtation with Clio: The Story of a Collaboration" (*Yale University Library Gazette*, XLVII [July, 1972]), Geoffrey Morley-Mower examines, with frequent reference to correspondence, the collaboration of Cabell and Florida historian A. J. Hanna in the writing of *The St. Johns* (1943).

### Theses and Dissertations

"Dissertations on Cabell" (*Cabellian*, I [Spring, 1969]) lists the eleven dissertations on Cabell written from 1954 through 1968.[21] In addition, the third edition of "Southern Literary Culture," edited by Jack D. Wages and William Andrews (*Mississippi Quarterly*, XXXI [Winter, 1978–79]), lists both dissertations and masters' theses written on Cabell in American universities between 1969 and 1975. Information on more recent graduate work can be obtained by consulting Volume 15 of the *Comprehensive Dissertation Index—1973–77* and the yearly supplements which follow it.

### Concluding Observations

In "Whatever Happened to the Cabell Revival?" (*Kalki*, VI, no. 2 [1974]), Robert Canary observes: "Dom Manuel has not yet returned; the Cabell revival has not yet taken place; and we must face the

---

21. Joe Lee Davis discusses extensively several of these dissertations in "Recent Cabell Criticism," *Cabellian*, I (Fall, 1968), 1–12, reviewed earlier in this section.

possibility that one is as unlikely as the other." Canary's observations are essentially accurate. There has been a Cabell revival of sorts, but it has been very modest and limited in its scope. A close look at the journals which publish articles on Cabell confirms the limited extent of critical interest. The overwhelming majority of articles have been published in the *Cabellian* and *Kalki*; one journal is now defunct and the other has a very small circulation. Most of the other articles have appeared in the *Mississippi Quarterly* and the *Southern Literary Journal*. Very few Cabell articles have been published in journals outside the South. Unfortunately Edmund Wilson's call for a reappraisal of Cabell's work has not provoked interest among a large enough number of critics of major stature. And one can hardly escape the conclusion that Cabell's national reputation has not in the long run been helped by making him the object of a kind of critical cult worship.

Perhaps, as Robert Canary suggests in another article reviewed in this section, Cabell will appear more frequently in our English curriculum if we can find a more appropriate critical context for discussing his work. If this idea has merit there would be no better place to work out its implications than in a biography. Indeed, the most obvious deficiency in Cabell scholarship today is the lack of a comprehensive and perceptive critical biography. A first-rate biography by a first-rate scholar would do more than anything else to rehabilitate Cabell in the eyes of America's literary establishment. Until this biography appears, one can hope that future Cabell scholarship will be more modest and less sweeping in the claims it advances for this interesting modern American writer.

# NOTES ON CONTRIBUTORS

MARK ALLEN is Assistant Professor of English at the University of Texas at San Antonio. His interest in Cabell is a result of contributions made to *The Fantastic Imagination*, an anthology of short fiction, and *Fantasy Literature: A Core List and Reference Guide*.

LESLIE A. FIEDLER is Samuel Clemens Professor of English at the State University of New York at Buffalo. His best known work of literary criticism is *Love and Death in the American Novel*. Two forthcoming books are *Olaf Stapledon* and *What Was Literature?*

JOSEPH M. FLORA is Professor of English and chairman of the department at the University of North Carolina at Chapel Hill. He frequently turns his attention to Cabell; recent essays include "From Virginia to Poictesme: The Early Novels of James Branch Cabell" and "James Branch Cabell's Tribute to H. L. Mencken and Their Era."

W. L. GODSHALK is Professor of English at the University of Cincinnati. Several of his essays on Cabell were collected in a volume, *In Quest of Cabell*.

EDGAR E. MACDONALD as a child was a neighbor of the Cabells; his doctorate in comparative literature from the Sorbonne is a tracing of Cabell's literary sources, and his articles on Cabell have appeared in *American Literature*, the *Southern Literary Journal*, the *Cabellian*, and the *Richmond Quarterly*. He is Professor of English at Randolph-Macon College.

LOUIS D. RUBIN, JR., is University Distinguished Professor of English at the University of North Carolina at Chapel Hill. His numerous works of literary criticism include *No Place on Earth: Ellen Glasgow, James Branch Cabell, and Richmond-in-Virginia* and *The Wary Fugitives: Four Poets and the South*.

DOROTHY MCINNIS SCURA is Associate Professor of English at Virginia Commonwealth University. She has published articles on Ellen Glasgow as well as *Henry James, 1960–1974: A Reference Guide*, an annotated bibliography of criticism on James.

RITCHIE D. WATSON, JR., is Associate Professor of English at Randolph-Macon College. He has published essays on William Styron and George Bagby and is writing a study of the Cavalier figure in southern fiction.

# INDEX

## DATE DUE

| | | | |
|---|---|---|---|
| | | | |
| | | | |
| | | | |
| | | | |
| | | | |
| | | | |
| | | | |
| | | | |
| | | | |
| | | | |
| | | | |
| | | | |
| | | | |
| | | | |
| | | | |
| | | | |
| | | | |

Demco, Inc. 38-293